'Goodbye, Spain?'

The Question of Independence
for Catalonia

The Cañada Blanch / Sussex Academic Studies on Contemporary Spain

General Editor: Professor Paul Preston, London School of Economics

Margaret Joan Anstee, *JB – An Unlikely Spanish Don: The Life and Times of Professor John Brande Trend*.

Richard Barker, *Skeletons in the Closet, Skeletons in the Ground: Repression, Victimization and Humiliation in a Small Andalusian Town – The Human Consequences of the Spanish Civil War*.

Germà Bel, *Infrastructure and the Political Economy of Nation Building in Spain, 1720–2010*.

Kathryn Crameri, *'Goodbye, Spain?': The Question of Independence for Catalonia*

Michael Eaude, *Triumph at Midnight in the Century: A Critical Biography of Arturo Barea*.

Francisco Espinosa-Maestre, *Shoot the Messenger?: Spanish Democracy and the Crimes of Francoism – From the Pact of Silence to the Trial of Baltasar Garzón*

Soledad Fox, *Constancia de la Mora in War and Exile: International Voice for the Spanish Republic*.

María Jesús González, *Raymond Carr: The Curiosity of the Fox*.

Helen Graham, *The War and its Shadow: Spain's Civil War in Europe's Long Twentieth Century*.

Angela Jackson, *'For us it was Heaven': The Passion, Grief and Fortitude of Patience Darton – From the Spanish Civil War to Mao's China*.

Gabriel Jackson, *Juan Negrín: Physiologist, Socialist, and Spanish Republican War Leader*.

Sid Lowe, *Catholicism, War and the Foundation of Francoism: The Juventud de Acción Popular in Spain, 1931–1939*.

David Lethbridge, *Norman Bethune in Spain: Commitment, Crisis, and Conspiracy*.

Carles Manera, *The Great Recession: A Subversive View*.

Olivia Muñoz-Rojas, *Ashes and Granite: Destruction and Reconstruction in the Spanish Civil War and Its Aftermath*.

Linda Palfreeman, *¡SALUD!: British Volunteers in the Republican Medical Service during the Spanish Civil War, 1936–1939*.

Linda Palfreeman, *Aristocrats, Adventurers and Ambulances: British Medical Units in the Spanish Civil War.*

Cristina Palomares, *The Quest for Survival after Franco: Moderate Francoism and the Slow Journey to the Polls, 1964–1977.*

David Wingeate Pike, *France Divided: The French and the Civil War in Spain.*

Hugh Purcell with Phyll Smith, *The Last English Revolutionary: Tom Wintringham, 1898–1949.*

Isabelle Rohr, *The Spanish Right and the Jews, 1898–1945: Antisemitism and Opportunism.*

Gareth Stockey, *Gibraltar: "A Dagger in the Spine of Spain?"*

Ramon Tremosa-i-Balcells, *Catalonia – An Emerging Economy: The Most Cost-Effective Ports in the Mediterranean Sea.*

Maria Thomas, *The Faith and the Fury: Popular Anticlerical Violence and Iconoclasm in Spain, 1931–1936.*

Dacia Viejo-Rose, *Reconstructing Spain: Cultural Heritage and Memory after Civil War.*

Richard Wigg, *Churchill and Spain: The Survival of the Franco Regime, 1940–1945.*

'Goodbye, Spain?'

The Question of Independence
for Catalonia

KATHRYN CRAMERI

sussex
ACADEMIC
PRESS
Brighton • Chicago • Toronto

Cañada Blanch Centre
for Contemporary
Spanish Studies

CATALAN
OBSER
VATORY LSE

2 4 6 8 10 9 7 5 3

First published in hardcover 2014, reprinted in paperback 2015, in Great Britain by
SUSSEX ACADEMIC PRESS
PO Box 139
Eastbourne BN24 9BP

and in the United States of America by
SUSSEX ACADEMIC PRESS
Independent Publishers Group
814 N. Franklin Street, Chicago, IL 60610

and in Canada by
SUSSEX ACADEMIC PRESS (CANADA)
24 Ranee Avenue, Toronto, Ontario M6A 1M6

Published in collaboration with
the Cañada Blanch Centre for Contemporary Spanish Studies and
the Catalan Observatory, London School of Economics.

British Library Cataloguing in Publication Data
A CIP catalogue record for this book is available from the British Library.

Library of Congress Cataloging-in-Publication Data
Crameri, Kathryn.
Goodbye, Spain? : the question of independence for Catalonia / Kathryn Crameri.
pages   cm
Includes bibliographical references and index.
 ISBN 978-1-84519-659-2 (hb : alk. paper)
 ISBN 978-1-84519-707-0 (pbk: alk. paper)
  1. Catalonia (Spain)—History—Autonomy and independence movements.
2. Nationalism—Spain—Catalonia—History—21st century. I. Title.
DP302.C68C73 2014
320.1'509467—dc23

                                                        2014005776

Typeset & designed by Sussex Academic Press, Brighton & Eastbourne.
Printed by Edwards Brothers Malloy, Ann Arbor, USA.
This book is printed on acid-free paper.

Contents

The Cañada Blanch Centre for Contemporary Spanish Studies

In the 1960s, the most important initiative in the cultural and academic relations between Spain and the United Kingdom was launched by a Valencian fruit importer in London. The creation by Vicente Cañada Blanch of the Anglo-Spanish Cultural Foundation has subsequently benefited large numbers of Spanish and British scholars at various levels. Thanks to the generosity of Vicente Cañada Blanch, thousands of Spanish schoolchildren have been educated at the secondary school in West London that bears his name. At the same time, many British and Spanish university students have benefited from the exchange scholarships which fostered cultural and scientific exchanges between the two countries. Some of the most important historical, artistic and literary work on Spanish topics to be produced in Great Britain was initially made possible by Cañada Blanch scholarships.

Vicente Cañada Blanch was, by inclination, a conservative. When his Foundation was created, the Franco regime was still in the plenitude of its power. Nevertheless, the keynote of the Foundation's activities was always a complete open-mindedness on political issues. This was reflected in the diversity of research projects supported by the Foundation, many of which, in Francoist Spain, would have been regarded as subversive. When the Dictator died, Don Vicente was in his seventy-fifth year. In the two decades following the death of the Dictator, although apparently indestructible, Don Vicente was obliged to husband his energies. Increasingly, the work of the Foundation was carried forward by Miguel Dols whose tireless and imaginative work in London was matched in Spain by that of José María Coll Comín. They were united in the Foundation's spirit of open-minded commitment to fostering research of high quality in pursuit of better Anglo-Spanish cultural relations. Throughout the 1990s, thanks to them, the role of the Foundation grew considerably.

In 1994, in collaboration with the London School of Economics, the Foundation established the Príncipe de Asturias Chair of Contemporary Spanish History and the Cañada Blanch Centre for Contemporary Spanish Studies. It is the particular task of the Cañada Blanch Centre for Contemporary Spanish Studies to promote the understanding of twentieth-century Spain through research and teaching of contemporary Spanish history, politics, economy, sociology and culture. The Centre possesses a valuable library and archival centre for specialists in contemporary Spain. This work is carried on through the publications of the doctoral and post-doctoral researchers at the Centre itself and through the many seminars and lectures held at the London School of Economics. While the seminars are the province of the researchers, the lecture cycles have been the forum in which Spanish politicians have been able to address audiences in the United Kingdom.

Since 1998, the Cañada Blanch Centre has published a substantial number of books in collaboration with several different publishers on the subject of contemporary Spanish history and politics. A fruitful partnership with Sussex Academic Press began in 2004. Full details and descriptions of the published works can be found on the Press website. A constant interest of the series has been the relationship of Catalonia with the political establishment in Madrid. This has been reflected in the volumes by Germà Bel, Ramon Tremosa and Olivia Muñoz-Rojas. In the run-up to Barcelona's proposed Autumn 2014 referendum on Catalan independence, bitterly opposed by Madrid, Professor Kathryn Crameri's *'Goodbye Spain?'* could not be more timely.

Preface by Geoff Cowling

When I retired from the Consulate General in Barcelona and from HM Diplomatic Service in 2005, the question of outright independence for Catalunya was hardly a burning issue, even for the Socialist-led coalition "Tripartit" government. The Tripartit had taken over power from the long serving CiU in 2003 and later appointed the pro-independence ERC President, Josep-Lluís Carod-Rovira, as Catalunya's Vice President. Responsible for Foreign Affairs, he had the foresight to establish a network of overseas Catalan Delegations in Paris, Brussels, New York and Berlin. So why is the subject of Catalan independence so important today? The answer to that question lies in Professor Kathryn Crameri's perceptive analysis – 'Goodbye, Spain?'

The preamble to an Act of Parliament (the *Estatut*) passed by the then Socialist Spanish Government in 2006 acknowledged that Catalans considered Catalunya to be a "Nation". This gave rise to Catalunya's claim to the right to self-determination under the UN Charter and provided a massive impetus to the concept of Catalan independence. The Constitutional Court in Madrid later challenged the *Estatut* on the grounds that it violated Spain's 1978 Constitution, which defined the integrity of Spain, itself ultimately defended by the Spanish Armed Forces. This challenge touched a raw nerve with mainstream Catalunya whose citizens took to the streets in July 2010 behind banners proclaiming "We are a Nation – We decide!" The reasons for the adoption of the campaigning slogan "El Dret de Decidir" – the right of Catalunya to decide its future – are analysed in surgical detail in Professor Crameri's chapters dealing with political parties and pro-independence groups.

From those demonstrations in 2010, the issue of Catalunya's "right to decide" its independence has snowballed. On 11 September 2012, *"La Diada"*, Catalunya's National Day and the anniversary of the day in 1714 when Barcelona was overrun by Spanish Bourbon forces, one and a half million Catalans packed Barcelona's streets waving the *Senyera* and the independent *Estelada* flags calling for independence. Influenced by this massive demonstration, parliamentary elections were brought forward by President Artur Mas. These resulted not in more support for the governing CiU, but in increased support for the pro-independence ERC, a relatively insignificant party ten years ago. This bottom-up drive for Catalan independence has surged from Catalunya's streets and taken the politicians by surprise, in contrast to the top-down call for Scottish independence from the Scottish National Party's leadership.

The forthcoming three hundredth anniversary of *"La Diada"* on 11 September 2014 has assumed huge importance. Emotions are running high and President Artur Mas has called for an independence consultation on 9 November. The right-wing Partido Popular government in Madrid is enraged, pointing to the illegality of such a move under Spain's constitution and its similarities with the illegal and unconstitutional referendum in the Ukraine. The mainstream Socialist PSOE is not thrilled either, and the weak PSC (Catalan Socialist Party) is split. Some senior military officers, whose formative years were under Franco, have made barely concealed threats to use the military's Constitutional obligation to defend Spain's territorial integrity as a pretext for removing the Catalan Government. One member of the armed forces publicly stated that the Fatherland was more important than democracy. Some PP politicians have tacitly supported the military view, pointing to the precedent set by the UK Government in imposing direct rule during the "Troubles" in Northern Ireland. Comments that Catalunya "belongs to Spain" and references to the Catalans as a "tribe" have done little dispel the perception that some in Spain maintain a colonialist attitude towards Catalunya.

Madrid has also been rattled by the progressive use of Catalan at all levels in Catalunya's education system, to the extent that the Spanish language is taught on the same level as English. Catalunya is the only one of Spain's 17 autonomous communities to have set up a government department to "recover the historic memory" of the Spanish Civil War. This policy has inevitably focussed on the actions against Catalunya's population by Franco's forces, and the historically ignored exodus of half a million refugees who fled across the Pyrenees in the winter of January 1939 on the fall of the Spanish Republic. These traumatic events are now commemorated by the moving Exile Museum at La Jonquera on the French Border.

The Catalan Government is currently mounting a sophisticated pro-independence campaign on Catalunya's TV3 Channel, which also televises *Polònia*, a popular political satire. A new lavish exhibition at El Born displays the excavated remains of a swathe of houses destroyed by the Bourbon Spanish in 1717. It chronicles the earlier siege, the retribution against the defending Catalan population and the crushing of Catalunya's democratic institutions, identity and language on Barcelona's capitulation in 1714. The siege added Rafael Casanova to the list of Catalunya's iconic heroes. His statue in Barcelona and burial place in Sant Boi de Llobregat are venerated each 11 September. Professor Crameri describes the relevance of this period in her chapter on Past Heroes and further develops how this homage is exploited in a subsequent chapter covering the media in all its complex aspects. For example, Catalan newspapers such as the pro-independent *Ara* are gaining ground both in print and on the internet. *El Periódico* and *La Vanguardia* now produce both Catalan and Spanish language editions. As always, Barcelona's world-renowned Football Club is a rallying point for all things Catalan. And YouTube is a source of extraordinary Flashmobs and "lipdubs" promoting independence, produced by Catalunya's innovative youth.

However, many questions concerning the real impact of independence go unanswered and are barely debated. Assumptions are made about continued EU membership and use of the Euro. Few people are asking the hard questions about the definition of Catalan citizenship, immigration policy, the division of Spain's debt and national assets, NATO membership, defence forces, coastal and fishery protection, air traffic control, relations with neighbouring France and Catalan-speaking Andorra, the Monarchy, electricity and water supply, the attitudes of large commercial investors such as Volkswagen and BASF, the ability of the Catalan state to back the assets of Catalunya's large banks etc. Some Catalans, preferring to face the future uninfluenced by Catalunya's historical past, feel they cannot voice their pragmatic views and doubts about the wisdom of independence for fear of being shouted down. Cava producers are vulnerable and subject to boycott when anti-Catalan feelings erupt in the rest of Spain. That said, in March 2014 Ferrari and Amazon announced major investments in Catalunya.

There are still many months to go before the November independence consultation, if it takes place. Attitudes are hardening. The Madrid government maintains its refusal to debate Catalunya's "right to decide" its future on the grounds that it violates Spanish law and the Constitution. Faced with such intransigence, President Artur Mas does not rule out a Unilateral Declaration of Independence if the independence consultation is in favour. The scene is set for a clash. An unanswered question remains the extent of support from other EU nations. Perhaps conscious of the Catalan language YouTube "libdubs" made by its own *Estelada-* and *Senyera*-waving Catalan population in Languedoc Roussillon, France has confined itself to saying that the issue of independence is a Spanish internal matter. If Madrid does impose direct rule on Catalunya, other EU countries, while "regretting" an internal coup d'état, may well adopt the same policy.

Professor Crameri's 'Goodbye, Spain?' explores these issues in great depth and marks a milestone in scholarship in Catalunya's long and turbu-

lent history. Whether the title of this book proves to be prophetic remains
to be seen. Perhaps Catalunya will be granted the "right to decide" its future
in 2014, or perhaps this will be denied, though one hopes not through military intervention. But irrespective of the outcome of the forthcoming
consultation, and the subsequent political engagement, the issue of independence is now so ingrained in the contemporary Catalan psyche (and
indeed in its equally strongly felt rejection by parts of mainland Spain) that
its potential could mark and sour internal Spanish politics for decades to
come.

GEOFF COWLING, HM Consul General, Barcelona 2002/2005
March 2014

Author's Preface

This book tackles a very recent, complex and ever-evolving phenomenon: the current rise in support for independence in Catalonia. It focuses on the period from 2005 (when support for independence started to rise during the debates on Catalonia's new Statute of Autonomy) to the end of 2013 (when this book was completed). Whatever may happen after this end point, it is hoped that the analysis of this period will stand as a useful contribution to the academic study of Catalan nationalism.

Given the topical nature of this subject, I am often asked about my own stance on Catalan independence (that is, if my interlocutor has not already jumped to their own conclusion). It therefore seems to me that a statement of my own position might be helpful to the reader at the outset. I believe in the Catalans' democratic right to decide their own territorial relationship with Spain, even though this research project has of course left me with no illusions about the manufactured nature of the discourse of the 'right to decide' itself.

However, I have no strong views on whether Catalonia should or should not be independent; some form of asymmetrical federalism would appear to be the best solution, but unlikely to come to pass. It seems to me that successive Spanish governments have not only failed properly to understand the Catalans, they have failed to make even a meaningful effort to do so. Some relatively minor concessions to Catalonia's sense of nationhood, a true acknowledgement of the Catalan language and culture as part of the rich heritage of the whole of Spain, and active acceptance of Catalans' desires to contribute to Spain's on-going political and economic modernisation could have prevented the escalation of Catalan frustrations that has led to the current situation.

Parts of chapter 4 of this volume were published in an earlier form as 'History Written by the Losers: History, Memory, Myth and Independence in Twenty-First Century Catalonia' (*Hispanic Issues Online*, 11 (2012)) and '"We Need Another Hero": The Construction of Josep Moragues as a Symbol of Independence for Catalonia' (*National Identities*, 13/1 (2011), 51–65 www.tandfonline.com). Initial research for this book was made possible by a travel grant from the Faculty of Arts and Social Sciences and the School of Languages and Cultures of the University of Sydney, and it was completed during a period of research leave generously given by the University of Glasgow.

All quotations originally in Catalan or Spanish are given in English translation, with the originals in footnotes; these translations are my own unless otherwise indicated. Names of institutions and groups are given in full with an English translation the first time they appear, and subsequently they are referred to using an appropriate abbreviation. Some of the books referenced are Kindle editions that have no page numbers, in which case Kindle locations are provided for quotations, with apologies to readers who might struggle to find the quotation in the printed version.

There are many people who have helped me in the long process of researching this book, but I would particularly like to thank Micaela Pattison for her enthusiastic help during her short stint as my research assistant, Marina Vidal for keeping me so well informed of the latest media coverage, and Alan Crameri for his proof-reading and confidence-boosting skills.

List of Abbreviations

All names are given in full, followed by a translation and the relevant abbreviation, the first time they arise.

AMI   *Associació de Municipis per la Independència*
Association of Municipalities for Independence

ANC   *Assemblea Nacional Catalana*
Catalan National Assembly

C's   *Ciutadans – Partido de la Ciudadanía*
Citizens – Party of the Citizenry

CCC   *Convivencia Cívica Catalana*
Catalan Civil Coexistence

CDC   *Convergència Democràtica de Catalunya*
Democratic Convergence of Catalonia

CEO   *Centre d'Estudis d'Opinió*
Centre for Opinion Studies

CiU   *Convergència i Unió*
Convergence and Union

CUP   *Candidatura d'Unitat Popular*
Popular Unity Candidates

ERC   *Esquerra Republicana de Catalunya*
Republican Left of Catalonia

EUiA   *Esquerra Unida i Alternativa*
United and Alternative Left

FE   *Federalistes d'Esquerres*
Left-Wing Federalists

ICV   *Iniciativa Per Catalunya Verds*
Initiative for Catalonia Greens

PP   *Partido Popular*
People's Party

PPC   *Partit Popular Català*
Catalan People's Party

PSC   *Partit dels Socialistes de Catalunya*
Socialist Party of Catalonia

PSOE   *Partido Socialista Obrero Español*
       Spanish Socialist Workers' Party
RI   *Reagrupament Independentista*
       Realignment for Independence
SI   *Solidaritat Catalana per la Independència*
       Catalan Solidarity for Independence
TVC   *Televisió de Catalunya*
       Television of Catalonia
UDC   *Unió Democràtica de Catalunya*
       Democratic Union of Catalonia

Cover Illustrations

FRONT: The demonstration organised by the Catalan National Assembly on 11 September 2012 was designed to constitute an unequivocal call for Catalonia's politicians to work towards independence. The Assembly's president, Carme Forcadell, made it clear before the march that anyone attending would be counted as a supporter of independence, regardless of the slogan or flag they displayed, and an estimated 1.5 million chose to participate on that basis. This suggested that a large segment of the Catalan public was prepared to take the extraordinary risk of moving towards independence even though the party in power had not directly encouraged such a bold step. At a meeting with the Leader of the Catalan Parliament after the march, Forcadell formally requested on behalf of the demonstrators that the parliament begin the process of secession from Spain. *Image from Wikimedia Commons (free media repository), titled "Casa Amatller (Barcelona)", posted 11 September 2012 by Pere prlpz.*

BACK: A motorway toll booth may seem an unlikely symbol of separatist struggle, but in May 2012 the booths on Catalonia's main trunk roads became just that. A campaign entitled 'We don't want to pay' (#novolempagar), organized on Facebook and Twitter and reported by the media, succeeded in causing long tail-backs as motorists politely refused to pay tolls. The campaign was launched on 1 May, with organised convoys of vehicles targeting various key points around the region, some of them bearing the *estelada*, an unofficial variation on the Catalan flag used by pro-independence groups. Subsequently, some motorists refused to pay whenever they used the toll roads and a number of fines were issued as a result. The motive for their refusal was that Catalonia has more toll roads – and Catalans therefore spend more of their money on tolls – than any other region of Spain, including Madrid. But this was not just a protest directed at the Spanish government: it was part of a growing movement calling for independence for Catalonia on the grounds that Catalans would be materially better off if they had their own state. *Image from Wikimedia Commons (free media repository), titled "Manifestació a Girona del No vull pagar, peatge Girona sud", posted 1 May 2012 by Arnaugir.*

Introduction

A motorway toll booth may seem an unlikely symbol of separatist struggle, but in May 2012 the booths on Catalonia's main trunk roads became just that. A campaign entitled 'We don't want to pay' (#novolempagar), organized on Facebook and Twitter and reported by the media, succeeded in causing long tail-backs as motorists politely refused to pay tolls. The campaign was launched on 1 May, with organised convoys of vehicles targeting various key points around the region, some of them bearing the *estelada*, an unofficial variation on the Catalan flag used by pro-independence groups. Subsequently, some motorists refused to pay whenever they used the toll roads and a number of fines were issued as a result. The motive for their refusal was that Catalonia has more toll roads – and Catalans therefore spend more of their money on tolls – than any other region of Spain, including Madrid. But this was not just a protest directed at the Spanish government: it was part of a growing movement calling for independence for Catalonia on the grounds that Catalans would be materially better off if they had their own state. How did something as banal as motorway tolls come to be associated with Catalan independence? Is this really what the recent rise in support for secession boils down to, the money in Catalans' pockets?

If so, this represents a significant shift from the Catalanist perspectives of the late twentieth century, which were mainly articulated around language, culture and identity. Cultural distinctiveness was, of course, used as an argument for political and administrative autonomy, but financial considerations were secondary and more regionalist than nationalist in character (Keating et al., 2003: 55). *Convergència i Unió* (CiU), the hegemonic party in Catalonia from 1980–2003, was very much governed by the philosophy articulated by its leader, Jordi Pujol, in his investiture speech as President of Catalonia's Autonomous Government on 22 April 1980: 'If there is one objective that a Catalan government has to prioritise it is the defence, strengthening and projection of those things that mean that, down the centuries, Catalonia has been Catalonia: its language, its culture, the experience of its history, sentiment and the collective consciousness, the defence of its political rights, the will to be . . . ' (Pujol, 2011: Kindle loc. 164).[1] Pujol's primordialist stance contrasts markedly with the later perspective of a different Catalanist leader, Josep-Lluís Carod-Rovira of *Esquerra Republicana de Catalunya* (ERC), who in 2008 applauded those who have come to desire independence influenced only by 'the pocket and the head, in other words, the desire for a better life' (Carod-Rovira, 2008: 55).[2] To use these extreme opposites as examples represents an oversimplification, of course, but they illustrate the main question: exactly why have Catalans come to support independence in much greater numbers over the last decade?

To date, this question has mainly been tackled by political scientists, on the basis of analyses of voting patterns and the correlation of different types of survey data, and by political theorists through studies of the strains in the constitutional relationship between Spain and Catalonia and the question of sovereignty. These approaches have produced some important contributions, but they need to be complemented by other forms of analysis drawing on the resources of a diverse range of academic disciplines. This is because in order to understand how particular forms of pro-independence discourse have unexpectedly become hegemonic we need also to take into account the cultural and emotional dimensions of the process. This Introduction will examine my reasons for asserting the importance of these dimensions, before giving a brief outline of the structure of the rest of the book.

Rationality, Ethnicity, Instrumentalism

Theorists of secession often treat the phenomenon in terms of a 'cost/benefit' analysis. For example, Viva Ona Bartkus describes secessionist movements as the product of the constant performance of such calculations: the cost of secession vs. the benefit of secession, and the cost of remaining part of the nation-state vs. the benefits of doing so (Bartkus, 1999: 4; see also Sorens, 2005). 'Costs' and 'benefits' might be either tangible (relating to economic well-being or political power), or intangible (for example, the freedom to deploy symbols or use an autochthonous language without interference). Any changes in political circumstances will shift the equation either towards or away from independence as a viable proposition at any given time. However, this does not make a choice between independence and the status quo a simple either/or proposition, since the cost/benefit calculations have different dimensions that – taken together – may give a result that is ambivalent or even conflicting. Furthermore, an actual attempt at secession might only be possible at an 'opportune moment' that might depend on factors beyond the secessionists' control (Bartkus, 1999: 145).

Jason Sorens argues that at the moment of making a decision to support independence the tangible always wins over the intangible: 'Secessionist parties in advanced democracies succeed not because they appeal to a primordial past but because they are able to present independence or wideranging autonomy as beneficial in political and economic terms' (Sorens, 2005: 307). For Sorens, rather than being the driving force behind the desire for independence, ethnic identity and national sentiment are tools that help secessionists to achieve important political and economic goals. His list of common 'risk factors' for secessionism includes perceptions of economic neglect by the state, relative affluence, a significant population, and geographical distance from the centre of power, all of which apply to Catalonia (Sorens, 2005: 309–10, 319–20). These need to be seen in the more general context of recent globalisation, and the increased autonomy offered to many regions by their central government as a response to this (Sorens, 2004).

According to Sorens, a strong sense of group identity is not in itself enough to persuade individuals that they should support independence, no matter what linguistic, cultural and kinship ties the group may enjoy. It appears, then, that even for nationalists, secession is not about the emancipation of an age-old nation, but the creation of a new state that satisfies contemporary needs.

However, this distinction between primordialism and instrumentalism, national sentiment and calculating reason, is too clear-cut and ignores the multiple dimensions of the nation itself. Sorens himself points out that Sardinia meets many of the conditions that could give rise to a strong secessionist movement and yet does not have one, and hypothesises that this is due to the relatively weak position of the Sard language and the lack of a sense of Sardinian national identity (Sorens, 2005: 322). We must therefore be careful to distinguish ethnic identity from national identity, since in most cases national identity has both ethnic and civic components (Smith, 1991: 13). Furthermore, Anthony D. Smith proposes that national identity must work on two different levels, the socio-political and the cultural-psychological (Smith, 1991: 70). Steven J. Mock highlights the tensions that can result from these different demands: 'the nation must be both preserved and invented insofar as, broadly speaking, it is the former that satisfies the cultural-psychological and the latter that addresses the sociopolitical' (Mock, 2012: 44). Mock considers that nationalists' attitudes towards their ethnic past represent neither authenticity (as primordialists would have it) nor invention (as suggested by modernists), but profound ambivalence. On a broader level, national identity as a whole is also underpinned by ambivalence, hence its complexity and capacity for adaptation (Mock, 2012: 280).

Mock's argument is partly based on the dialogue between modernist and ethno-symbolist approaches to nationalism. In a nutshell, the key area of dispute between the two approaches is the extent to which a pre-existing ethnic community, or 'ethnie', genuinely conditions the modern nation, rather than simply providing material that nationalists may draw upon at will for their own purposes. This debate extends specifically to motivations for secession and ethnic violence: is ethnicity inherently and perpetually conflictive?; or is it in fact epiphenomenal, 'a mere "spin" that politicians put on events so as to mask their true motives'? (Hale, 2008: 2, 30–1); or something in between? Mock suggests that the modernist/ethno-symbolist debate is best resolved by side-stepping it: if the members of a nation believe its founding myths and revere its symbols, then it does not matter whether these are invented or not (Mock, 2012: 281–2). Dismissing their beliefs, even after thorough intellectual scrutiny of them, is not going to help us to solve nationalist conflicts. My own opinion is very similar: arguing about the rights and wrongs of Catalan discourses on national identity, or their Spanish counterparts, would not be productive in a study of this kind, nor would focusing purely on their construction. Instead, what is needed at this point is an understanding of the way that long-term discourses about national identity interact with contemporary events and concerns, the ambivalence and anxiety this generates in those who are weighing up Catalonia's possible political futures, and how this might translate into political action.

My argument, then, is that cultural products allow us to explore dimensions of these questions that a purely political focus does not. Literature, film and television will therefore be used here alongside a more politically-orientated discussion of recent events and shifting political discourses. There are primarily two reasons for doing so. Firstly, it allows a deeper understanding of the notion of ambivalence, which is more easily expressed through culture. (Political rhetoric is of course normally used to provide certainties rather than to explore areas of uncertainty.) Secondly, it sheds light on the role of Catalonia's cultural and intellectual elites in generating support for independence. In general terms, nationalist cultural elites in stateless nations tend to play the role of promoters of the national culture, creating a distinctive cultural community that fosters a sense of solidarity, and attempting to mobilise others outside their own circles (Guibernau, 1999: 93–4). In Catalonia, the prominence of elite forms of regionalism/nationalism since the nineteenth century has led to the characterisation of the movement as primarily bourgeois (Balcells, 1996: 23). One major exception to this can be located in the 1930s, when class-based Catalanist struggle supported by various factions on the left of politics briefly became hegemonic before being crushed by the Franco regime (Balcells, 1996: 87–105). As we will see, one of those forces – Catalan republicanism – has also become a lynchpin of the current drive for independence. Moreover, some of the impetus for independence has been taken out of the hands of the political parties altogether, by civil pro-independence groups that cut across party lines. This has led to claims that the struggle for independence in Catalonia is primarily a bottom-up rather than a top-down movement (Guibernau, 2014).

However, this characterisation operates on only one dimension (political parties↔civil society), ignoring the crucial intersecting factor of the activities of the cultural and intellectual elites. It also hides the fact that one of the key elements in their own influence is their close relationship with the pro-independence (or at least 'pro-referendum') sectors of the Catalan print and broadcast media, which is reciprocally beneficial. This book therefore also touches on issues related to what Manuel Castells calls 'communication power', one aspect of which is 'how social movements and agents of political change proceed in our society through the reprogramming of communication networks, so becoming able to convey messages that introduce new values to the minds of people and inspire hope for political change' (Castells, 2009: 8). The multidimensionality of these power networks and 'the rise of the interactive production of meaning' problematise the very idea of 'top-down' and 'bottom-up' movements, suggesting that instead of trying to fit our analysis into such a one-dimensional model we should be alert to the indicators of complexity: unpredictability, instability and 'butterfly effects' (Castells, 2009: 132; Urry, 2005: 237). On one hand, this very complexity must surely account for some of the dynamism of the pro-independence movement. On the other, we also need to be alert to the emotional impact of such unpredictability, including the potential effects on political behaviour of the uncertainty and anxiety it produces in the general public.

Emotion, Affect, Anxiety

Jaume Lorés describes the general sense of Catalanism that existed after the Franco regime as 'non-specific, but very heartfelt' (Lorés, 1985: 60).[3] This lack of specificity was not surprising given that political expressions of Catalanism had been banned for several decades, while cultural expressions were severely limited in their scope because of restrictions on the public use and institutional promotion of the Catalan language. Jordi Pujol managed effectively to fill this void after 1980 with his particular vision of a Catalan nation that was inclusive but at the same time based on inherited cultural characteristics. One of his party's key achievements was to shift Catalans' perceptions so that the majority began to think of Catalonia as a nation rather than a region.[4] Nevertheless, this was accompanied by the establishment of a regional bureaucracy that crystallised institutional Catalanism into a form that may have been more specific but was not so conducive to nationalist sentiment (Crameri, 2000). This led some commentators to complain that people were becoming 'tired' of Catalanism, which therefore needed to reinvent itself (Strubell i Trueta, 1997). On the other hand, more recent events have stimulated forms of what Michael Billig calls 'hot nationalism' (Billig, 1995). Emotion – or 'passion' – is a vital component of hot nationalism (Billig, 1995: 44), and this is certainly true of the recent rise in support for independence in Catalonia, where for many people their commitment to the nation has once more become 'heartfelt'.

Academic interest in the role of the emotions in social and political life has increased substantially in recent years and produced a number of significant publications (e.g. Ahmed, 2004; Neuman et al., 2007a; Nussbaum, 2013). Two strands emerge from this work that are of interest for the present discussion, one related to the role of what we might call 'collective' emotions, and another related to affect. The term 'collective' is of course misleading, since as Sara Ahmed puts it, 'shared feelings are not about feeling the same feeling' (Ahmed, 2004: 11). The idea of a shared national sentiment is actually a product of 'collective misrecognition', because this sentiment becomes reified – or 'fetishised'– through a discourse that negates the conditions of its production and circulation (Bourdieu, 1991: 153; Ahmed, 2004: 11). This means that if we ask nationalists about the emotions that motivate them to act on behalf of the nation, they will not possess the required level of self-consciousness to step outside this discursive construct, and will instead use the question as an opportunity for self-justification (Barbalet, 2001: 67). Unless we are specifically interested in examining these self-justifications, therefore, it is more productive to analyse the ways in which 'emotions become attributes of collectives, which get constructed as "being" through "feeling"' (Ahmed, 2004: 2).

In this way, the study of discourses related to collective emotions can provide a useful perspective on the role of nationalist sentiment in the current rise in support for independence in Catalonia; an examination of the role of affect provides another. The term itself is only slightly less problematic than 'collective emotion', since it has various definitions that derive from different theoretical approaches and posit different distinctions between affect, feeling and emotion (6 et al., 2007: 5–6). Nevertheless,

Neuman et al. are able to give a relatively straightforward definition that underpins the work presented in their edited volume on the role of affect in political thought and behaviour: '*Affect* is the evolved cognitive and physiological response to the detection of personal significance' (Neuman et al., 2007b: 9). Despite the fact that affect is therefore a phenomenon firmly located in the individual, it is quite possible that a particular object or event will provoke similar responses in a very large number of people, thereby making it possible to speak of affect as something that reveals common patterns (Marquis, 2012: 427). Indeed, Ahmed draws attention to the fact that affect accumulates around an object or sign specifically as the result of circulation (Ahmed, 2004: 45). Affect therefore has a collective structural dimension that is inherently dynamic, and this too can be studied in relation to the influence of affect on the areas of political decision-making that involve questions of national sentiment.

In *Communication Power*, Manuel Castells picks up on one particular aspect of the recent work on affect: affective intelligence theory (Castells, 2009: 146–50; Cassino and Lodge, 2007). He describes its importance for an understanding of the link between reason and emotion in political decision-making:

> The theory of affective intelligence provides a useful analytical framework that inspires a diversified body of evidence in political communication and political psychology supporting the notion that emotional appeals and rational choices are complementary mechanisms whose interaction and relative weight in the process of decision-making depend on the context of the process. (Castells, 2009: 146)

The crux of the theory is that an individual's judgement is conditioned by pre-existing affective dispositions (Cassino and Lodge, 2007: 101). Positive or negative affective responses to particular stimuli then produce 'affective tags' which attach to the object in question. These act as shortcuts, conditioning subsequent responses to comparable stimuli (102–4). This process has an effect on our political decision-making because it 'tends to alter the processing strategy of the individual to ensure a certain outcome, generally the maintenance of the current affect' (105). In contrast, individuals who feel anxious about a particular issue and have no strong affective predisposition to guide their thinking look more closely at the contextual information available to them before reaching a judgement (ibid). The conscious exercise of rationality therefore tends to be reserved for unexpected or uncertain situations (Mackuen et al., 2007: 127).

Castells also highlights research that indicates that the relationship between material interests and political choices is nowhere near as straight-forward as might be supposed (Castells, 2009: 153–4). In fact, he states quite categorically that 'values shape citizens' decisions more often than their [material] interests do' (Castells, 2009: 154). Even in extreme situations such as an economic crisis, when material interests become more salient, voting behaviour will tend to reflect emotional rather than rational responses to the crisis (ibid). This has two important implications for our analysis of Catalonia: it calls into question some of the more instrumentalist interpretations of recent developments, while at the same time inviting us to look at what might produce the emotional responses that steer Catalans' reactions to messages about the desirability of independence.

This book will therefore examine elements that help to constitute the on-going construction of national sentiment and how they relate to more transient questions about the costs and benefits of independence. In other words, I am interested in how the symbolic interacts with the pragmatic. Brubaker and Cooper's distinction between categories of practice (used by 'lay' people implicated in the practice itself) and categories of analysis (used by theorists) is helpful here (Brubaker and Cooper, 2000). They warn that theorists should avoid 'uncritically adopting categories of practice as cate-gories of analysis' (Brubaker and Cooper, 2000: 5). Since concepts such as 'identity', 'ethnicity' and 'nation' fall into both camps, it is easy to fall into the trap of reproducing the way that they are reified by those who employ them to signal something fundamental about their everyday experience (Brubaker and Cooper, 2000: 4–5). To avoid this,

> We should seek to explain the processes and mechanisms through which what has been called the 'political fiction' of the 'nation' – or of the 'eth-nic group,' 'race,' or other putative 'identity' – can crystallize, at certain moments, as a powerful, compelling reality. (Brubaker and Cooper, 2000: 5)

My aim is therefore to analyse how the categories of practice employed by Catalan nationalism have shifted over a defined period of time, high-lighting the complexities and disjunctions revealed by these shifts. On one hand, mainstream Catalanism is moving towards a discourse based around what we might call 'the right to be materialist', centred on demands for the democratic recognition of what the majority of Catalans want even if this happens to be primarily motivated by a desire for material benefits. On the other hand, many of the specific manifestations of this discourse reveal a continuing attachment to the traditional symbols of nationalism, most of which are derived from conceptions of the nation as an ethnic group. These contradictory factors give rise to tensions when the hegemonic Catalanist discourse of inclusivity and voluntary identification with the nation clashes with symbols whose origins in primordialist conceptions of the nation have largely been erased by the discourse itself. Whenever this erasure comes to light (as it frequently does during debates between proponents and opponents of independence), this gives rise to questions about its positive or negative effects. Is it a necessary step for the creation of an inclusive and cohesive community, or a way of disguising the imposition of a particular concept of Catalonia on any residents who do not share it? The components of identity normally associated with ethnicity therefore have the potential to act as both an integrating and disintegrating force in the current context of Catalonia.

The discussion in this volume therefore focuses on three main questions, all of which are interrelated: (1) to what extent is the current secession movement in Catalonia driven by instrumentalism and opportunistic cost/benefit calculations?; (2) what is the role of nationalist sentiment, public emotion and affect in producing active support for independence?; and 3) what is the role played by cultural and intellectual elites in stimulating public support for the political project of independence? These questions partly arise out of the movement's own self-characterisation as one which is civic in nature, inclusive, profoundly democratic, not primarily motivated by questions of identity, and largely driven by the will of the people (in other words, 'bottom-up'). Indeed, one of the aims of this book is to demonstrate how this narrative has been constructed. However, if we are fully to understand recent events in Catalonia we also need to examine the contradictions and gaps that are papered over by this narrative.

As has already been noted, some of these contradictions provide obvious points of attack for opponents of Catalan independence. Thus Catalans are accused of instrumentalism (in the form of the manipulation of nationalist values by political elites in order to gain power and material advantage) and ethnic particularism (through the 'imposition' of the Catalan language and culture, and of a nationalist discourse that silences other voices). Such attacks have become increasingly blunt and virulent, especially in certain sections of the Spanish right-wing media, which have gone as far as equating Catalanism with totalitarianism (e.g. Anonymous, 2013a) – a charge that has been circulating widely in inflammatory comments posted by individuals on the web and social media. Reasoned opposition to the idea that Catalans have the right to choose independence is increasingly being displaced by insults and exaggerations. Although not analysed in detail in this book, this anti-Catalanism needs to be borne in mind because of the widening gap it produces between Catalans' self-image and public image, and the complex ways in which this process stimulates shifts in identity and identification (Guibernau, 2013: 16–17; Maalouf, 2000: 11–13).

According to Richard Jenkins, even though a group's self-image and public image do not bear any necessary relation to one another, there will always be at least some kind of interaction between the two: 'some process of conscious or unconscious adjustment in the ongoing making and re-making of social identity' (Jenkins, 1997: 59). Furthermore, the ethnic categorisations that lie at the heart of this process not only lead to stereotyping in everyday discourse, they also become institutionalised (Jenkins, 1997: 61). This is why, as Rogers Brubaker puts it, 'Categorization and classification in [. . .] formal and informal settings are increasingly seen as not only central to but as *constitutive* of ethnicity, race and nationhood' (Brubaker, 2009: 32–33). Naturally, Catalans have always tended to construct their national identity by categorising themselves as different from other Spaniards. What is less often acknowledged is that Spaniards also constitute their national identity with reference to their differences with the Catalans (Muro and Quiroga, 2004). This process is necessarily ambivalent, in the sense that much Spanish nationalist rhetoric is based on a denial that there are any substantial differences, in order to argue that Catalans should accept that they are fundamentally Spanish and stop pushing for cultural and political recognition as a separate group. Nevertheless, the process by which Catalans are categorised by other Spaniards is constitutive of both Catalan and Spanish identities.

Henry E. Hale extends the idea of categorisation in order to give a new twist to arguments about the role of ethnicity, by proposing a conceptual separation of ethnicity and ethnic politics. Like Sorens, he believes ethnicity is not a sufficient motivation for secession, but rather than seeing it simply as a tool to be drawn upon at will by ethnopolitical entrepreneurs, he posits that it does have a conditioning effect, although not in the way defended by ethno-symbolists. Instead, he views ethnicity as 'a mechanism for uncertainty reduction' that is needed because uncertainty has negative emotional consequences (Hale, 2008: 62). He also suggests that it provides a way of interpreting the world that precedes conscious thought and action (48). This is because ethnicity becomes a 'category-based rule of thumb', producing automatic responses in a similar way to affective tagging, as described above (although Hale suggests that schemata based on ethnicity precede both emotion and cognition and would therefore condition the tagging process itself) (48). Ethnicity therefore also 'precedes the politics of interest, helping make the pursuit of interest possible' (33), and it is this 'pursuit of interest' that we see played out within ethnic politics. In turn, the conflict that this generates is a result of the desire for uncertainty reduction, since the ethnic divides that are solidified by categorisation 'make it both easier for those in a region to act together and also more difficult for them to trust the centre' (Breuilly et al., 2011: 682).

Hale's theory has several aspects that have the potential to illuminate recent events in Catalonia, including his insistence that the passion often displayed by separatists springs from their recognition that independence could give them a materially better life, thus linking rather than separating the emotional and the economic (Hale, 2008: 85). However, before making use of his view of ethnicity, specifically, we first need to ask whether ethnicity actually provides a good 'rule-of-thumb' for Catalans. The hegemonic Catalanist discourse of the post-Franco era has always disavowed ethnicity as the basis of belonging. While this discourse might obscure problems encountered by foreign immigrants, for example, we should not jump to the conclusion that Catalans hypocritically pay lip service to civic nationalism while secretly retaining ethnically-based beliefs.[5] In fact, Catalan ethnicity is relatively 'thin', in the sense that it 'organizes relatively little of social life and action' (Cornell and Hartmann, 1998: 73–4), especially now that Catalonia is so ethnically diverse. Hale, on the other hand, specifically bases his theory on situations where there are thick ethnic divides. However, he also points out the importance of territory, saying that ethnicity plays a significant role in reducing 'uncertainties based on territorial relationships and the distribution of goods that are important for people's life chances' (Hale, 2008: 78). If, as is the case in Catalonia, ethnicity would be a problematic 'rule of thumb' for many because of its thinness, then perhaps territory itself can become a kind of 'post-ethnic' substitute. Indeed, Michael Keating describes territory as one of 'two structuring features of nationality claims' (identity being the other), and argues that in recent years 'territory has become *more* important as a basis for political legitimacy' (Keating, 2001: 16; my emphasis). There are also echoes of this in the way that the boundaries of the Autonomous Community of Catalonia have become the accepted limits of the independence movement despite their arbitrary nature and the resulting exclusion of some who would wish to be included (i.e. a minority of the residents of contiguous Catalan-speaking areas).

Territory can only operate as a substitute mechanism for uncertainty reduction if it is accompanied by some sense of group identity, because otherwise it could not generate the necessary trust. However, Montserrat Guibernau argues that people are surprisingly willing to trust others with whom they feel they have something in common, making it relatively easy to engage a group of disparate individuals in a common project – through social networking, for example (Guibernau, 2013: 103). Indeed the idea of Catalonia as a project was a mainstay of Pujol's discourse (Pujol, 2012a: Kindle loc. 1351). Other aspects of ethnic identity might then find their own substitutes in mechanisms that connect people within a certain territory and rely on processes of identification and 'belonging by choice', rather than identity (Guibernau, 2013: 26–49). Nevertheless, the residual lure of ethnicity remains strong, which brings us back to the profound ambivalence of nationalist movements described by Steven Mock.

In order to explore different dimensions of this ambivalence, this book is broadly structured around an argument that moves from a primarily political to a primarily cultural focus. **Chapter 1** provides necessary background information on the political parties and civil groups that have been active in the independence debate since 2005. It is mainly designed for readers who may not already be familiar with the Catalan context, but also includes a discussion of the importance of the internet and social media in permitting civil society to play such a dynamic role in the pro-independence movement. **Chapter 2** takes the form of an analysis of key events from 2005–2013 that either have changed the focus of the debate or appear to have motivated more Catalans to support independence. **Chapter 3** looks at the way certain elements of the political discourse around independence have shifted and crystallised over the same period. Both of these chapters also delve further into subjects presented in this Introduction: instrumentalism; identity and identification; anti-Catalanism; and the interface between rational and emotional reasons for supporting independence.

The next three chapters focus on particular cultural phenomena that demonstrate the role of Catalan cultural and intellectual elites in engaging public support for independence. **Chapter 4** looks at the use that is being made of Catalonia's past, focussing on the events associated with the loss of Catalonia's autonomous institutions as a result of the War of Succession. 2014 is the three-hundredth anniversary of the end of the war after the siege of Barcelona, and messages about the deeds of its heroes form a potent rallying-cry inviting Catalans to fight for the creation of a twenty-first century Catalan state. **Chapter 5** examines the role of television in engaging the public in current debates on independence, both through presenting rational arguments and by stimulating particular affective responses. Finally, **Chapter 6** examines a group of novels that imagine a future Catalan state in an attempt to reassure the reader that such a thing is both possible and desirable. The differences and similarities in their approach further illustrate the ambivalence generated when relating a nation's past identity to hopes for a renewed future.

Chapter 1

Political Parties and Civil Pro-Independence Groups

Until very recently, the vast majority of Catalan nationalists have tended not to espouse separatist views (Conversi, 1997: 259–60). However, from as early as the end of the nineteenth century there have been identifiable but small groups of Catalans who did hope for independence (Llorens Vila, 2005; Rubiralta i Casas, 2004). Jordi Llorens Vila describes these groups as manifesting an emotional rather than a rational form of separatism, which coexisted with the development of Catalan autonomism and federalism but was unable to form itself into any kind of alternative political project (Llorens Vila, 2005). In terms of properly organised separatist groups, the first of any real political significance was *Estat Català* (Catalan State), founded in 1922 by Francesc Macià (Rubiralta i Casas, 2004: 11). During the political turmoil of the 1930s, which saw the brief existence of the Spanish Second Republic, two different declarations of Catalan sovereignty within a federalist framework were made. First, Macià (at that point the leader of ERC) took advantage of his party's win in the 1931 local elections to declare Catalonia a Free Republic which he hoped would become part of a Spanish confederation. However, once the Second Republic was established, Macià was forced to settle for autonomy. In 1934, his successor as President of Catalonia's Autonomous Government – Lluís Companys – responded to the victory of right-wing forces in the Spanish elections by declaring Catalonia a State within the Federal Republic of Spain, which led to his imprisonment and the suspension of Catalonia's autonomy.

During the Franco dictatorship (1939–75), Catalan nationalism was politically fragmented even though it was united in its opposition to the regime (Guibernau, 2004: 50–69). In the early years of the dictatorship, the *Front Nacional de Catalunya* (National Front of Catalonia) was formed in order to combine resistance to the Franco regime with a clear pro-independence agenda, but it was unable to achieve its goal of uniting all of Catalonia's separatist forces against the regime (Díaz i Esculíes, 2005). In the early 1970s, Catalan separatism regrouped itself around the recently-founded *Partit Socialista d'Alliberament Nacional* (Socialist Party for National Liberation) (Rubiralta i Casas, 2004: 133–4). It was also at this time that a small number of separatists decided to turn to armed struggle, beginning a phase of minor terrorist activity that was to continue until 1995 (Pagès i Blanch, 2005).

Any semblance of unity between pro-independence groups forged in the last days of the Franco regime did not last long, and fragmentation has been a perpetual characteristic of Catalan separatism up to the present day. Autonomy and federalism were therefore the main strands to emerge from the Catalanist movements of the new democratic period (post-1975), and the dominant forms of Catalanism have been the non-separatist varieties represented by the *Partit dels Socialistes de Catalunya* (Socialist Party of Catalonia – PSC), and CiU under their first leader Jordi Pujol. This dominance is now being challenged by increased support for ERC, which has come to play an important role in both the *Generalitat* (Autonomous Government) and local politics. Furthermore, parts of CiU itself have now moved towards support for independence, while a fluctuating collection of minor separatist parties have been joined by civil groups in an increasingly broad spectrum of pro-independence organisations. This chapter will look in detail at these developments, providing necessary background information for the discussions to follow.

To begin with, however, it is worth putting this discussion into context by looking at some of the available statistics on the evolution of support for independence since 2005. The main source here is a series of statistical reports published by the *Generalitat de Catalunya* itself through its *Centre d'Estudis d'Opinió* (Centre for Opinion Studies – CEO), created in 2005. Previous statistics collected by other bodies such as the *Institut de Ciències Polítiques i Socials* (Institute for Political and Social Sciences) show that there was a rise in support for independence towards the end of José María Aznar's presidency of the Spanish government (1996–2004), which fell again with the change of government in 2004 (Belzunces, 2008: 3). By 2005, figures were comparable to what they had been during the 1990s.

Initially, the CEO asked respondents to select between a range of different options for their preferred model of Catalonia's relationship with Spain. This included options ranging from 'Region' (i.e. with fewer powers than Catalonia currently holds), through 'Autonomous Community' and 'Federal State' to 'Independence'. From a base of 13.6% in June 2005, support for independence had risen to a massive 47% by 2013 (Centre d'Estudis d'Opinió, 2005: 15; Centre d'Estudis d'Opinió, 2013a: 28). Meanwhile, support for federal options had fallen from 31% to 21%, and

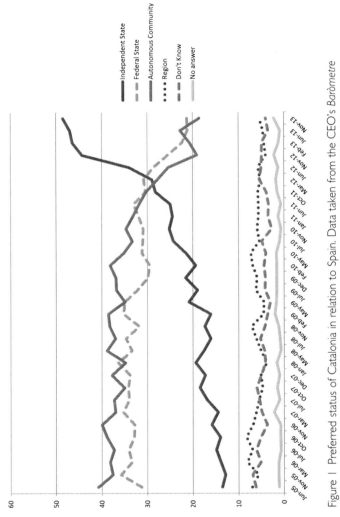

Figure 1 Preferred status of Catalonia in relation to Spain. Data taken from the CEO's *Baròmetre d'opinió política* ('Barometer of Political Opinion'). (Generalitat de Catalunya, 2005–13)

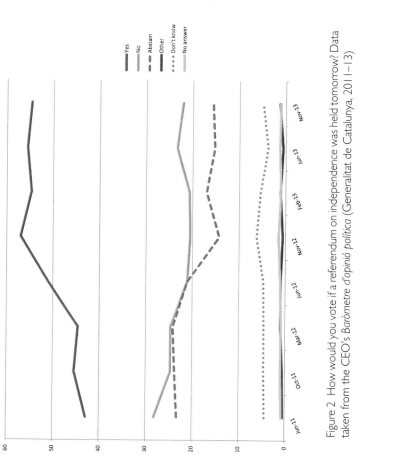

Figure 2 How would you vote if a referendum on independence was held tomorrow? Data taken from the CEO's *Baròmetre d'opinió política* (Generalitat de Catalunya, 2011–13)

for the status quo as an Autonomous Community from 41% to 23%. Despite some minor fluctuations, these trends are clearly present throughout the thirty iterations of the survey, with the most significant leaps in support for independence coming between March and November 2012 (see Figure 1).

In 2011, the CEO introduced a new question to complement this existing one, asking how respondents would vote if a referendum on independence were held tomorrow. The decision to include this question in a government-sponsored report is significant in its own right. The first time it was asked, 43% said they would vote in favour, with 28% against and another 23% saying they would not vote (Centre d'Estudis d'Opinió, 2011: 28). By 2013, the percentages had risen to nearly 56% in favour, with only 23% against and 15% of abstentions (see Figure 2) (Centre d'Estudis d'Opinió, 2013a: 28). To put this in context, in mid-2013 support for Scottish independence was standing at 37% with those against totalling 46%.[1] When asked why they would vote for independence, the most popular reasons given in 2013 were wanting Catalonia to have control of its own resources, and because Catalonia would be generally better off, followed by the feeling that the rest of Spain did not understand Catalonia (Centre d'Estudis d'Opinió, 2013b: 24). Those who would vote against were most concerned with preserving the unity of Spain and their own dual identity.

It is always assumed that there is a high degree of correlation between having been born in Catalonia and having Catalan parents, on one hand, and supporting radical nationalist options on the other. This is true to some extent: Ivan Serrano's study of CEO data from 2011 shows those who identify themselves as solely Catalan or more Catalan than Spanish are definitely more likely to think that Catalonia should be an independent country (Serrano, 2013a: 526). However, Serrano's analysis also proves that regarding oneself as solely Spanish or more Spanish than Catalan does not automatically exclude independence as the preferred option, with small numbers in each of these groups saying that they would vote 'yes' in a referendum (Serrano, 2013a: 526–7). Similarly, among recent arrivals to Catalonia of any origin, 19% supported independence, as did nearly 25% of first-generation Catalans (Serrano, 2013a: 530). As we will see, this also affects the distribution of support for independence among political parties, which is spread more broadly than the parties' main constituencies might suggest.

Political Parties since 1980

Convergència i Unió

CiU was initially a coalition of two parties: *Convergència Democràtica de Catalunya* (Democratic Convergence of Catalonia – CDC) founded by Jordi Pujol in 1974, and *Unió Democràtica de Catalunya* (Democratic Union of Catalonia – UDC), which has a much longer history, dating back to 1931. The parties federated in 2001 but retain distinct characteristics. CiU has either been in power or in opposition in the *Generalitat* since its full re-establishment in 1980, and has been an important force in local politics. It has also consistently won a small but significant number of seats in the Spanish parliament. Its two most influential leaders have been Jordi Pujol and Artur Mas, both of whom have been Presidents of the *Generalitat* (Pujol from 1980–2003 and Artur Mas from 2010 to the present). Both men came from CDC – the more influential partner – although UDC's leader Josep Antoni Duran i Lleida is the federation's Secretary General and spokesperson for the Catalan Group in the Spanish parliament.

It is perhaps helpful to divide CiU's attitude to self-determination into three periods: Pujol's presidency of the *Generalitat* (1980–2003), Artur Mas's leadership in opposition (2003–10), and Mas's presidency (December 2010-present). Pujol had always made it clear that neither he nor the party he founded had any kind of separatist agenda. Instead, his aim was to gain the kind of autonomy that would allow him and his fellow Catalans to 'live fully' as Catalans, a desire that he did not see as incompatible with maintaining a dual Spanish identity (Pujol 2012a: Kindle loc. 3835). As a result, Pujol concentrated on winning gains to Catalonia's autonomy whenever the climate was right for him to do so – for example, when CiU's votes in the Spanish parliament were needed by the party in power. This led to his party's approach being described as 'peix al cove' or 'pragmatic possibilism' (Dowling, 2013: 135).[2] There is no doubt that this did strengthen Catalonia's autonomy, but it left both Catalonia and CiU at the mercy of political machinations beyond their control.

When Pujol decided not to stand for re-election in 2003, he hoped to ensure a smooth transition, grooming Artur Mas well in advance as his successor. However, CiU's reputation at that point had been damaged by its 'pact of convenience' with the Spanish ruling party the *Partido Popular* (People's Party – PP), which was cultivating an increasingly strong Spanish nationalist discourse at that time (Dowling, 2009: 188). Mas's rival for the presidency was Pasqual Maragall of the PSC. Maragall was the popular former Mayor of Barcelona who had narrowly failed to defeat Pujol in 1999, winning more votes but fewer seats (Giordano and Roller, 2002: 102). In the event, this pattern repeated itself in 2003, but with a controversial outcome (Madí, 2007): a three-way coalition cobbled together by the PSC saw Maragall installed as President at the head of a 'tripartite' left-wing government.

This meant a (not entirely unexpected) period in opposition for CiU, during which Mas would need to establish his authority within the party as well as improving his public image (Madí, 2007: 41, 44, 58). In order to do this, he stuck broadly to the route that had been mapped by Pujol while at the same time developing his own specific pathways: for example, by supporting the idea of a new Statute of Autonomy for Catalonia that Pujol had formerly rejected (Lo Cascio, 2008: 329; Mas, 2003: 125–31; Pujol, 2012a: Kindle loc. 1254). Mas played a pivotal role in negotiations on the Statute despite CiU being in opposition at the time. He also devised his own political programme and ideology, based on what he termed 'la Casa Gran del Catalanisme', or 'the Big House of Catalanism', an attempt to lead the construction of a consensus based on CDC's understanding of Catalanism that would appeal to all residents of Catalonia, whatever their origins. Most importantly, this was accompanied by statements supporting the right of Catalans to decide their own political future (Mas, 2007).

Nevertheless, Mas's move towards a sovereigntist position lagged well behind the views of some other members of CDC. Its youth wing *Joventut Nacionalista de Catalunya* (Nationalist Youth of Catalonia) had long been more inclined to independence, and some of the former members of this organisation who were now coming up through the ranks of CDC refused to sacrifice their earlier aspirations. Other rising stars of the party were also open about their support for secession, including one of Jordi Pujol's sons, Oriol Pujol. However, UDC retained its preference for a confederal solution, and Duran i Lleida found himself increasingly trying to put the brakes on Mas's drift towards an independent Catalonia. In 2010, CiU were finally able to reclaim power in the *Generalitat*. The events surrounding CiU's return to power and its re-election in 2012 will be examined in chapter 2, while the shift in CiU's position on independence between 2005 and 2013 will be further analysed in chapter 3.

Esquerra Republicana de Catalunya

ERC was born in 1931 out of a merger of left-wing forces that included Macià's *Estat Català*. Macià himself was its first leader, and – as has already been noted – it achieved resounding success in the local elections in the very year of its formation. Both Macià and his successor Lluís Companys played pivotal roles during the period of Catalonia's autonomy under the Second Republic, although as we have seen their attempts to engineer the creation of a confederal Spain were unsuccessful. Companys himself was forced into exile towards the end of the Civil War, only to be arrested by the Nazis at Spain's request and sent to Madrid to face a firing squad. Surviving as best it could during the Franco regime, ERC was one of the clandestine political parties that worked to ensure autonomy for Catalonia was part of the political agenda for the restoration of democracy. However, its gains in the first years of democratic elections were disappointing given its hegemonic position in Catalan nationalism in the 1930s, and it did not appear able to broaden its appeal.

According to Klaus-Jürgen Nagel, this was partly because of the party's inability properly to distinguish itself from CiU, one cause of which was its 'disorientation' on the question of independence (Nagel, 2010: 136). Without a clearly-articulated stance, ERC existed in a grey area between its traditional confederal position and demands for reform of the system of autonomy, while neither ruling out nor committing to the possibility of independence (ibid.). This changed in 1987 when new faces Àngel Colom and Josep-Lluís Carod-Rovira attempted to galvanise the party into adopting independence as one of its core aims. By 1991, under the leadership of Colom, ERC had declared itself independentist, becoming the principal institutional representative of this form of Catalan nationalism (Rubiralta i Casas, 2004: 203). However, the internal frictions continued, with Colom leaving in 1996 to form his own, unsuccessful independence party (Dowling, 2013: 134). He was succeeded as General Secretary by Carod-Rovira, who remained the party's major figure until 2008.

ERC certainly has solid credentials as an independentist party, and as we will see in chapters 2 and 3, Carod-Rovira has been crucial in projecting an attractively calm, inclusive and rational vision of Catalan separatism. However, the party has endured numerous electoral ups and downs as well as coping with internal dissent. Gaining institutional power as part of the 'tripartite' coalition governments of 2003–10 proved both a blessing and a curse, spelling the end of Carod-Rovira's association with the party and a hunt for a new leader. This mantle passed briefly to Joan Puigcercós, before settling on Oriol Junqueras in 2011. Wary of repeating the experience of the *tripartit,* Junqueras refused an offer of a coalition with Mas after the 2012 elections, preferring to remain in opposition while supporting (and galvanising) Mas's push for a referendum on independence.

Partit dels Socialistes de Catalunya

The PSC was officially created in 1978, but draws on a much longer tradition of Catalan and Spanish socialism. In Spanish elections it is federated with the *Partido Socialista Obrero Español* (Spanish Socialist Workers' Party – PSOE), and shares its basic social-democratic approach. However, the two have traditionally differed substantially in their views on the organisation of the Spanish state (Roller and Van Houten, 2003: 13–14). The PSC favours a federal Spain that would allow for the recognition of Catalonia's differences and the consolidation of its self-government. On the other hand, until very recently the PSOE had shown no genuine enthusiasm for federalism, although it was of course instrumental in creating the current shape of the State of Autonomies while in power in Madrid from 1982–1996 and 2004-2011.

The PSC has normally performed much better in Spanish general elections and local elections than at the level of the Autonomous Community (Dowling, 2013: 132–3). Even when it managed to lead the *Generalitat* from 2003–10 this was only achieved in a three-way coalition. The party is mainly perceived as appealing to those whose family origins lie outside Catalonia and therefore have dual identities, to Catalans who 'believe that federalism *per se* is a superior political orientation' (Lluch, 2012: 452), and to those who put class issues before matters of identity. However, by 2013 a significant number of PSC voters – 22% – were prepared to vote 'yes' in a referendum on independence (Centre d'Estudis d'Opinió, 2013a: 37). Moreover, a federal Spain was not the preferred option of PSC voters, with 40% instead preferring some form of autonomy, only 34.5% opting for federalism, and nearly 15% seeing independence as the best solution (Centre d'Estudis d'Opinió, 2013a: 35).

This split has also become apparent within the party's leadership, and in the PSC's relationship with the PSOE. As we will see in chapter 3, pessimism about the real possibilities of Spain adopting a federal framework has grown markedly in recent years, to the point where many commentators now dismiss the idea as not even worth considering. Nevertheless, the PSC affirmed its commitment to federalism by the selection of Pere Navarro as its candidate for the Presidency of the *Generalitat* in the 2010 elections. The elections themselves were a disaster for the PSC, which won only 18% of the vote. In 2012 this percentage fell even further, to 14%, adding to the ignominy of having lost power in Barcelona's City Council in 2011 for the first time in the democratic era.

The party's official opposition to independence has not deterred many of the town councils under its control from joining the *Associació de Municipis per la Independència* (Association of Municipalities for Independence – AMI), an umbrella group whose aim is to coordinate the struggle for independence at the level of local government. The PSC has also expressed qualified support for Catalonia's 'right to decide', a move which led it into direct conflict with the PSOE in February 2013, when 13 of the PSC's 14 members of the Spanish parliament voted in favour of motions on this issue presented by other Catalan parties, defying the PSOE's instructions to vote against them. These internal splits and the seriousness of the situation in Catalonia have finally led the PSOE to make a more serious commitment to federalism. A statement released by the party in July 2013 criticised the re-centralising tendencies of Spain's *Partido Popular*, laid out the issues with the current system of autonomy, called for a reform of Spain's constitution, and declared that 'federalism should be the definitive model for our territorial organisation' (Consejo Territorial, 2013: 7).[3] It is too early to tell whether this will breathe new life into the federalist project, or convince those members of the PSC who have already moved towards other positions (causing divisions not just with the PSOE but within the PSC itself). More will be said in chapters 2 and 3 about the PSC's actions during the era of the *tripartit* and the PSOE's role in limiting the reform of Catalonia's Statute of Autonomy, but the main point to note here is that up to now PSC-PSOE has been incapable of providing a credible federalist alternative.

Partido Popular

The PP positions itself as a centre-right party and has a clear commitment to the territorial unity of Spain based on the provisions for this in Spain's Constitution of 1978 (Balfour and Quiroga, 2007: 114–17). Its branch in Catalonia is now known as the *Partit Popular Català* (Catalan People's Party – PPC), and was formed at the same time as the main party in 1989 following a change from the previous name of *Alianza Popular* (People's Alliance). The PP has generally resisted giving any further autonomy to the regions, although it was forced to make some concessions in the late 1990s to ensure CiU's support in the Spanish parliament. Its former leader José María Aznar (Prime Minister of Spain from 1996–2004) is an outspoken critic of Spain's peripheral nationalisms, as is its current leader, and Spanish Prime Minister since 2011, Mariano Rajoy. Given this pedigree, it is unsurprising that the PPC is a minority force in Catalonia, generally winning between 9 and 13 per cent of the votes in elections to the *Generalitat* and holding power in only a handful of local councils. Nor does the PP make up for this in Spanish general elections: in 2011, it enjoyed a landslide victory in the rest of Spain but three of Catalonia's four provinces voted CiU while the fourth – Barcelona – voted PSC-PSOE. The resulting electoral map shows a quite dramatic split in political preferences between Catalonia and the rest of Spain, reminiscent of the Labour/Conservative division between Scotland and England during the Thatcher era.

The PPC treads a difficult line between the PP's centralism and an acknowledgement of some of Catalonia's cultural, social and economic differences. Nevertheless, it is a staunch critic of Catalonia's linguistic immersion policies in education and an advocate for the rights of Spanish speakers in Catalonia. Its leader since 2008 is Alicia Sánchez Camacho, now one of the most recognisable female figures in Catalan politics. Her influence is greater than the PPC's share of the votes might suggest, partly because of the PP's importance in Spain as a whole, and partly because she has a high media profile: she is both an easy target for criticism and a reliable source of controversial comment.

Nevertheless, the PPC's support for Spanish unity has been much less of a factor in the independence debate than the effect of the PP's actions in Madrid. As we will see later, it was the PP that initiated the most comprehensive of the legal challenges to the new Statute of Autonomy. Since coming to power in 2011, Mariano Rajoy has flatly refused to engage in discussions about either greater fiscal powers for Catalonia or a referendum on independence, and has proposed recentralisation of some of the functions of the Autonomous Communities as an answer to Spain's economic woes. Meanwhile, his Education minister José Ignacio Wert has set about trying to downgrade the position of autochthonous languages in the school curriculum, and to ensure that all Spanish school children are exposed to 'appropriate' forms of knowledge about Spain's history and identity as a nation. This has pleased the right-wing Spanish media (most notably the newspapers *ABC* and *La Razón* and the television channels *Telemadrid* and *Intereconomía*), which has become an ever more enthusiastic critic of Catalan nationalism. The effect of this double political and media assault is, as we will see, one of the main driving forces behind the Catalan independence movement.

Other Parties

A number of smaller political parties deserve a mention here, mainly because they illustrate the fragmentation of party-political forms of Catalan nationalism and the difficulty of establishing consistent electoral support outside the main parties. *Iniciativa Per Catalunya Verds* (Initiative for

Catalonia Greens – ICV) is a left/Green party that formed the third member of the *tripartit* along with the PSC and ERC. It houses supporters of both independentism and federalism – the latter differentiated from the PSC's version by its more radical, asymmetrical character (Lluch, 2012: 446, 449). *Candidatura d'Unitat Popular* (Popular Unity Candidates – CUP) is an anti-capitalist and pro-independence political grouping that initially concentrated its efforts on fielding candidates in local elections, where its representatives have grown substantially in number since a very modest start in 2003. In 2012, it put up candidates for the first time in the elections to the *Generalitat*, gaining three seats and thus adding to the total number of pro-sovereignty members of the parliament.

Other pro-independence groups have come and gone in the period 2005–2013. 2009 saw the launch (with much fanfare) of *Reagrupament Independentista* (Realignment for Independence – RI), a group that had split from ERC under the leadership of Joan Carretero and was intended as an agglutinating force for diverse pro-independence sectors. Its political programme had only two basic aims, independence and a complete reform of the democratic process, with no position on the left-right spectrum. Despite gaining some support, *Reagrupament* won no seats at the 2010 election, where its thunder was stolen by *Solidaritat Catalana per la Independència* (Catalan Solidarity for Independence – SI). SI was jointly led by the former president of FC Barcelona, Joan Laporta, whose support for the independence movement had made him a figure coveted by different pro-independence parties, including RI. Preferring to form a new group, Laporta joined forces with other well-known independentists (Alfons López Tena, Uriel Bertran and Toni Strubell) to form SI, winning seats for each of them in the 2010 elections. However, Laporta later left SI, retaining his seat as an independent member of parliament. SI won no seats in the 2012 elections.

Another quite different party also needs to be mentioned here: *Ciutadans–Partido de la Ciudadanía* (Citizens–Party of Citizenry – C's). Formed in 2005/6 at the height of debates over Catalonia's new Statute of Autonomy, C's is opposed to Catalan independence and the promotion of Catalan over Spanish in the region. It differentiates itself from the PPC by calling itself 'anti-nationalist' (thereby claiming not to be a Spanish nationalist formation), and centre-left rather than centre-right in its social and economic policy. Its support base is mainly located in Greater Barcelona, where it has won the majority of its votes. In 2012, it achieved nine seats in the Catalan parliament, winning some of the protest votes against independence that might otherwise have gone to the PPC.

Political Disillusionment and the Rise of Civil Movements

Since Spain's transition to democracy, party politics has provided the main outlet for expressions of autonomist, federalist and separatist views in Catalonia. However, over the last few years there has been a shift in focus away from the parties and towards civil action in support of independence, i.e. from political to 'sociological' Catalanism (Lluch, 2010: 341). This is not an entirely new phenomenon, as it draws on a long tradition – some would say myth – of Catalan civil society as the guardian of Catalonia's spirit and identity at times when political action was difficult (Ucelay Da Cal, 2008). However, the level of commitment and organisational professionalism currently being shown by groups not aligned with specific political parties most certainly is unprecedented, and points to an enhanced sense among many Catalans of what Rogers Brubaker calls 'groupness' (Brubaker, 2004: 12–13).

One of the main reasons for this swing away from political parties as the locus of pro-independence mobilisation is an increasingly widespread disillusionment with modern democratic processes in Spain. There are many factors in this disillusionment, some of them relating of course to the global financial crisis that began in 2008, which left many people in Western democracies cynical about the power of their elected governments to control the actions of multinational businesses and banking institutions. The Spanish government under both the PSOE and PP has been unable to deal effectively with the economic crisis, and there is a widespread perception that they have protected elites while making life harder for ordinary people. Constant cases of corruption at different levels of government in Spain – state, regional and local – have also made Spaniards extremely cynical about their politicians.

However, there is also a specific motivation for discontent in the case of Catalonia: the process by which Catalonia's new Statute of Autonomy was drafted and approved. None of the Catalan or Spanish parties emerged unscathed from the protracted wrangling over the contents of the Statute, which gave rise to widespread apathy among voters and a low turnout in the ratifying referendum held in 2006. The effects of this conflict were then prolonged for another four years by the challenge to the Statute in Spain's Constitutional Court. All this will be analysed in detail in chapter 2, but here it is worth noting the conclusions reached by Silvina Vázquez, who carried out a qualitative study on disillusionment with politics in Catalonia from 2008–10. Rather than a generalised disenchantment, by that time the phenomenon in Catalonia had become specifically related to 'Spain as a *polit-ical nation*' (Vázquez, 2011: 62). Moreover, the initial apathy evidenced by the vote on the statute had passed, giving rise to a new mobilisation around the desire for 'recognition'.[4]

Given the widespread cynicism about politicians, it is therefore not surprising that Catalans should have turned to other forms of organisation to achieve this aim. This is not to say that there is a strict split between civil action and party politics, since in many cases the support and involvement of the parties is welcomed or even necessary. However, the impetus for action increasingly comes not from the parties but from other organisations, as was shown to spectacular effect with the demonstration on 11 September 2012 organised by the *Assemblea Nacional Catalana* (Catalan National Assembly – ANC), in which around 1.5 million Catalans participated. Events such as this will be treated in the next chapter; meanwhile, the aim here is to provide necessary background information on some of these organ-isations.

Before doing so, we need to consider briefly the crucial impact that the internet and access to social media have had on the capacity of Catalan civil groups to organise events, recruit supporters, and spread messages. In this respect, Catalanist activism is no different to other kinds of contemporary social movement organisation, since as Manuel Castells puts it, 'alternative media are at the core of alternative social movement action' (Castells, 2009: 343). Specifically, though, I would argue that without social media and the internet, the Catalan independence movement could not possibly have progressed so far in such a short space of time, and even with the same chain of political events, levels of pro-independence activism and voter support would have been much lower at this stage.

One of the key media outlets for the pro-independence movement has been the newspaper ARA, which was founded in November 2010. Referring to it as a newspaper probably makes it appear as though the discussion here has suddenly turned to the traditional print media, but this is not the case. ARA's main strength is the way it integrates traditional and new media into an innovative multiplatform environment, including print, interactive web content, video and social media (Parreño Rabadán, 2010). On its third anniversary in 2013 it reported average daily sales of 27,520 print copies but more than 1.7 million online views, with 22,000 subscribers, 100,000 Facebook 'likes', and nearly 150,000 followers on Twitter.[5] These figures show that the reach and influence of ARA go far beyond its actual sales, partly because of its emphasis on participation and dialogue with its readers. This dynamic is also reflected in its wide range of commercial activities and cultural patronage, which includes: an online store selling books, wine, T-shirts and DVDs (among other things); 'ARA Films' which allows people to view Catalan cinema online for a fee of around 2–4 Euros per film; and schemes to provide copies of literary classics in Catalan to schools and libraries.

ARA was founded by a group of media professionals that included Carles Capdevila, Antoni Bassas, and Toni Soler, all of whom have strong connections with Catalan radio and television and were already well known at the time ARA was launched. It is largely aimed at well-informed and well-educated young Catalan speakers, who are (or will be) professionals and the leaders of Catalonia's political and civil associations (Giménez, 2010). Its active support for the independence movement is hinted at, but not explicitly stated, in its original mission statement:

> ARA wants to contribute to the debate, talking about everything without dogmas or limits, so that Catalonia can look to the future with all its ambition and energy, and soon become one of the most prosperous and contented European societies, capable of generating non-material and material wealth for its citizens in a permanent and sustainable way.[6]

Not only is its editorial stance pro-referendum/pro-independence, it has also actively supported the organisation of demonstrations and other events. For example, it helped to mobilise the population to take part in the *Via Catalana* demonstration of 11 September 2013 (when a human chain was formed that stretched from the northern to the southern borders of Catalonia), even offering free subscriptions for a month to anyone who took part. The relationship between ARA and the independence movement is symbiotic: ARA generates support for pro-independence activities, and is rewarded by ever-increasing sales and influence among those who see it as the main mouthpiece for their views. Furthermore, its regular contributors are excellent examples of the power of the Catalan cultural and intellectual elite to shape the debate on Catalonia's future independently of the political parties.

As well as ARA's contribution to garnering support for pro-independence activities (and the campaign against road tolls discussed in the Introduction), there are countless other examples of 'e-mobilisation', on both large and small scales. Mass demonstrations such as those that took place in Barcelona on 10 July 2010 and 11 September 2012 relied on both civil and political groups to organise their supporters using their own email lists and websites, but they were also able to draw in unaffiliated individuals through the sharing of information about the events via the web and social media. To give just one example, in 2012 a short publicity video to garner support for the 11 September demonstration was produced by the ANC and uploaded to YouTube. It used a poem by Salvador Espriu written to protest about Catalonia's subjugation during the Franco regime (part of *La pell de brau* (The Bull Hide), 1960). The poem was recited by various recognisable personalities from the world of Catalan politics and culture, translating Espriu's cry for freedom during the dictatorship into a present-day call for independence (Danés, 2012). At the time of writing (a year later) this had received over 63,000 views, although it is not possible to calculate in retrospect how many of those came in the short period between publication (1 September 2012) and the demonstration itself. A version with English subtitles had received over five thousand views.

Jennifer Earl and Katrina Kimport argue that one of the major changes brought about by new technologies is to broaden the range of participants, and the definition of what counts as activism or participation, while at the same time requiring much less organisational effort (Earl and Kimport, 2011). 'Drastically small teams' can now mobilise large numbers of people who have no formal connection to a social movement organisation, and the resonance of their actions can be even greater than before (Earl and Kimport, 2011: 163). There are indeed numerous examples of localised actions in Catalonia organised by small teams that have achieved massive dissemination before and after the event.

A representative example would be the 'Lipdub for Independence' that took place in Vic in October 2010, with 5,771 participants. (This was claimed as a world record lipdub, although *The Guinness Book of Records* does not actually recognise the category). The entire event was coordinated through Facebook and a Wordpress blog by a small collective whose names were generally not revealed, although individual spokespeople sometimes gave press conferences on the group's behalf. On the day itself, participants were filmed in the streets of Vic's old quarter lip-synching to a song called 'La flama' by the contemporary Valencian group *Obrint Pas*. Many of the participants belonged to cultural groups, which provided scenes involving Catalan dances and other forms of traditional culture. All material relating to specific groups or parties was banned, although people were encouraged to bring either the official Catalan flag or one of its pro-independence variations. According to Oriol Freixenet Guitart, not only was there massive participation in the event itself, but the video of it attracted half a million hits on YouTube in just a week, along with fifteen thousand comments (Freixenet Guitart, 2010). By August 2013, the official version on YouTube had been viewed more than two million times (Youcat, 2010).

Catalonia's civil groups find it easier than the political parties to gather a broad spectrum of supporters for such events, especially where – as with

the 'Lipdub for Independence' – there are no visible signs of different political allegiances. Mobilising under the unqualified banner of 'independence'
greatly facilitates short-term coalition building, a process supported by the
internet's power to underpin such 'loose and temporary connections' (Earl
and Kimport, 2011: 151). Civil groups also seem to be better at devising
innovative, fun activities in which people wish to participate, lipdubs being
one example, flashmobs another. However, what seems most important
here to explain mass participation in such events is the increased desire for
recognition, as highlighted in Vázquez's study of political disillusionment
(Vázquez, 2011: 62–3). Peter Dahlgren sees the demand for recognition in
liberal democracies as relating both to questions of individual self-esteem
and new conceptions of citizenship, which give rise to a desire for political
agency that cannot be satisfied by party politics (Dahlgren, 2007: 56, 58).
These connections seem to be confirmed by recent events in Catalonia,
where civil groups that originally formed around issues of language, identity and culture have increasingly been radicalising into pro-independence
organisations. If previous efforts by political parties and institutions have
not been enough to guarantee recognition by the Spanish state (Vázquez,
2011: 63), then citizens may take these matters into their own hands.

Òmnium Cultural

Òmnium Cultural was founded in 1961, during the dictatorship, and is therefore by far the oldest organisation that will be mentioned here
(www.omnium.cat). Its Latin name indicates that it is a cultural organisation 'belonging to everyone', and in this spirit its core mission has been to
promote knowledge of the Catalan language and its associated culture as
widely as possible. Over the decades, it has built up a portfolio of activities
including administering literary prizes, organising a wide variety of
cultural events, and promoting the use of the Catalan language in various
settings. It currently has more than thirty thousand members and 28
branches.

Over the last few years, *Òmnium* has progressively become more and more
directly implicated in the pro-independence movement. From 2009, its
branches helped in the organisation of local consultations on independence.
In 2010, it was the main organiser of the 10 July demonstration in support
of Catalonia's new statute, under the banner of the 'right to decide'. Not
only did over a million people participate in the march, but its impact was
broadened significantly by the organisers' use of the web and social media
to create what they dubbed Catalonia's first 'Demonstration 2.0' (Òmnium

Cultural, 2010).[7] Live updates could be sent via Twitter using the hash tag #*somunanacio* ('we are a nation'), and the same keyword could be used when uploading photos to Flickr. This was facilitated by the creation of a temporary free Wi-Fi network along the route of the march. Interested non-participants and the media could therefore easily follow the progress of the demonstration, which also received live television and radio coverage.

Òmnium's current statutes (dating from 2011) list as one of the organisation's objectives 'the full collective recuperation of the identity of the Catalan nation', but make no direct reference to working for a Catalan state.[8] Nevertheless, since 2012 it has openly committed itself to supporting Catalan independence, for example by working with the ANC in the organisation of the pro-independence demonstration on 11 September 2012. On 29 June 2013 it was the main organiser of a 'Concert for Freedom' in Barcelona FC's *Camp Nou* that was specifically designed as a call for a referendum on independence to be held in 2014. Despite some organisational difficulties that caused delays for those heading into the stadium, around ninety thousand people attended the concert, which was also broadcast on Catalan television.

Plataforma per la Llengua

Like *Òmnium Cultural*, the *Plataforma per la Llengua* (Platform for the Language) has become significantly more visible and radical over the last few years. Founded in 1993, as the name suggests the aim of *Plataforma* is to support and promote the Catalan language, working especially with new arrivals to Catalan-speaking regions (www.plataforma-llengua.cat). It also acts as a pressure group whenever legislation on language is being discussed at any level of government, and in commercial settings such as promoting the dubbing of films into Catalan and the use of the language in product labelling. One of its main concerns in recent years has been the attempts by the PP to challenge the use of Catalan in education. It publishes studies on these topics as well as guides designed to help Catalan speakers exercise their linguistic rights in everyday situations. In April 2011 it organised a lipdub of its own in Barcelona to highlight the role of Catalan as a language of social integration.

While the overall aims of the *Plataforma* have remained rooted in issues to do with the Catalan language, it has also given its support to pro-independence activities such as the *Via Catalana* (see above and Chapter 2). Unsurprisingly, many of its members support independence because they feel that the survival of the Catalan language depends on having the power of a Catalan state behind it. A statement from the *Plataforma* after the Constitutional Court's ruling on the Statute reflects this without being an unequivocal call for independence: 'This ruling confirms that the Catalan language cannot have its own legal framework and bars the way to equality of linguistic rights in Spain. From now on, in order to guarantee these rights we must devise a radical change in the legal framework – either through a reform of the Spanish Constitution or through the creation of a new Catalan state within the European Union – which comes from the citizens of Catalonia and respects their right to decide on such a central element for social and cultural cohesion as is the Catalan language' (Plataforma per la Llengua, 2010).[9]

Assemblea Nacional Catalana

One of the founders of the *Plataforma per la Llengua* subsequently became the founding president of the ANC. Carme Forcadell Lluís, a Catalan philologist and teacher, was elected president at the ANC's constituent assembly in March 2012. Forcadell is also a member of *Òmnium Cultural*; it is not unusual for activists to be members of several such organisations either sequentially or simultaneously, but Forcadell is a particularly good example because of the influence she has wielded within these associations over the years. The prior experience of Forcadell and many other members of the executive explains how the ANC was able to organise the largest demonstration in Catalonia's history just a few months after it was officially constituted as an association.

The statutes of the ANC, as revised in 2013, commit the organisation to promoting the political and social conditions necessary for Catalonia to become an independent state, working to bring together groups and individuals with the same aim (Assemblea Nacional Catalana, 2013: 3–4). The reasons for this are explained in its founding document, approved in April 2011, which states that the autonomic model for Spain has failed and there only seem now to be two options: to remain with a united Spain that continues to be characterised by 'unifying and homogenising Castilian objectives', or to seek independence (Assemblea Nacional Catalana, 2011).[10] The document also describes Catalan civil society's rejection of 'the current process of economic destruction and cultural genocide', its disappointment with the way it is represented by political institutions, and the increasing number of actions in favour of independence that have resulted.[11] Like all the other associations mentioned here, the ANC retains a scrupulous commitment to democratic means of protest and action.

Other Associations

So far, the ANC has achieved great success with its activities, as measured by participation, media and political impact, and the number of different associations with which it has successfully collaborated. However, the panorama of pro-independence groups springing from civil society is in many ways as fragmented as the political parties. Keeping alliances strong is the main challenge facing any organisation attempting to act as a pro-independence umbrella group, whether in the civil or political sphere. It should come as no surprise, therefore, that the associations listed so far represent only the tip of a very large iceberg. Other examples include: *Sobirania i Justícia* (Sovereignty and Justice), founded in 2009 and mainly active in the Barcelona area; *Sobirania i Progrés* (Sovereignty and Progress), created in 2006 with the support of many well-known figures including Oriol Junqueras; *Catalunya Sí* (Catalonia Yes), which is a bridging organisation between party politics and civil society, whose primary aim is to support ERC's particular vision for independence; and the *Plataforma pel Dret de Decidir* (Platform for the Right to Decide), another umbrella group which since 2005 has organised demonstrations and publicity campaigns and helped to run the popular consultations on independence, although some of its members have now moved to the ANC. Supporting the work of these activists are a number of groups whose concern is to collect information in support of arguments for independence – e.g. the *Cercle d'Estudis Sobiranistes* (Circle for Sovereignty Studies) founded in 2007 – or to raise awareness of Catalonia's situation both inside and outside the region – e.g. *Col·lectiu Emma* (Emma Collective), which collates and disseminates news about Catalonia from and to interested parties throughout the world.

Two other organisations worth mentioning are the *Cercle Català de Negocis* (Catalan Business Circle, founded in 2008) and *Fundació Catalunya Estat* (the Catalonia State Foundation, created in 2011). These are particularly significant because of their orientation towards the business world. Historically, while many Catalan businesspeople – especially the owners of SMEs – have been sympathetic to cultural nationalism, they have seen Spain as the natural economic ambit for their business activities (Cabana, 2007). In contrast, over the past few years increasing numbers of businesspeople have started to argue that the protection of the Spanish state is no longer necessary or sufficient for Catalonia's economy to flourish (Canadell, 2013). The next two chapters will explore some of the reasons for this, including the perception that Spain has neglected Catalan business needs by, for example, failing to provide adequate infrastructure in key areas such as transport despite the high proportion of tax revenues gathered in Catalonia.

The *Cercle Català de Negocis* has been campaigning specifically on these issues and trying to win support from businesspeople. The remit of *Fundació Catalunya Estat* is broader in the sense that businesspeople are just one of its target groups, but it is important to note that one of its aims is to raise money from the business sector to support the pro-independence activities of other associations.

One of the main points raised in this chapter has been the on-going fragmentation of the Catalan independence movement, which has severely limited its political impact in the past. As we have seen, this fragmentation continues to affect both political parties and civil groups, with different formations constantly coming and going, integrating and splitting. It will be interesting to see whether the ANC can avoid this fate and genuinely act as the cohesive force it wishes to be – in the same way that we wait to see whether the pro-independence parties that currently have seats in the Catalan parliament can put aside their other differences if Catalonia's secession crisis finally comes to a head. However, it does seem that the negative effects of this fragmentation have been somewhat mitigated – at least in the civil sphere – by the power of the Internet to mobilise both committed activists and sporadic participants around specific events. In this sense, fragmentation could turn out to be an advantage as much as a disadvantage, since people do not have to commit to membership of any one organisation and can choose to participate (or not) on an event-by-event basis, thus very much increasing the pool of possible participants (Earl and Kimport, 2011: 93). As a result, organisers wield significant 'network-making power', capitalising on the dynamic nature of the civil movement to make multiple connections and exploit fleeting synergies (Castells, 2009: 47).

Furthermore, fragmentation and fluctuating memberships do not appear to affect the capacity of participants to trust either each other or the event organisers. As Montserrat Guibernau points out, people are generally quick to trust others when they feel they belong to a 'community of equals', because together they 'construct a shared illusion of forming a community created to fight for what they regard as a just common cause' (Guibernau, 2013: 103). If we add this to other factors such as an increased desire amongst ordinary Catalans for recognition and political agency, frustration at Spain as a political entity and at Catalonia's political parties, and independence as a rallying cry that glosses over other differences, it is not surprising that so many people have been drawn into active support for the independence movement.

The core membership of all of these organisations is mainly drawn from the middle classes: teachers, lecturers, lawyers, doctors, businesspeople, local councillors, civil servants and journalists. Nevertheless, participation in specific pro-independence events involves a much broader spectrum of the population, especially in terms of age profile – many activities will draw whole family groups, which is one reason why they remain peaceful. Anecdotal evidence also suggests that a fair number of participants are 'new Catalans', although it is difficult to get an accurate picture. Attention is generally drawn to particular cases, such as the English-born author and journalist Matthew Tree, who has lived in Barcelona since 1984 and whose active support for independence has made him a key asset. The collaboration of household names such as writers, actors, singers, and media and sports personalities is an important factor for the success of publicity campaigns prior to any event, and for ensuring media coverage during and afterwards.

This membership profile suggests that the civil pro-independence movement is – like its political counterpart – largely directed by a core of educated middle-class Catalan speakers. This leads commentators such as César García and Thomas Jeffrey Miley to conclude that Catalanism is a form of elite-led ethnic nationalism dressed in more inclusive civic clothing (García, 2010; Miley, 2007; Miley, 2013a). Miley, for example, claims that 'working-class Castilian-speakers' preferences are being effectively blocked from articulation within the channels provided by political society', because even in parties such as the PSC, elected politicians are much more likely to identify as Catalans/Catalan-speakers than the constituency they represent (Miley, 2013a: 16). This then begs the question as to why these groups have not formed civil associations of their own to counter the work of Catalan nationalist organisations.

If the answer is that the working class will necessarily find it harder to form organisations than the middle classes, then we can ask why the existing civil group *Convivencia Cívica Catalana* (Catalan Civil Coexistence – CCC) has not become more of a rallying point for alternative views (García, 2010: 12). CCC was founded in 1998 as a response to the increasing dominance of Catalan within the education system, and is therefore the civic counterpart to the more recently-created political party *Ciutadans*, mentioned above. CCC has been able to take various actions against Catalonia's policy of linguistic immersion in the education system, but has not generated large numbers of active supporters or broadened its remit in the light of the new debates around independence. García argues that this is because those who disagree with the hegemonic views disseminated by Catalan nationalists are caught up in a 'spiral of silence', which marginalises dissent and forces such people to resign themselves to having no political representation (García,

2010: 13, 15). He also supports Miley's thesis that Catalonia suffers from an 'ethno-linguistic divide' that is carefully hidden under a civic veneer (Miley, 2007: 7).

However, Ivan Serrano criticises this conclusion as over-simplistic, as it ignores 'the multifaceted relation between national identity and its political expressions' (Serrano, 2013a: 529). His own analysis of CEO data suggests that the recent increase in support for independence has not been underpinned by an ethnic polarisation of national identification: as we saw earlier, there are those who identify themselves as more Spanish than Catalan who would still be prepared to vote for independence (Serrano, 2013a: 527). We therefore need to look closely at the political circumstances that explain this disjunction.

Chapter 2

The Path to a Pro-Independence Consensus

There is no doubt that the pivotal moment in the recent growth in support for independence has been the process of creating and ratifying Catalonia's updated Statute of Autonomy, which was approved by referendum in 2006. Although this is not by any means the only relevant event, the Statute of Autonomy and the subsequent challenge to its legitimacy in Spain's Constitutional Court represent – as Jaime Lluch points out – a 'central state constitutional moment' of the kind that 'sets in motion the process that leads to the founding of a new political and constitutional orientation within a [sub-state] national movement' (Lluch, 2010: 355, 342). This happens because 'constitutional moments are interpreted by the minority nationalists as an instance of majority nation nationalism, and, thus, these constitutional events impact the intersubjective relations of reciprocity between minority nationalists and majority nation nationalism' (342). They thus function as points at which groupness may 'crystallize', or at least achieve temporarily higher levels (Brubaker, 2004: 12).

Both Lluch and Brubaker stress the contingency of the evolution of nationalist movements, rejecting narratives that ascribe overly coherent or deterministic trajectories to them. Lluch points out that 'temporal variation within national movements is an important and yet under-theorized area in the study of nations and nationalism' (Lluch, 2010: 338). What is missing is an awareness of 'the element of contingency in political life, and the interdependency of human actions within and across spatial contexts' (Lluch, 2010: 339). It is precisely this issue of interdependency that Brubaker addresses with his concept of 'groupness as an *event*' (Brubaker, 2004: 12). Rather than arising naturally from ethnic similarity, a sense of groupness may actually arise only in situations of inter-group conflict, may need to be manufactured by elites, or may even fail to cohere despite the best efforts of ethnopolitical entrepreneurs (12–13). Even when groupness does crystallise it is 'variable and contingent rather than fixed and given' (12).

Brubaker and Lluch's stress on the importance of contingency in nationalist movements rightly challenges primordialist accounts of national identity as 'age-old and enduring' (Lluch, 2012: 437). As noted in the Introduction, we might therefore be tempted to explain Catalonia's current situation using instrumentalist accounts of nationalism, which focus not on ethnicity as a 'given' but on the interests it is 'alleged to serve' (Özkirimli, 2010: 88): i.e. those of the elites within particular ethnic groups. In this kind of account, ethnic identification – far from being based on inherent characteristics – is 'epiphenomenal', or a by-product of the quest for power (Lluch, 2012: 436). Sajjar Ahmad, for example, labels the recent rise in support for secession in Catalonia a clear-cut case of instrumentalist nationalism, based on political rather than ethnic factors (Ahmad, 2013). Ivan Serrano's call for analysts to separate national identification from support for independence also makes it clear that the political must not be assumed to proceed directly from the ethnic (Serrano, 2013a). However, this does not automatically mean that we should assume that the reverse is true – that the ethnic proceeds directly from the political (Hale, 2008: 2–3). As Özkirimli says, such assumptions should be tested in relation to 'empirical insights based on "real-life" cases' (Özkirimli, 2010: 219).

This chapter looks at the key events that have shaped attitudes to independence since the beginning of the process of negotiating the new Statute of Autonomy (2005). For instrumentalists (like Ahmad), this relation of events will confirm the view that the current move towards secession responds to material concerns generated by contemporary political circumstances. Primordialists, on the other hand, might see it as confirmation of an inherently conflictive situation in Spain resulting from the millennial coexistence of different ethnic groups (Lluch, 2012: 437). Rather than responding to contingent political circumstances, then, a Catalan with a primordialist understanding of his/her identity might view this narrative of events as confirmation of a deeper truth, perhaps pointing to secession as the inevitable outcome of lengthy historical processes. Meanwhile, Spanish nationalists – most of whom have an equally primordialist take on nationalism – will seize on any discordant notes in this narrative (such as the low turnout for the referendum on the Statute) as proof of the illegitimacy of the whole Catalanist project. With these contradictory potential interpretations in mind, we now turn to an examination of these events.

The *Tripartit* and the New Statute of Autonomy

The year 2003 marked a new era in Catalan politics, with the installation of Pasqual Maragall as President of the *Generalitat* at the head of a three-way coalition of PSC, ERC and ICV. One important consequence of this was the elevation of ERC and its then leader Josep-Lluís Carod-Rovira to a position of considerable influence within the *Generalitat*. It was also during the coalition's first term in office from 2003–6 that the first act in the drama of Catalonia's attempt to strengthen its Statute of Autonomy played itself out.

Before the 2004 general elections, the leader of the PSOE, José Luis Rodríguez Zapatero, announced that if they won the election, all of Spain's Autonomous Communities would be invited to update their statutes of autonomy if they wished to do so (Colino, 2009: 268; Keating and Wilson, 2009: 540–1). This was partly a response to the Catalans' and Basques' frustration with the increasing Spanish nationalism and hostility to further regional autonomy that were hallmarks of the PP's second term in government from 2000–2004 (Balfour and Quiroga, 2007: 109–11; Guibernau, 2014). In an attempt to win Catalan votes, Zapatero apparently promised to accept whatever might be contained in any statute passed by the Catalan parliament, although he subsequently denied that this was an unconditional promise (Requejo, 2010: 160; Ridao, 2006: 165; Rusiñol and Cué, 2003). The Catalan parliament lost no time in producing a draft, which it overwhelmingly approved in 2005. However, according to the procedure laid down in the Spanish Constitution of 1978 this was only the first stage: as a Spanish Organic Law, the draft needed to be approved by the parliament in Madrid, which could make changes to the text approved by the Catalans. Zapatero had already announced that in fact he would support the statute only if it was fully constitutional (Ridao, 2006: 115), while the *Partido Popular* made it very clear that they would not tolerate the inclusion of articles such as one that defined Catalonia as a nation. Their leader Mariano Rajoy described the statute as 'a nightmare' (Ridao, 2006: 128).

There followed a series of negotiations between Zapatero and the Catalan parties to produce a draft that could be endorsed by the Spanish parliament (Keating and Wilson, 2009: 543–5; Maragall, 2008: 280; Ridao, 2006: 162–5). Artur Mas ended up playing a key role here even though he was leader of the opposition, which had the effect of undermining the credibility of the *tripartit* (Madí, 2007: 161–7). The result of these machinations was a watered-down statute that removed key clauses on finance and language (Colino, 2009: 273). Additionally, an article in which it was stated that Catalonia was a nation was replaced by a much vaguer statement in the preamble (where it had no legal force), to the effect that Catalans consider Catalonia to be a nation. The statute that was put to a referendum in Catalonia on 18 June 2006 was therefore much weaker than the one that had been approved by a massive majority in the Catalan parliament, but still contained substantial new powers for Catalonia (Colino, 2009).

This side-stepping and back-tracking had several major consequences. Firstly, ERC said that they were unable to endorse the revised statute and, after initially deciding that they would ask their members to abstain in the referendum, finally advised them to vote 'no' (Martínez-Herrera and Miley, 2010: 26; Ridao, 2006: 192–4, 207). This made their position within the *tripartit* untenable (see below and Orte and Wilson, 2009: 429). Secondly, the lengthy process of negotiation was accompanied by heightened anti-Catalanism from the PP, the right-wing Spanish media, and even ordinary Spaniards (Keating and Wilson, 2009: 543–4; Madí, 2007: 186–7; Strubell i Trueta, 2008: 27, 41). One of the most tangible manifestations of this was the campaign to boycott *cava* (Catalan champagne). This strategy had been used before in reaction to Carod-Rovira's statement in 2004 that Catalans should not cooperate with Madrid's attempt to secure the Olympic Games, and returned in 2005 as a way of protesting against 'unreasonable' Catalan demands in the Statute. A few shops withdrew *cava* altogether, while others printed signs directing shoppers to 'non-Catalan' alternatives.

Thirdly, it produced a sense of apathy and frustration among Catalans, who – tired of witnessing so much political manoeuvring for so little result – failed to support the vote on the referendum in anything like the numbers that the political parties would have wanted (Madí, 2007: 179). Although voters endorsed the statute by a clear majority, turnout was a disappointing 48.9% (Martínez-Herrera and Miley, 2010: 27). There were several reasons for this apparent lack of interest on the part of the Catalan electorate. The referendum came at a time of increased frustration with the political process in general, which had led to high levels of dissatisfaction and abstention among Catalan voters (Lago et al., 2007; Ferran Sáez, 2011a). The vicissitudes of the *tripartit,* and the political manoeuvres resulting from the hung parliament of 2003, generated a climate of weariness among the Catalan electorate, whose predominant attitude was therefore one of apathy, resulting in 'exit' rather than active participation and collaboration. Also, the 'yes' and 'no' campaigns were very much phrased in party-political terms, with the two major parties CiU and PSC both recommending 'yes' votes to their supporters and only minority parties proposing abstention or 'no' votes; this cut firmly across 'ethnic' cleavages.[1] Despite the anti-Catalan rhetoric of certain Spanish politicians and journalists and the over-hyped *cava* boycott, Catalans had not yet reached the point of exasperation that was to come after several more years of such attacks. In fact, jibes about the poor turnout in the referendum hurt because they were pointing to an uncomfortable reality: Catalans had indeed failed to take the opportunity presented by the statute to express a clear sense of group solidarity.

Finance, Infrastructure and the Challenge to the Statute

By the end of 2006 the Statute was in force and sales of *cava* had largely returned to normal (Valero, 2006). However, the coalition was in tatters, an early election had been called, and Maragall had been removed as the PSC's candidate for the Presidency.

The relationship between the PSC and ERC had always been problematic. Maragall was forced to sack Carod-Rovira as a result of scandals surrounding his meeting with representatives of the Basque terrorist group ETA, and ERC later withdrew the rest of its *consellers* (ministers) from the government because of disagreements over the Statute (see above). Partly as a result of the damage done to the PSC by the media storm surrounding Carod-Rovira's meeting with ETA on a day when – ironically – he was Acting President, Maragall found himself under increasing scrutiny from the leader of the Spanish socialists José Luis Rodríguez Zapatero. When Maragall accused CiU of having taken a 3% 'commission' on contracts for public works, lack of proof forced him into an embarrassing climb-down that also damaged his credibility. It was at this point that José Montilla came into the picture as a replacement for Maragall. Montilla was a minister in Zapatero's government and was regarded as a much safer pair of hands to lead the PSC than the erratic Maragall.

Not only was Montilla closer to Zapatero, he also had a very different personal and political background to Maragall. Having moved to Catalonia as a teenager, much of the initial reaction to the announcement of his candidacy for the presidency revolved around the 'novelty' of him being an immigrant Catalan. Montilla had never worn his love for Catalonia on his sleeve as did Pujol and Maragall, and was more of a 'party man'. This was one factor in helping CiU win the election in 2006 both in terms of number of seats and votes, since Mas was more of a known quantity to the swing voter (Pallarés and Muñoz, 2008: 450–1). However, CiU were not able to achieve an absolute majority and were once again out-manoeuvred by the PSC when it came to negotiating the support of other parties (Madí, 2007: 273–7; Pallarés and Muñoz, 2008: 460–1). This allowed the PSC back into power but left them dependent once again on ERC and ICV in a renewed version of the *tripartit* that had failed during the previous parliament. Carod-Rovira's position in fact became even stronger than before, since Montilla was forced to name him Vice-President, a post that had not previously existed in the modern era of the *Generalitat*. Despite being removed from the leadership of ERC in 2008, his role as Vice-President ensured him public visibility and political influence right up until the next elections in November 2010.

The approval of the Statute was by no means the end of the challenges the *tripartit* would face on this matter. The financial framework set out in the Statute had to be fleshed out with a proper agreement on the actual amount that Catalonia would receive each year. Theoretically, this should have been a straightforward process given that it would involve the Spanish socialist government negotiating directly with their PSC counterparts in Catalonia. However, tensions between the two federated parties that were caused by the process of negotiating the statute were in fact raised to new heights by the process of agreeing the finance deal (Orte and Wilson, 2009: 430, 433). This was supposed to be finished by the end of 2008 but was actually ratified a whole year later. In the end, ERC and its new leader Joan Puigcercós claimed the credit for brokering the deal, which saw Catalonia granted an extra 3,855 million Euros per year (after a transitional period). However, this did not solve the problem of perceived financial neglect by the state.

There are two main aspects to Catalan financial grievances. The first is the lack of true fiscal autonomy: Catalans look with envy at the Basque Country's Economic Accord (*Concierto Económico*) by which they collect their own taxes and pay an agreed proportion to the state. On the other hand, Catalonia – like the majority of Autonomous Communities – is dependent on an allocation of funds by the state, so that even though they collect part of their own revenue, this is topped up by the state to a set amount. The second issue is a widespread annoyance that Catalonia hands over more in taxes than the amount it receives back in services and investment. This imbalance is perceived to be directly responsible for major shortcomings in any form of infrastructure that requires Spanish investment, especially transport.

This sense of grievance explains why, over the last few years, and especially during the negotiations on the new Statute of Autonomy and the finance agreement that followed this, two phrases came to be repeated *ad nauseam* in public debate in Catalonia: 'fiscal deficit', and 'infrastructure crisis'. The phrase *dèficit fiscal* refers to the 'fiscal imbalance of Catalonia with the Spanish state', which 'has supposed a systematic outlay of wealth estimated between 7–9% of Catalan GDP in recent years' (Pons i Novell and Tremosa i Balcells, 2005: 1456). ERC had been using the *dèficit fiscal* as an argument in favour of independence for many years, and there was an increase in CiU-initiated studies on the phenomenon from the late 1990s onwards. (These mainly consisted of attempts to quantify the extent of the deficit from the incomplete information available.) However, it was not until debates began on the new Statute of Autonomy in 2005 that the phrase really entered the consciousness of the general public (Albert Sáez, 2005: 94–5). The issue was the extent to which Catalonia could be legitimately asked to show financial 'solidarity' with the rest of Spain, allowing part of its taxes to support the needs of less wealthy regions. Many Catalan commentators argued that it was the extent of the deficit, rather than having a deficit *per se* that was the problem (Ros et al., 2003: 105). However, despite this concentration on a reduction rather than an elimination of the deficit, the argument came across badly in the rest of Spain where, for many, it simply confirmed the 'lack of solidarity' of the Catalans, or even their 'meanness' (Dowling, 2009: 190; Pujol, 2007). The *Partido Popular* was especially fond of using this accusation to discredit Catalan demands during the negotiations on the Statute and the new funding regime (Dowling, 2009: 195–6).

The fiscal deficit is of course directly related to the 'infrastructure crisis'. Carod-Rovira succinctly expressed the relationship as follows: 'we pay Scandinavian taxes and receive Latin American infrastructures' (Carod-Rovira, 2003: 18). The problem relates to any form of infrastructure that is either administered directly by the state or requires state funding, but its effects are most noticeable in the area of transport. Major complaints include the following: Barcelona's *El Prat* airport is not encouraged to function as a hub for intercontinental flights, which means having to add an expensive internal flight to Madrid on to the cost of many long-haul journeys; Catalonia has the highest number of toll-roads in Spain and its road users therefore have substantially higher costs than other Spaniards, whose roads are mainly publicly funded; the development of high-speed rail links from Barcelona both to Madrid and to France has been given an extremely low priority, with detrimental effects not only for passengers but also for freight (Tremosa i Balcells, 2006: 250); the state-owned rail company RENFE, which ran most local train services around Barcelona until 2010, had failed to invest properly in these services, leading to frustrating delays and poor service for commuters. The direct effect of these shortcomings on the general public as well as on businesses explains why the 'infrastructure crisis' was of much more interest to Catalans than the rather academic debates on the fiscal deficit (Balcells, 2008: 161).

The second factor that heightened tensions in this period was the long wait for a judgement on the Statute by Spain's Constitutional Court. Spain's system for resolving conflicts between the State and the Autonomous Communities involves *ex post facto* challenges that are heard by a Constitutional Court made up of twelve politically-appointed judges. This meant that even though the Statute had passed through all the necessary stages and was in the process of being implemented, it could be challenged retrospectively by interested parties on the grounds of unconstitutionality. Unsurprisingly, it was the PP that produced the most comprehensive challenge, hoping that the Court would repeal no fewer than 128 of its 223 articles. The matter proved so difficult to resolve that it took four years, and was so bitter that it called into question the legitimacy of the 12-member tribunal itself. In November 2009, a suspicion that the judgement was about to be released led twelve newspapers based in Catalonia to run the same editorial, entitled 'Catalonia's Dignity' ('La dignitat de Catalunya').[2] The editorial pointed out that only ten of the tribunal's members were available to pass judgement because one had died and another had been recused. Moreover, four members had technically come to the end of their term of office but had not been replaced. The newspapers called on the Court to recognise that its judgement would have far-reaching consequences for Spain's future as a plural society, and asked it to respect the will of the Catalan people as expressed in the referendum on the Statute. Many Spanish newspapers – especially those with right-wing stances – responded by criticising the editorial as an illegitimate attempt to put pressure on the Constitutional Court.

The sentence finally released on 28 June 2010 found only 14 articles unconstitutional and ordered the 'reinterpretation' of 27 more. However, many of these were considered fundamental by Catalans, including article 6.1 that referred to the Catalan language as the 'preferred' language of public administration, communication and education; and article 206.3 that freed Catalonia from the obligation of providing financial support for other autonomous communities if these were not making 'a similar fiscal effort'.[3] As expected, the reference to Catalonia as a nation, in the preamble, was left untouched – but the judgement stressed that it had no legal effect and that Spain was the only nation recognised by the Constitution. The full text of the judgement was released on 9 July 2010, and the next day over one million Catalans marched through Barcelona in protest. The demonstration (organised by *Òmnium Cultural*) was supposed to be in support of the Statute (i.e. of Catalonia's rights within the Spanish State), but there was a significant presence of separatist groups as well as individuals with pro-independence flags and banners. As *El País* put it, 'From babies to senior citizens. From Girona to the lands of the Ebro. Born in Catalonia or in Africa. Yesterday's demonstration in Barcelona was dominated by variety' (Carranco and Vallespín, 2010).[4]

The continuing controversies surrounding the statute in the years following the referendum had obviously roused Catalans from their apathy. If the initial cuts by the Spanish parliament had generated a sense of disillusionment that was reflected in the referendum turnout, the sentence of the Constitutional Court managed to energise Catalans into overt displays of their frustration, which in turn produced further instances of anti-Catalanism from Spanish politicians and the media. As a result, the public image of the Catalans within Spain became increasingly at odds with the Catalans' own self image (Jenkins, 1997: 59). As José Montilla put it, 'They made us out to be a privileged, mean people who only do what suits us best at the expense of the rest of Spain' (Strubell i Trueta and Brunet, 2011: 51). Catalans responded to such attacks with a widespread annoyance that other Spaniards showed so little willingness to understand their point of view, a phenomenon which, for some, only proved Catalonia's 'incompatibility' with the rest of Spain (Ridao, 2007: 153–4; Strubell i Trueta, 2008). This produced a heightened sense of 'solidarity under fire', one tangible manifestation of which was the massive turnout at the pro-statute demonstration.

The Fiscal Pact and the Popular Consultations on Independence

The November 2010 elections saw CiU return to power with a respectable – although not absolute – majority. This finally allowed Mas to attempt to restore CiU's political hegemony in Catalonia, but also set the scene for further conflict in the relationship between the Catalan and central governments. With the PSOE in power in Madrid and the PSC in Catalonia, the relationship between Spain and Catalonia had actually got worse rather than better, leading even Montilla to warn of the increasing disaffection of the Catalans with Spain (Montilla, 2007). Mas had little time to forge a working relationship with the PSOE – in the context of Spain's ever-deepening economic crisis – before they were swept aside by the PP in November 2011, since which time relations between the two governments have gone from bad to worse.

Mas's main preoccupation at this time was the poor financial position of Catalonia, which had not been in any way alleviated by the new financial arrangements resulting from the Statute. This was partly because of delays in transferring agreed funds, but as the economic crisis began to hit even harder, the focus increasingly fell on the Autonomous Communities as the preferred target for cuts in public spending, and they were forced to agree to drastic measures to reduce their deficits. Not only this, but when the PP came to power they made no secret of the fact that they were considering how some of the functions of the ACs could be re-centralised, ostensibly because of problems of duplication and inefficiency.

It was in this context that Mas attempted to gain support for a bilateral fiscal relationship with the Spanish state, known as the *Pacte Fiscal* (Fiscal Pact). The origins of this idea lie in the Basque Autonomous Community's *Concierto Económico*, mentioned earlier, which allows it to collect and retain most of its own tax revenue: 'the best fiscal deal by far in all of Spain' (Martínez-Herrera and Miley, 2010: 16). (Navarre has a similar system, but these are the only two ACs to do so.) Although the *Concierto* has historical precedents, it was not a foregone conclusion that the Statute of Autonomy the Basques negotiated during the transition to democracy would include it, and some determination was necessary to make sure that it did. In his memoires, Jordi Pujol reflects on the reasons why Catalonia did not make a similar claim at that time. He alleges that CDC did push for this but was overruled by the Catalan branches of state-wide parties (PSOE, UCD), because they thought the Basque system problematic and out-dated (Pujol, 2011: Kindle loc. 2676–2711). Pujol tried to better Catalonia's fiscal autonomy throughout his term of office, and a parliamentary study on the possibility of a *Concierto Económico* was carried out in 1999. It is therefore not surprising that – given the general dissatisfaction with the fiscal provisions in the new Statute – Mas should have tried to move forward with the idea after coming to power in 2010.

In 2011, following a joint proposal from CiU and ERC, Catalonia's parliament commissioned a cross-party study of a potential new financial model based on the idea of the *Concierto Económico*. The final report begins with extracts from various parliamentary resolutions approved between 2000 and 2011 that called for a new fiscal relationship between Catalonia and Spain (Butlletí Oficial del Parlament de Catalunya, 2011). It is interesting to note that the specific term 'pacte fiscal' appears in a resolution from 2000 and then disappears again until 2011, indicating that the negotiations around the new Statute had taken a different tack – one that would have been perceived as less threatening by the Spanish government. The wording of the resolution passed in October 2011 was however quite categorical: 'The Parliament of Catalonia notes the necessity of achieving a fiscal pact for Catalonia outside the system of the common regime and multilateral negotiation'.[5] The study looked at the German *Länder* as well as the

Basque Country and Navarra, and heard from a number of expert witnesses (mainly academics). Its conclusions were then used as the basis of a formal proposal that, after three months of negotiations, was approved by CiU, ERC and ICV, with support from PSC for some but not all clauses. Thus, the Catalan government was mandated by the parliament to seek negotiations with the Spanish government on a fiscal pact. Rajoy and Mas met to discuss the *Generalitat*'s proposal on 20 September 2012, just a few days after the massive pro-independence demonstration of 11 September. Unsurprisingly, Rajoy roundly rejected the possibility of such a pact, citing its unconstitutionality.

Although the *Cercle Català de Negocis* was a keen supporter of the push for a fiscal pact, the actions of other civil groups at this time tended to be more concerned with matters to do with sovereignty in general terms. This included a concerted effort to organise unofficial local referenda on independence in as many parts of Catalonia as possible. The event that began this trend was held in the small town of Arenys de Munt on 13 September 2009. The initiative came from a local group, the *Moviment Arenyenc per a l'Autodeterminació* (Arenys Movement for Self-Determination, founded in 2005), and was supported by the local council after a proposal to do so was put forward by CUP councillors. Although a legal challenge later meant that the council had to withdraw from active participation in the event, it went ahead with volunteer organisers and achieved a turnout of 41% of the registered local electorate (Muñoz and Guinjoan, 2013: 50). The 'yes' vote was 96.2%, which suggests that the symbolic and non-binding character of the poll meant those who might have voted 'no' saw no reason to bother to take part.

Nevertheless, the symbolism of this figure, the media coverage the event received, and the realisation that it afforded an opportunity to exercise some form of agency prompted other municipalities to organise their own consultations. Another 167 were held on 13 December of the same year, with more following over the next sixteen months, until a total of 552 had been organised throughout Catalonia by April 2011 (Muñoz and Guinjoan, 2013: 52). They had a combined turnout of 18.12% and a 'yes' vote of 91.7%. The last wave included Barcelona, an obvious risk since its more cosmopolitan population made a low turnout and lower 'yes' vote a distinct possibility, as well as being more difficult to organise because of the sheer number of potential voters. In the event, the turnout was very slightly above average and the 'yes' vote came in at nearly 90%. Even the Spanish newspaper *El País* praised the level of commitment and organisation needed to achieve this (Roger, 2011).

Muñoz and Guinjoan's analysis of how the unofficial referenda spread across Catalonia shows that municipalities with high levels of support for ERC and CiU were most likely to organise a vote, and having an established pool of activists to draw on was also a crucial factor (Muñoz and Guinjoan, 2013: 59, 64). Similarly, 'the turnout rates achieved [. . .] can be explained by the intensity of the mobilization efforts, as well as by pre-existing motivations and the participatory tradition of the municipality' (Muñoz and Guinjoan, 2013: 64). Like Serrano and Lluch, they also warn against a simplistic equation of support for independence with ethnic origin:

> while the percentage of the population born outside Catalonia was an important factor, its effect vanished after we took into account political factors (turnout and vote). This result points to the fact that we should not conceptualize political differences among different origin groups as 'essentially' linked to the national or ethnic background of each individual group, but rather related to party affiliation and therefore contingent to the political process. (Muñoz and Guinjoan, 2013: 64)

In other words, it is what happens after immigrants arrive – such as 'weak political integration in Catalonia' (ibid.) – that explains any lack of engagement with the process, rather than their origins *per se*.

The increased level of civil mobilisation achieved with the popular consultations went hand in hand with the creation and expansion of civil organisations over the same period, as described in chapter 1 of this volume. Much of their rhetoric at this time was couched in terms of the Catalans' 'right to decide', and even many of the unofficial referenda were promoted as an expression of this right rather than specifically as a call to vote for independence (Muñoz and Guinjoan, 2013: 50–1). It was therefore particularly significant that the demonstration organised by the ANC for 11 September 2012 was designed to constitute an unequivocal call for Catalonia's politicians to start a process of secession. As we have noted, Mas's energies at this time were locked into the *pacte fiscal*: a battle that was being fought very much in the political rather than the civil arena. His views on independence itself were not clear, and CiU as a whole harboured a mixture of independentist and other visions for Catalonia's future. Also, the popular frustration attached to the Constitutional Court's verdict on the Statute had been enhanced by the deepening of Spain's economic crisis. Specifically, many Catalans were angered by the need to ask Spain for extra funds to support the provision of basic services when Catalonia had long been a net contributor to Spanish coffers, especially if that meant accepting increased fiscal controls and even a reduced level of political autonomy.

As a result, as Carme Forcadell put it, 'The people are prepared, and we need our government and institutions to take a step forward, because we want a free and sovereign country, we want independence' (VilaWeb, 2012a).[6] Forcadell made it clear before the march that anyone attending would be counted as a supporter of independence, regardless of the slogan or flag they displayed, and an estimated 1.5 million chose to participate on that basis. Notable attendees included Jordi Pujol and several ministers of the *Generalitat*, although Artur Mas did not attend – he said – because his institutional position as President stopped him from doing so. Despite Forcadell's clarity on the purpose of the event, Mas also encouraged attendance by those who wished to support the *pacte fiscal* rather than independence, demonstrating once again the ambiguity of his personal views (ARA, 2012). The ANC had asked for a delegation to be received by the President after the march, but in fact it was the leader of the Parliament who did so. During this meeting, Forcadell formally requested on behalf of the demonstrators that the parliament begin the process of secession from Spain.

The clarity of, and level of support for, this message was somewhat surprising. In essence, it signified that a large segment of the Catalan public was prepared to take the extraordinary risk of moving towards independence even though the party in power had not directly encouraged such a bold step. This would appear to disprove the theory that the Catalan public is being manipulated by political elites (Martínez-Herrera and Miley, 2010). There are, however, several caveats that should be applied here. Firstly, despite the ANC's clear message that participating meant being counted as a supporter of independence, there will no doubt have been attendees with other agendas (e.g. the fiscal pact, federalism, or simply a desire to express anger at Catalonia's political and economic situation). Secondly, although the theme of the march was 'Independence in Europe', it is impossible to know how many of the demonstrators would have had a real grasp of what that might mean. As we will see in the next chapter, by this time the word 'independence' had become a cry of liberation that in some senses meant 'anything but the status quo'. Similarly, the soothing idea of remaining under the European umbrella begs questions about the process of being able to do so. As a survey published by *El Periódico* shows, support for independence drops by around 10% when the European element is removed, although 40% of those polled in 2012 were still willing to contemplate this (El Periódico, 2012). Nevertheless, the 11 September demonstration does confirm that the relationship between Catalan politics and civil society is both complex and reciprocal.

The Road to Referendum?

The 11 September 2012 demonstration was a watershed in Catalan politics in the same way that the march of 10 July 2010 can be seen as a pivotal point for the galvanisation of civil society. Its most obvious effect was on Artur Mas, who – after receiving confirmation from Rajoy that the idea of a fiscal pact would not prosper – took the gamble of calling early elections specifically in order to gain a mandate for a referendum on independence. Two days after the elections were announced, the Catalan parliament passed a resolution calling for whoever won them to hold a public consultation on independence some time in the next legislature.

The election took place on 25 November, but did not produce the result Mas had hoped for. Rather than rallying around CiU as the new champion of 'the right to decide', voters split their pro-independence votes between CiU and ERC (and to a lesser extent CUP and ICV). CiU lost twelve seats while ERC gained eleven. The Spanish media portrayed this as a setback to the referendum project as a whole, but this was certainly not the case. Added together, pro-independence parties now made up two-thirds of the parliament. However, it appears that many voters saw parties other than CiU – especially ERC – as a safer choice to ensure that a referendum would actually happen, given the recent conversion of Mas to the cause. Furthermore, the choice of Oriol Junqueras as ERC's candidate for the presidency reinstated some of the credibility for the party that had been lost in the era of the *tripartit*. Junqueras knew that ERC's support would be crucial if Mas was to try to organise a referendum, but was wary of the potential pitfalls of too close a relationship. Despite being offered a partnership with CiU, ERC instead chose to take up its place in opposition (having won more votes than the PSC), but to support CiU on matters relating to Catalonia's sovereignty. This would allow them to express their disagreement on other matters, such as welfare cuts.

Other than allowing Mas to be confirmed as President, the first major outcome of this agreement was the drafting of a 'Declaration of Sovereignty and the Right to Decide of the People of Catalonia', presented to the new parliament at its first sitting in January 2013. The text makes a clear claim to Catalan sovereignty: 'The Catalan people have, by virtue of democratic legitimacy, the character of a sovereign political and legal subject'.[7] It also repeatedly uses the phrase 'right to decide', committing the parliament to beginning a process that would allow the citizens of Catalonia to exercise this right. The declaration was supported by CiU, ERC, ICV and one member of CUP. The PSC – with its renewed commitment to federalism under Pere Navarro – had ordered its members to vote against, but a quarter of its deputies did not cast votes so as not to have to do so. In Madrid, the PP's initial reaction was to state that the Declaration had no legal effects and was therefore unimportant, but nevertheless it eventually decided to put up a challenge in the Constitutional Court. As a result, in May 2013 the Court suspended the Declaration while it began the process of studying its constitutionality.

Meanwhile, pressure was building on Artur Mas to set a timeframe for a referendum. The resolution passed by parliament before the elections had simply stated that it should take place during the next term, but the obvious date for any kind of consultation was the autumn of 2014. Not only was this to be the date for the Scottish referendum – potentially enhancing international interest by exploiting the coincidence of two such momentous events – , it would also be the three-hundredth anniversary of the loss of Catalonia's autonomy. Not surprisingly, ERC were keen to push for this, and Mas therefore found himself agreeing to hurry preparations along. In July 2013, he sent a letter to Rajoy asking to begin negotiations on how a referendum might take place, as if in a final attempt to find a consensual way forward. When this initiative failed, the Catalan parliament set about devising its own process for holding a referendum, which was nevertheless based partly on the idea that under article 150.2 of the Spanish Constitution the Spanish government would be able to transfer to Catalonia the power to hold a legal referendum (Mateos, 2013). Attempts to involve the PSC in these plans were unsuccessful, causing further internal dissent among the Catalan socialists, many of whom would personally have wished to support the idea of a legal consultation (González, 2013). Meanwhile, preparations for independence began in earnest with the constitution of an advisory group of experts, and plans for a strengthened tax-collecting body to be in place ready to take over all Spain's functions at the point of independence.

At the level of local government, the *Associació de Municipis per la Independència,* founded in September 2011, continued to increase its membership, reaching 670 local councils and 36 other local government entities (including two provinces) by September 2013. Many of these also declared themselves 'Free Catalan Territories', following a precedent set by the village of Sant Pere de Torelló in September 2012. While this obviously had no legal effect, the declaration was intended to spur the *Generalitat* into action on independence by stating that the municipality's allegiance to the Spanish Constitution and law was temporary, until Catalonia had such instruments of its own. A year later, around one fifth of Catalonia's municipalities had followed suit.

Civil organisations were also keeping up the pressure, since there was obviously a danger that public support might be lost if the momentum gained in 2012 could not be carried forward. Once the elections were over, the independence debate had become somewhat confined to the political sphere, but two large-scale civil events were being prepared: *Òmnium Cultural*'s 'Concert for Freedom', mentioned in chapter 1, and the ANC's human chain or *Via Catalana* (Catalan Way). This took place on 11 September 2013, and was inspired by a similar event in which the capitals of Estonia, Latvia and Lithuania were linked by a human chain in 1989 during their own independence struggles. Rather than trying to better the turnout at the demonstration in 2012, the organisers set a much lower target for participation based on the number that would be needed to form a chain from the French border in the north to Valencia in the south, passing through Girona, Barcelona and Tarragona. Once again, an impressively thorough organisation saw the different parts of the route being filled by asking participants to sign up in advance on the ANC's website. In the end, an estimated 1.6 million people took part, just beating the number of participants in September 2012.

Two opposing dynamics emerged in the period after 2005: the strengthening of the pro-independence consensus, and the reactive emergence of various forms of opposition to this. What Lluch terms 'the intersubjective relations of reciprocity' between a large number of Catalans and the Spanish government and media were ruptured by the conflict around the Statute (Lluch, 2010: 342). The fissure then widened every time an event occurred that Catalans could attribute to the neglect or contempt of them by the State. Sociologist and pro-independence campaigner Salvador Cardús stresses that pro-independence sentiment in Catalonia 'is not just something born of the here and now [. . .]. On the contrary: it is the result of a long, continuous and well-documented process of disappointment' (Cardús, 2010: 14).[8] Nevertheless, it is clear that the number of Catalans sharing this sense of disappointment was increased substantially by the events outlined in this chapter. One of the factors that facilitated this was the deliberate attempt by pro-independence ideologues to prise apart questions of identity and support for independence – a process that will be the subject of the next chapter.

Chapter 3

Political Discourse

The Triumph of Rationality?

As was noted in the Introduction to this volume, Viva Ona Bartkus theorises secession movements in terms of the constant performance of 'cost/benefit' calculations (Bartkus, 1999: 4; see also Sorens, 2005). A change in the political context will shift the equation either towards or away from independence as a viable proposition at any given time. Even a long history of grievances is not enough in itself to produce an active attempt at secession. Rather, 'For a community to decide to secede, it must perceive a change in its circumstances and its political alternatives' (Bartkus 1999: 8). While I disagree with elements of Bartkus's specific analysis of the Catalan situation in the period in which she was writing,[1] the concept of cost/benefit calculations does help us to understand the current rise in interest in independence in Catalonia, since recent events have focussed Catalans' minds on just such calculations.

Naturally, these events speak for themselves only up to a point, and political discourse is central to the process of making Catalans aware of their apparent new political alternatives and the factors they should take into account in their calculations. Politicians and pundits set out to give their 'expert' view, claiming 'to be not only "right" in a cognitive sense, but "right" in a moral sense' about what these alternatives and factors are, and how Catalans should act on them (Chilton, 2004: 117). Just as importantly, they need to make people care enough about the subject to bother to listen to their claims at all, especially those who have not traditionally recognised themselves as being interpellated by separatist discourse. As Bartkus points out, 'leaders cannot instigate a [secession] crisis without mass support' (Bartkus, 1999: 5); moreover, the demonstrable size of this support is directly related to the perceived legitimacy of the secessionist movement. Leaders also need to be able to persuade the public that any attempt at secession would not carry too heavy a price.

The analysis in this chapter will therefore focus on political discourse, as expressed through speeches and published writings, and as reported in the media. Its purpose is to show how, over the period from 2005 to 2013, a series of simplified messages about independence has been generated, transmitted, and widely accepted – to the point of being accepted as *doxa* (Bourdieu, 1986: 471) – even in some cases by Catalans who do not support independence. Behind this process lies a stress on the *rationality* of the idea of secession, distancing the pro-independence movement from sentimental or identitarian arguments, which are often instead attributed to the anti-independence constituency. This chapter will focus on three key claims: (1) that one does not have to feel a strong sense of Catalan identity to want independence, and arguments relating to welfare and the economy are just as legitimate; (2) that autonomy is fundamentally inadequate and federalism is not a viable alternative, therefore the only solution is independence; and (3) that Catalans have the democratic right to decide their own future. All three arguments rely on explicit cost/benefit calculations, some of which relate to economic well-being or political recognition, and some of which draw on more intangible aspects such as democratic rights. However, the stress on taking a rational approach to these calculations cannot hide the fact that they also have a clear moral and emotional resonance for many Catalans, a subject that is briefly examined in the final part of this chapter.

From Identity to the Economy?

As we noted in the Introduction, Catalan ethnic identity is comparatively 'thin', although that does not make it unimportant (Cornell and Hartmann, 1998: 73–4). Individuals still have a strong sense of what it means to them to self-identify as Catalan (Brubaker, 2004: 42), but it is hard to define the term in such a way as to indicate a coherent ethnic category, let alone a group (Brubaker, 2004: 12–13). Furthermore, mainstream, contemporary Catalan nationalism has always consciously defined itself in civic rather than ethnic terms (Brubaker, 2004: 134–5; Conversi, 1997: 192–6, 208–21). Where particular identity markers can be said to have both ethnic and civic features, it is the civic element that is stressed, especially by framing this within a discourse of inclusivity.

The prime example of this is the Catalan language, which has long been viewed as a mechanism of integration for new Catalans (Conversi, 1997: 194–6). The primacy of language as a marker of groupness has generally compensated for the lack of an ethnically-based definition of who is or is not Catalan. Indeed, as a collective noun, 'Catalans' would be something of an empty signifier if it were not for the association of being Catalan with speaking Catalan (Fernàndez, 2008: 234; Serrano, 2013b: 146). During the

Franco dictatorship, Catalans had been forced to relegate key aspects of their identity to the private sphere, because of restrictions on language, culture and the political expression of non-Spanish identities. Not only this, but a large number of immigrants from the south of Spain had entered Catalonia in the 1960s and 70s, changing the linguistic balance of Barcelona and some other major towns, and prompting a need for a new discourse of inclusivity that would also encourage these people to learn Catalan and become involved in Catalan culture (Conversi, 1997: 208–17).

With the advent of democracy and Catalan autonomy, Jordi Pujol and CiU therefore formulated a discourse that spoke primarily of language, identity, and the desire to construct an inclusive and prosperous Catalan society. Part of this discourse involved the rejection of separatism, and the assertion that the demand for autonomy was primarily based on the need to protect and enhance Catalan identity, rather than on political and economic factors (Conversi, 1997: 172; MacInnes, 2006: 687). This became the hegemonic discourse in Catalan nationalism at the time, although it was of course criticised from both inside and outside Catalonia: by some non-Catalans who felt that the insistence on identity was being used hypocritically to cover up Catalan material greed, and by the Catalan political parties who were trying to challenge Pujol's hegemony.

One of these parties was ERC. From 1989 to 1996, under the leadership of Àngel Colom, the party had developed a clear pro-independence stance, couched in terms of identity and nationhood – i.e. within the same basic parameters as Pujol's non-separatist discourse. According to Jaime Lluch, 'the social and political economy axes were non-existent in ERC's discourse during the period of Colom's leadership' (Lluch, 2010: 352). It was not until Josep-Lluís Carod-Rovira took over the leadership in 1996 that ERC's discourse was re-focussed onto the perceived economic and political benefits of secession. While certainly not dismissing language and identity, his view (as expressed in his 2003 book *El futur a les mans* (The Future in Our Hands)) was that these were not enough as the basis of a political project. Instead, he advocated a 'new Catalanism of well-being' (Carod-Rovira, 2003: 91),[2] and later expressed this even more starkly as a Catalanism that comes from the head and the pocket, rather than the heart (Carod-Rovira, 2008: 55). In other words, Catalans should be seeking independence because they will be materially, rather than 'spiritually', better off.

It is worth looking in detail at Carod-Rovira's thoughts because many of the ideas he expressed several years ago now form part of the standard arguments in favour of independence. In particular, his book *2014*, published in 2008, has been influential in contributing to the independence debate and the pressure for a referendum. This is partly because of the publicity it generated at the time of publication (when he was Vice-President of the *Generalitat*), which included the publication of some extracts in *El Periódico* and a review in *El País* (Vilaregut, 2008). The ideas presented in the book were reinforced and further developed in a speech given in November 2009 with the title 'Goodbye nationalism, long live the nation!' (Carod-Rovira, 2009).[3] As has already been noted, the most interesting feature of his discourse at this time was the downplaying and even dismissal of matters of identity as a reason for supporting independence: a radical departure from the legacy of Pujolism.

Carod-Rovira's intention was to separate support for independence from nationalism, and identification with pro-independence arguments from feelings related to Catalan identity. Although it is sometimes repetitive and unstructured, the book makes numerous clearly understandable statements along those lines, indicating that it is not just aimed at readers who generally follow political debates but is attempting to reach a wider audience. Carod-Rovira makes his basic position clear early on: it is not necessary to consider oneself a nationalist to want independence for Catalonia, 'it is only necessary to want a better life for yourself and your loved ones' (Carod-Rovira, 2008: 16).[4] He then constructs an argument that urges Catalans to think with their heads about independence, rather than their hearts or their 'guts' (27). In his view, the kind of pro-independence sentiment that is born of a gut reaction against 'Catalanophobia' from the rest of Spain is 'adolescent', and has had the unfortunate consequence of making Catalans suspicious of the state as an institution (27, 43). On the contrary, he claims, 'the only thing that stops you having to give explanations as to why you are as you are, do what you do, speak how you speak and want what you want is to have a state' (49).[5] There is therefore no shame in wanting independence for economic reasons, since this is a perfectly rational position (55). Furthermore, Catalans should need no further justification for asking for independence other than the fact that they want it, and those who are in favour of independence should dedicate their time to make sure that this desire becomes hegemonic (85).

Carod-Rovira then goes on to suggest that when support for independence becomes a matter of rationality rather than sentiment, it also ceases to be inextricably bound up with identity. 'Loving Spain from Catalonia, being and feeling *also* Spanish in Catalonia, *more or much more* Spanish than Catalan in Catalonia – perhaps even *just* Spanish – is perfectly compatible with arguing for Catalan independence' (156).[6] Identities are complex and multi-layered, and therefore identification with Catalonia is more important than an inherited identity in constructing a shared sense of belonging (159–62). Neither identity nor nationalism are therefore necessary or sufficient conditions for supporting independence: all that is required is to want a better quality of life (258).

Carod-Rovira calls this 'practical sovereigntism', and in his review of the book Ricard Vilaregut labels it 'pragmatic independentism' (Carod-Rovira, 2008: 258; Vilaregut, 2008). The idea is not of course Carod's alone, although he does seem to have taken it further than others. His ERC colleague Joan Ridao, for example, explicitly disagreed with the idea that it is possible to be in favour of independence without also being a nationalist: since a desire for independence is a desire to see the state become congruent with the nation, 'all independentism is consubstantially nationalist' (Ridao, 2005: 174).[7] Even so, he seems to disagree more with the way in which Carod-Rovira phrases the concept, rather than with its substance: he suggests it is just a clumsy way of asserting the voluntarist form of nationalism over the organicist form (178). Carod-Rovira appears to concede this point in his speech of 4 November 2009 by continually speaking of 'essentialist nationalism' rather than 'nationalism' *tout court* (Carod-Rovira, 2009). He makes it clear in the speech that banishing essentialist discourses of identity and nationalism is a prerequisite for finding the kind of broad-based support necessary for an independent future (Carod-Rovira, 2009: 15).

What Carod-Rovira is advocating, then, is a collective push for independence based not on an abstract notion of the nation itself but on the welfare of each individual member. Catalans are being encouraged to act in their own best interests, and to safeguard the everyday elements with which they most identify rather than the continuation of a supposedly immutable identity. If their concerns are primarily about living standards and the future prospects for themselves and their family, then this is just as legitimate as wanting to protect their right to have their children educated in Catalan or to call Catalonia a nation. This 'practical sovereigntism' of 'the pocket' is indeed one of the directions that the dominant pro-independence discourse in Catalonia has taken – although not of course through Carod-Rovira's efforts alone. A survey in 2009 listed economic factors as the second most mentioned reason for supporting independence (by 62.3% of respondents) (Universitat Oberta de Catalunya/Instituto DYM, 2009), with a 2011 survey putting them first (Centre d'Estudis d'Opinió, 2011: 28–9). Arguments relating to identity are still given by respondents to both surveys, but they come some way down the list. In contrast, those who had responded that they would vote against independence were actually more likely to attribute their decision to opinions about identity or 'sentiment/conviction', with 60.8% citing the latter in the 2009 survey (Universitat Oberta de Catalunya/Instituto DYM, 2009).

Of course, this lays Catalans open to the charge that the short-term economic situation of Spain is a more important factor in the rise in support for independence than any other. Pro-independence campaigners tend to refute this charge by pointing out that Catalonia's economy has fundamentally different characteristics to other areas of Spain and has never been properly supported by the economic policies of the state (Canadell, 2013). The current crisis therefore highlights an existing reality rather than creating a new one. It could also be argued that the desire for independence for economic reasons is a logical extension of the regionalist discourse espoused by CiU under Pujol. As Rodríguez-Pose and Sandall point out, decentralisation is increasingly being viewed (globally) as 'simply the means to an end, a technical solution to the problem of economic organisation', and treating it in this way has made it easier for central governments to give concessions to separatists without losing too much credibility (Rodríguez-Pose and Sandall, 2008: 58, 61). Catalans originally put their faith in this route but have been increasingly disappointed by its results. Independence thus becomes the 'technical solution' to the economic problems that decentralisation has failed to address, if only because of the apparent impossibility of achieving a deal on greater fiscal autonomy. However, these arguments are more relevant to the elites than to an average Catalan. On the other hand, Carod-Rovira is careful to address himself primarily to those who are concerned about getting by from day to day and providing for their family's future. This is of course consistent with ERC's left republican ideology, and is one reason why the more business-orientated CiU was unable to capture more pro-independence votes in the 2012 elections. Nevertheless, both the 'elite' and 'popular' versions of the economic argument depart from the same basic premise: that Catalans would be financially better off if Catalonia were independent.

Alfons López Tena provides an example of the more exaggerated rhetoric stemming from this discourse in his book *Catalunya sota Espanya* (Catalonia Under Spain):

> Now the Catalan national project can be appealing not just to those who feel Catalan, and therefore mistreated, but also to those who feel both Spanish and citizens of Catalonia, and therefore mistreated; because this mistreatment is also felt, not nationally through the imposition of the Spanish nation, but through economic and fiscal mistreatment, and, in the last instance, as a result of the domination of a majority over a minority. [. . .] The Spanish discriminate against them as Catalans, even if they do not regard themselves as such.[8] (López Tena, 2007: 162)

Evidence that this message is getting through to new sections of the community is provided by the creation in 2013 of the organisation *Súmate*, which represents Catalans whose first language is Spanish but who are nevertheless in favour of independence, primarily for economic reasons.[9]

The increasing acceptance of economic concerns as a legitimate argument for independence in terms similar to those advocated by Carod-Rovira (since well before the financial crisis) has brought into the open economic cost/benefit calculations that might previously have been considered undesirable because of the danger of reinforcing the long-standing stereotype of Catalans as mean and selfish (Pujol, 2007). Pro-independence campaigners are now happy to air these arguments, claiming that one of the costs of remaining in Spain is to accept limitations on Catalonia's capacity for economic growth which in turn have a detrimental effect on the well-being of all Catalans. One of the benefits of secession, therefore, would be the capacity for a new Catalan state to enact policies that are tailor-made to Catalonia's economic needs and strengths, thus benefitting all of its residents, whatever their origins. The effectiveness of this message is confirmed by Ivan Serrano's analysis of data from the surveys carried out by the *Generalitat*'s Centre for Opinion Studies, which shows that support for fiscal autonomy has 'an independent and positive effect on attitudes towards independence even among groups with dual identities' (Serrano, 2013a: 541).

However, despite the popular appeal of these arguments – especially during a time of mass unemployment, wage and welfare cuts, and austerity measures – questions relating to identity remain important. As Rodríguez Pose and Sandall note, although economic justifications are becoming increasingly central in demands for decentralisation and self-determination across the world, these have a complex relationship with traditional identity discourses and are not simply replacing them (Rodríguez-Pose and Sandall, 2008). As Silvina Vázquez remarks, Herderian ideas of the primordial nature of the national culture and identity are still used to justify the argument that Catalonia is a nation and therefore deserves differential treatment within the state (Vázquez, 2011: 57). Furthermore, this vision of Catalonia as a 'natural' entity is often contrasted with a discourse that sees the state as a purely political construct or even an 'imposition' (57), with the implication that independence would restore Catalonia to its true, organic nature – not in ethnic terms but as a polity. In contrast, interviewees in Vázquez's study who were not in favour of independence regarded the idea as an unnatural 'breaking' of an entity that is coherent as it is (the Spanish state) (58). Vázquez's research was not designed to look more closely at these ideas of identity, but nevertheless she concludes that identity remains at the heart of questions related to self-government and is still a crucial determining factor in pre-disposing Catalans towards support for independence (63). A quantitative study carried out by Muñoz and Tormos in 2012 supports this view, and indicates that those with the strongest preference for independence are the most likely to justify this with reference to their Catalan identity (Muñoz and Tormos, 2012: 31). Economic arguments have therefore added to, rather than detracting from, pre-existing dispositions based on identity, broadening the appeal of independence without losing existing supporters.

The Disappointment of Autonomy and the Impossibility of Federalism

One of the problems with economic arguments for independence is that they necessarily have to be accompanied by reassurances that Catalonia would indeed be better off, and that any short-term economic decline caused by the secession process would be brief. Of course, this is very hard to prove because of the lack of comparable precedents, as well as uncertainty over key issues such as continued membership of the EU and the generosity or otherwise of the settlement with Spain. Fears related to these questions may make potential supporters of independence look for less risky alternatives (Hale, 2008: 76), which is why it is important to accompany any reassurances about the benefits of independence with arguments as to the unfeasibility of any other potential avenues. Pro-independence campaigners therefore devote significant effort to convincing their fellow Catalans that neither enhanced autonomy nor federalism are viable options. In both cases, the basis of the argument is that there is no likelihood of any Spanish government agreeing to implement a meaningful version of either. Nevertheless, there is a difference in the way that the two are described: Spain's 'experiment' with autonomy is couched as a failure and disappointment that belongs firmly in the past, while federalism – especially of the asymmetrical variety – is an impossible dream that could only come to pass in a utopian future.

As far as enhanced autonomy is concerned, the enforced changes to Catalonia's new Statute of Autonomy before it was approved in Madrid and the ruling of the Constitutional Court in 2010 are presented as concrete proof that Catalonia cannot achieve what it wants within the framework of Spain's State of Autonomies. Similarly, the mass demonstration on 10 July 2010 is portrayed as a sign that the majority of Catalans are already convinced of this fact (Sobrequés i Callicó, 2013: 124). Indeed, statistics from the CEO do show a marked fall in support for the option of autonomy after mid-2010 (Serrano, 2013b: 128). Despite being able to take advantage of these clear landmarks, commentators still engage in detailed analyses of the failure of autonomy in order to prove that this was caused by fundamental problems in the design of the Spanish state. This is to show that the events surrounding the new Statute in 2005–10 were not simply attributable to unfavourable short-term circumstances which might be rectified in future, and to confirm that Catalonia will never find a comfortable place in Spain on its own terms (Strubell i Trueta, 2008: 89).

There is no doubt that during the process of drafting the Spanish Constitution of 1978, there was no intention of creating the generalised system of autonomy that eventually resulted. As Javier Tusell puts it 'no one had even an approximate idea of what would be the final result of the process of decentralisation' (Tusell, 1999: 172).[10] The initial aim was to solve the specific problem of Basque and Catalan demands for a degree of self-rule, but what actually resulted was a complete regionalisation of Spain. Moreover, as Juan Pablo Fusi argues, there was only a limited understanding of the precise nature of the Basque and Catalan demands themselves. In *España: La evolución de la identidad nacional* (Spain: The Evolution of its National Identity) he comments that the provisions in the Spanish Constitution could never have 'solved' the problem of Basque and Catalan nationalism that they were ostensibly designed to tackle, 'because the nature of Catalan and Basque nationalism had nothing to do with the way the state was structured' (Fusi, 2000: 275).[11] It was assumed that reversing Francoist centralisation was the key to solving the problem of Basque and Catalan alienation. What was missing was an understanding that Basque and Catalan identity were 'historical realities, springing from long processes of consolidation and reinforcement of their own personality or differentiated cultural identity' (276).[12] Since Basque and Catalan nationalism were not simply products of Spain's centralising tendencies, they would not disappear as a result of decentralisation.

Given that the State of Autonomies was created largely by accident, it is not surprising that – as Salvador Cardús puts it – Spain 'felt threatened by its own invention' (Cardús, 2013: 97). As a result, for more than 30 years the central government's attitude to the regions has been characterised by a dynamic that couples administrative decentralisation with a preference for the homogenisation of regional powers (Serrano, 2013b: 59). This approach had the benefit of putting Spain in a better position to cope with 'new regionalist' agendas that were gaining momentum in Europe in the 1980s and 90s (Keating, 2000). However, it also put paid to the idea that the Catalans, Basques and Galicians could expect special treatment based on their historic differences. Many Catalanists view this as a betrayal and say that Catalonia's high level of support for the Constitution was based on the assumption that it provided for asymmetrical devolution.[13] Furthermore, they argue that the state is increasingly encroaching onto competencies that the Constitution originally reserved for the Autonomous Communities (López Tena, 2007: 98–9).

Not only have successive central governments fought against giving further powers to the Basque Country and Catalonia, other Autonomous Communities also worry that they will be left behind if certain regions have powers that they do not. Part of the problem here is that the ACs that do not claim a differentiated national identity have been unable to articulate a successful regionalist discourse without borrowing from the nationalist rhetoric of the 'historic nations'. Balfour and Quiroga correctly state that the regions feel that they need to be seen to have a strong identity in order to justify the existence of their regional institutions (Balfour and Quiroga, 2007: 74–5). However, there are many justifications for regional government that have nothing to do with identity but are based on arguments about good governance and economic viability, although these carry more weight from a top-down than from a bottom-up perspective (Rodríguez-Pose and Sandall, 2008).

Furthermore, as Margaret Moore points out in relation to Canada, many residents of territories with no sense of a sub-state national identity tend to be in favour of a strong nation-state, but instead they are presented with ever-stronger regional government, at the insistence of their regional political elites who personally benefit from this greater power (Moore, 2001: 118). The attitudes of regional political elites in Andalusia, Valencia and the Community of Madrid appear to confirm Moore's suggestion that 'granting political autonomy to groups when this is not required from a peace and stability perspective may create an institutional basis for exaggerating differences in order to expand power and jurisdiction' (ibid). Not only are regional politicians dependent on the central government for the legitimisation and expansion of their powers, but the main parties – especially the PP and PSOE – depend on their representatives in the ACs to support their state-wide policies and help to enhance their popularity with the Spanish electorate. This mutual dependency makes it difficult for the central government to give any concessions to a particular region without ensuring that the same is given to all of the ACs. Nor has the central government shown much of a desire to give such concessions. In fact, Luis Moreno goes as far as to say that 'The greediness of the centre towards the periphery may have been the most evident of the misguided tendencies of the country's political modernization' (Moreno, 2001: 138).

In this context, it is relatively easy to dismiss the idea of enhanced autonomy as a way forward (even in a future not conditioned by the particular brand of Spanish nationalism of the current PP government). Indeed, many of the same arguments can be applied to federalism, since this too would only come about with the consent and goodwill of the Spanish state. This is why the apparently more radical solution of independence is viewed by many as the only practical way forward, since this could be a unilateral decision (Cardús, 2010: 33; Carod-Rovira, 2008: 135–45). Once again it is interesting to take Carod-Rovira's thoughts in *2014* as an example of this argument, especially bearing in mind his role in moving ERC from a (con)federal to an independentist position. First, he points out that the only mention of federalism in the Constitution is a prohibition on the federation of ACs, which was specifically aimed at stopping Catalonia from attempting to negotiate formal links with the other Catalan-speaking territories. There is therefore no possibility of creating a federal Spain without passing first through the laborious process of devising a totally new Constitution (Carod-Rovira, 2008: 137). Secondly, it is far from clear what the constituent units of a federal Spain would be, with possibilities ranging from a federation based on all the existing ACs and Autonomous Cities, to an alliance with far fewer units that would be defined culturally and linguistically rather than by current politico-administrative borders.

Carod-Rovira criticises the PSOE for paying lip-service to the idea of federalism while doing absolutely nothing to implement this when in power, and concludes that even if it did undertake a federal reform this would only result in a new version of the current stress on homogenised powers (known as 'coffee all round') (Carod-Rovira, 2008: 139). Catalonia is the only region where federal ideas have a long political tradition, and there is very little genuine support for federalism in the rest of Spain. Catalan attempts to 'fix Spain', for example by proposing the use of languages other than Spanish in the Senate, are dismissed by Carod-Rovira as 'pathetic' and 'ridiculous'. Here, he develops an extended seafaring metaphor, mocking Catalan desires 'to have a place on the ship's bridge', which

> have been dashed time and time again against the rocks of cyclopean intolerance, uniformity and centralism. There is nothing else for it but to change the ship, the sea and the destination port. Any other route is destined, from the outset, to end in shipwreck, and this is clear even before setting sail. The next vessel we charter must be entirely ours, from the ship's identification number to the flag it flies. And if we have to share the bridge with someone, this can only be with the EU, not with Spain.[14] (141–2)

Carod-Rovira also dismisses asymmetrical federalism by asserting that anywhere this has been tried it has failed, citing the USSR, Yugoslavia and Czechoslovakia as prime examples, and making specific points relating to the cases of Quebec and Belgium. Indeed, many academic experts would agree with him, although John McGarry and Brendan O'Leary attribute this failure to the poor design of the states rather than to the idea of asymmetrical federalism itself (McGarry and O'Leary, 2007: 192). McGarry and O'Leary's 'recipe' for a successful design includes a commitment to 'consociational government at the centre' (McGarry and O'Leary, 2007: 198), an element that is also stressed by Ronald L. Watts: 'effective autonomous "self-rule" by itself is insufficient. Institutions and processes for effective "shared rule" have been equally essential in order to provide the glue to hold the different national groups within a federation together' (Watts, 2007: 231). The seeming impossibility of achieving this condition in Spain has led even the prominent former federalist and internationally-renowned academic Ferran Requejo to declare that he has 'stopped being an idiot' and now supports independence (Sallés, 2012).

The growing strength of this dismissal of federalism prompted an attempted fight-back in the run-up to the 2012 elections by a group of left-wing intellectuals, and the subsequent creation of an association called *Federalistes d'Esquerres* (Left-Wing Federalists – FE). While Carod-Rovira had poured scorn on federalism as a 'magic' (i.e. impossible) solution to Catalonia's troubles, the joint letter that prompted the formation of FE used the same adjective to dismiss the option of independence (Carod-Rovira, 2008: 136; Albert, 2012). The one-hundred signatories state that the economic arguments for independence are based on false premises and draw attention away from the real issue, which is the dual Spanish and Catalan identity of most of the population. Their own analysis has led them to conclude that 'a comparison of social benefits and costs is much more favourable in the case of a better federal position for Catalonia within Spain and Europe than in the case of independence'.[15] Nevertheless, they recognise the real challenges involved in achieving this:

> We are not unaware of the difficulties of what we are proposing and the genuine sensation up to the present of a certain failure of this proposition. On one hand, because the majority Spanish left has not wanted to play this card in any significant way, and on the other because the Spanish right is profoundly nationalist and takes refuge in constitutional immobilism whenever it is convenient to do so.[16]

Their specific call for voters not to abandon left-federal options in the

November elections was followed by the foundation of FE and a further determination to keep federal options alive in public debate in the run-up to the next Spanish general elections, scheduled for 2015. Nevertheless, at the time of writing FE had not been able to come up with anything like the kind of forceful argument in favour of federalism that others had found for dismissing it.

The weakness of this pro-federal discourse and the internal disarray of the PSC – examined in chapter 1 – have made it easier for pro-independence campaigners to claim that the only choice is between independence and the status quo. Nevertheless, in 2013 a new player entered this game when the leader of UDC Josep Antoni Duran Lleida began openly to press for a 'third way', despite the potential damage this might cause to the unity of CiU. Alarmed at Artur Mas's conversion to the pro-independence cause and the influence of ERC in pushing for a referendum, Duran proposed an alternative solution based on a fiscal pact, full cultural/linguistic sovereignty including control over education, Catalan participation in international institutions, and a reform of the Constitution to recognise the Catalans' 'right to decide' (Barbeta, 2013). Duran's idea was to find a compromise that would address the main grievance of the Catalans – the denial of Catalan sovereignty – while appeasing the PP by taking the focus off independence. Artur Mas gave the proposal a polite but dismissive response that was also addressed to the PSC's support for federalism: 'I'm not saying no to third ways, but the fact is that the third way is the one we have always taken, and if we are where we are it is because third ways have not worked' ((Agències), 2013).[17]

Despite the difficulty of making a convincing argument for federalism in the present circumstances, Silvina Vázquez's study reveals a high level of support for the concept of federalism *per se* among ordinary Catalans (Vázquez, 2011: 54–5). Interestingly, those with a higher level of formal education tended to think of federalism in asymmetrical terms, while those with fewer studies equated it with an enhanced version of 'coffee all round' that might bring more competencies but would not have any particular benefits for Catalan identity (Vázquez, 2011: 54). This might be explained by the complex nature of the idea of asymmetrical federalism and the lack of successful models with which Catalans can easily identify, in contrast to the symmetrical versions of Germany and the USA cited by those with lower levels of education. Another of Vázquez's findings is that as well as having a high level of education, those who supported asymmetrical federalism were also generally satisfied with the functioning of democracy, whereas this variable made no difference in support for symmetrical federalism. This seems logical, given that in the current climate, plumping for asymmetrical federalism requires a higher degree of faith that the fundamental democratic conditions would be solid enough for this to come about if a majority supported it.

Vázquez's 'political satisfaction index' was derived from the CEO's data, as reported in their thrice-yearly studies on political opinion (Vázquez, 2011: 13). This is a fairly broad-ranging index that does not differentiate between elements of satisfaction/dissatisfaction related specifically to the Catalan political context and those that derive from wider political and economic factors (Vázquez, 2011: 65). However, when Jaime Lluch analysed attitudes towards the central state, specifically, in Catalonia and Quebec, he reached a slightly different conclusion: nationalists with

> highly decentralizing political orientations [. . .] have negative or neutral attitudes toward the central state and the perceived nationalism of the 'majority nation', while less-decentralizing nationalists (federalists and teleological autonomists) have positive or neutral attitudes toward the central state and have no grievance against 'majority nation' nationalism. (Lluch, 2012: 454).

This suggests that an individual's shift from a federalist to a secessionist position is most likely to be motivated by a change in attitude towards the central state, possibly as a direct reaction against 'majority nation' nationalism. In other words, the balance of the cost/benefit analysis associated specifically with the state swings from an emphasis on the benefits of remaining a member, to a preoccupation with the costs of doing so.

Viva Bartkus views the perception that there has been a significant reduction in the benefits of membership as more salient to secession movements in democratic nation-states than an escalation of the costs (Bartkus, 1999: 168–9). While a reduction in benefits is certainly a key factor, the power of discourses relating to the cost of membership should not be underestimated, especially in persuading supporters of federalism and enhanced autonomy to switch their preference to independence. Although phrased in different ways, the primary message currently being transmitted by supporters of Catalan independence is that continued membership of the Spanish state entails an unacceptable cost: that Catalans cannot be everything they should be, politically, economically and culturally. Furthermore, both federalism and enhanced autonomy are portrayed as ineffective methods for reducing these costs.

The Right to Decide

If one of the attractions of independence over other alternatives is that it could come about as the result of a decision made by the Catalans alone, then this pre-supposes the existence of a mechanism for taking such a step. While arguments in favour of a unilateral declaration are gaining ground within pro-independence circles, this is still largely seen as a last resort because of international reluctance to concede its legitimacy (Serrano, 2013b). The emphasis remains on the use of a referendum to determine the will of the Catalan people, with the Scottish example serving as an indication of how this might become a reality.

In political discourse, arguments for the legitimacy of a referendum have largely coalesced around the issue of the Catalans' 'right to decide'. While influenced by the use of this concept in other nationalist movements (most obviously in the Basque Country (Keating and Bray, 2006)), Catalans have made it their own ever since the debates around the new Statute of Autonomy. It signifies an assertion that Catalonia is a sovereign entity and therefore has the democratic right to hold a referendum. However, the Spanish Constitution recognises only Spain as a sovereign entity, and this fact is used by the Spanish government to block any possibility of a referendum. As we have seen, this attitude has been a primary factor in mobilising Catalan civil society and was the direct target of the *Via Catalana* protest of 11 September 2013. Moreover, under Spanish law, only the state can call a referendum of any kind, and so any attempt by the Catalan Parliament to organise one would be illegal. The raft of local consultations sparked by the first one held by Arenys de Munt in 2009 were therefore organised by volunteer groups without any institutional involvement, despite often having the 'moral support' of local councils. A 'Law of Popular Consultations by Referendum' was passed by the Catalan Parliament in March 2010, but this makes clear that the law operates only in the areas that are within the competence of the *Generalitat* (independence not, of course, being one of them) and that the authorisation of the state is necessary for any consultation to take place.[18] Towards the end of 2013 a different approach was therefore being planned based on two possible routes: a petition to the state to devolve to Catalonia the power to hold a referendum on independence; and a new Law of Consultations in Catalonia to provide for a non-binding vote if this petition was unsuccessful.

The discourse of the 'right to decide' is clearly a claim for Catalan sovereignty in the face of these restrictions, but it also functions as a unifying force in an otherwise fragmented nationalist movement. Terms such as 'independence', 'sovereignty', 'self-determination' and 'l'Estat propi'[19] are used in different ways by different political parties and are subject to conflicting interpretations. On the other hand, 'the right to decide' encompasses all of these terms; or to cite Salvador Cardús's critical way of putting it, it is 'a comfortable refuge so as not to have to call things by their name' (Cardús, 2010: 145).[20] More importantly, though, it is the 'right to decide' that has now become the hegemonic nationalist discourse in Catalonia, replacing the identity/language discourse of the Pujol years (as is evident in the fact that it became the basis of CiU's election campaign for the 2010 Catalan elections). It is used and defended by ERC, CDC, UDC, CUP, ICV and a plethora of civil organisations. The PSC initially rejected the concept: for example, they were uncomfortable with the idea of marching behind a banner proclaiming the right to decide at the head of the demonstration on 10 July 2010, and instead opted for a secondary position behind a giant Catalan flag. However, just before the November 2012 elections, their discourse shifted to state explicit support for the right to decide, although with the understanding that this meant that all options – including federalism – would be on the table. The pro-independence newspaper *ARA* described this as 'the most rapid U-turn in their history', claiming that it had been made as a result of public pressure and political expediency (S. González, 2012).[21] Despite this, the PSC refused to form part of the *Pacte Nacional pel Dret a Decidir* (National Pact for the Right to Decide) launched by Artur Mas in June 2013 as a platform intended to bring together civil and political groups in support of a referendum.

One of the by-products of this stress on the right to decide has been a relative lack of public debate about what might be the actual decision to be made: in other words, what is actually meant by the term 'independence'? There is in fact little agreement on this issue, other than a general understanding that it would involve membership of the EU and a close commercial and cultural relationship with whatever was left of 'Spain'. Thorny questions such as whether other Catalan-speaking territories such as Valencia and the Balearic Islands could be included in an eventual independent state are tackled only by the bravest of commentators (e.g. Bertran, 2007: 79, 134–6). Intellectuals and party-members do sometimes debate the finer details, such as whether Catalonia would be a monarchy and even retain Spain's King Juan Carlos as head of state (López Tena, 2010), whether Catalonia would need its own army (Carod-Rovira, 2008: 274) and whether the Spanish language would still have a privileged status (Bertran, 2007: 147; Carod-Rovira, 2008: 70–3). However, the public debate as conducted in the media has tended not to focus on these questions. It concentrates instead on the reasons why Catalonia might benefit from independence and the political process that might allow it to achieve this.

It is no surprise, then, that Silvina Vázquez's interviews revealed that the term 'independence' caused more debate and disagreement amongst contributors than any other in her survey (Vázquez, 2011: 56).[22] In her analysis, she divides participants' reasons for supporting independence into two basic categories: (1) economic – Catalonia would be better off if independent; and (2) as a way of resolving a stalemate with Spain – a kind of 'last resort'. The first group is described as having no real grasp of the issues beyond the simple equation of independence with wealth: 'a type of pragmatic discourse that does not ask itself how, when or – least of all – why' (Vázquez, 2011: 56).[23] In contrast, the second group is clear on the 'why', although not the 'how' or 'when': independence would only be necessary when all other avenues of persuading Spain to recognise Catalonia's difference, and the rights that are perceived to derive from that, have failed (56–7).

The important thing to note about demands for the recognition of Catalan sovereignty is that they are constantly placed (by those who articulate them) in the context of the Spanish government's refusal to properly acknowledge the plurality of Spain. They claim that Spain's reluctance even to discuss the issue of Catalan independence indicates a 'democratic deficit', or political immaturity, that is not present in other multinational states such as the UK.[24] This deficit is explicitly contrasted with the democratic purity of the Catalan independence movement (Cardús, 2010: 66), as encapsulated in the very phrase 'the right to decide'. It is therefore not surprising that in a survey of Catalans conducted in 2009, 85.7% of respondents agreed with the statement that 'any decision [about Catalonia's political future] made democratically by the citizens of Catalonia must be respected by the institutions of the State' (Ferran Sáez, 2011b: 310).

As Ivan Serrano says, despite the ambiguity of the concept of the 'right to decide', 'it has managed to incorporate into political language a call for self-recognition as a *demos*, that is, as a subject of political decision-making, in an intelligible way' (Serrano, 2013b: 137).[25] Its force therefore lies in convincing more Catalans that Catalonia is a naturally sovereign entity without having to engage directly with a concept as complex as sovereignty. Indeed, its ambiguity beyond that is a distinct advantage, papering over some of the fundamental cracks in the pro-independence movement.

The Emotive Properties of Rational Argument

We have seen here how three particular arguments have evolved into easy-to-understand forms with widespread appeal: everyone would be better off in an independent Catalonia regardless of their origins; independence is the only genuine option to achieve this improvement; and Catalan citizens have the democratic right to decide their own future. These arguments are under-pinned by notions of strict rationality and democratic acceptability. Moreover, they are not formulated as expressions of ethnic politics but as political arguments *tout court*.[26]

However, there is a negative side to this apparent reasonableness, since the *doxa* of rationality and democracy allows those who argue against these statements to be easily dismissed as irrational and undemocratic, without needing to engage in detail with their arguments. Furthermore, political discourses which stress the rationality of the pro-independence position disguise the fact that many of these arguments still appeal directly to partic-ular emotions or sentiments. One simple example of this is the way that the phrase 'dèficit fiscal' – which represents a technical argument based on financial data – has increasingly been replaced by the loaded term 'espoli fiscal': 'fiscal plunder'. This transfers the emphasis from the effect to the agent, and carries an inherent condemnation of the practice as immoral. To speak of 'espoli fiscal' is therefore to engage in 'emotive coercion', inviting the hearer to respond with anger (Chilton, 2004: 118). Such coercion takes advantage of the fact that, as Hale puts it, 'people can become passionate about national independence in part *because* it is associated strongly with long-term economic expectations that they see as having very direct and important effects on their life chances' (Hale, 2008: 85).

Carod-Rovira wanted to consign to the past the figure of the *català emprenyat*, the 'angry Catalan' whose support for independence is born of a knee-jerk reaction against injustices perpetrated by 'Madrid' (Carod-Rovira, 2008: 27). However, the notion has actually become even more relevant since the PP came to power in November 2011, because of the increase in the number of direct attempts to curb Catalan powers. Whereas the original *català emprenyat* was largely motivated by the infrastructure crisis (Fancelli, 2007), this later version is responding to the PP's Spanish nationalism and dismissal of the Catalans' 'right to decide'. Nevertheless, this anger has much deeper roots related to the concept of other Spaniards' anti-Catalanism, which has a very long history. Joan Ramon Resina draws parallels with anti-Semitism: 'From the mid-19th century onwards, the Catalans have tended to be portrayed as the Jews of Spain' (Strubell i Trueta and Brunet, 2011: 65). Moisès Broggi identifies anti-Catalanism as one of the key causes of the Spanish Civil War (104), while Eugeni Casanova and Jordi Llisterri complain of profound and on-going anti-Catalanism within the hierarchy of the Spanish Catholic Church (128). However, the key element relates to attacks on the Catalan language, especially – in the current context – its use in education, although once again this is seen as only a recent manifestation of a trend going back to the eighteenth century (see, for example, Ganyet, 2013).

Complaints of deep-rooted anti-Catalanism tend to be met in return by allegations of Catalan 'victimism', especially from the right-wing Spanish media. Use of this accusation has become widespread as a way of disqualifying Catalan claims for differentiated treatment and it is often deployed by members of the public in comments on blogs and news sites. All this means that the public image of the Catalans within Spain has become increasingly at odds with the Catalans' own self image (Bel, 2013: 61–95). In some cases, in fact, the two are diametrically opposed: Catalans see themselves as industrious and entrepreneurial while others see them as money-grabbing; they see Catalan nationalism as inclusive and civic while others see it as exclusive and ethnic (Miley, 2007); they see the Catalan language as an open route to integration in Catalan society whereas others see it as a deliberately-enforced social, political and economic barrier (see Lodares, 2005; and Marfany, 2006). Catalans have reacted to these negative images with intense frustration, but not – in the main – with hatred: rather they complain of not being understood and being unfairly disliked as a result (Castro, 2013). Collective actions such as lipdubs or demonstrations then turn this frustration into the more positive emotions of pride and belonging, and what we might call 'enacting being Catalan' becomes associated with joyfulness, a sense of community, and enthusiasm.

Beyond Politics

As we have seen, Thomas Jeffrey Miley and César García accuse Catalan elites of trying to assimilate others into their ethnic group, marginalising and silencing those who will not do so, while Ahmad views them as using ethnicity as a tool in a fundamentally political conflict, and for instrumental purposes (Miley, 2007; Miley, 2013a; García, 2010; Ahmad, 2013). Yet the form of secessionist rhetoric that has now become hegemonic in Catalonia specifically rejects ethnicity as a discursive resource. It is of course true that variations within the separatist movement mean that the figure of the ethnopolitical entrepreneur has not been banished entirely, and indeed some people will respond as if they are being addressed as part of an ethnic group even when they are not. Nevertheless, as we have seen in this chapter, acceptance of non-ethnic arguments is already generalised and still growing. A sense of groupness – which is vital to the secessionist project – therefore needs to be achieved in other ways.

An examination of the persuasive techniques used by pro-independence politicians can only go so far in illustrating how this sense of groupness is being generated and propagated. Nor does it do much to clarify the relationship between elite actors and 'bottom up' mobilisation. As Viva Bartkus says, 'Due to the often diffuse nature of disaffection with the ruling regime among members of the community, their motivations for protest and even for secession cannot easily be determined' (Bartkus, 1999: 5). It is therefore not surprising that the analysis of political discourse undertaken in this chapter still leaves us with fundamental questions and contradictions. For example, Lluch argues that instrumentalist or materialist perspectives cannot properly explain the fact that 'those nationalists who pose the greatest challenge to the institutions of the central state assert that a calculus of their material well-being, or economic considerations in general, are not a primary or even a secondary consideration for them' (Lluch, 2012: 455). Yet we saw from the survey data cited above that the general public rates material questions high on the scale of their motivations for secession. Do their responses reveal the genuine reasons behind public support for independence, or are they in fact just an easier way of rationalising their motivations than trying to explain deep-seated feelings related to identity that they may not fully understand themselves (Barbalet, 2001: 67; Muñoz and Tormos, 2012: 19; Vázquez, 2013: 72)?

While some of these variations can probably be explained by the presence of particular stimuli at particular times, they also point to the kind of 'contradictions inherent to the construct of the nation itself' suggested by Steven Mock (Mock, 2012: 280). Examining them only from the point of view of political discourse therefore provides a limited one-dimensional picture of the problem. Cultural and intellectual elites have been central to the success with which pro-independence messages have been circulated and adopted, and so cultural products must be part of any analysis of the 'moving picture' of this particular secession movement (Bartkus, 1999: 5). It is my contention that the focus of such an analysis needs to be on what Paul Chilton calls 'the strategic stimulation of affect' (Chilton, 2004: 46), and the ways in which cultural products do this work in an environment where the political discourse is predominantly one of rationalism. Without such an analysis we cannot fully understand how discourses such as those examined in this chapter become '"sedimented" over time', or how they function to heighten the sense of risk attached to remaining part of the Spanish state (Özkirimli, 2010: 208; Hale, 2008: 78–80). The next three chapters therefore focus specifically on cultural products and the kinds of secessionist discourse with which they engage.

Chapter 4

Past/Present Heroes and the Future Catalan State

Catalonia's past has become a constant presence in twenty-first century debates about independence. In the last few years we have seen Catalonia's history explored in numerous television and radio programmes, historical novels, public talks, academic publications and conferences, YouTube videos, and the websites of associations whose *raison-d'être* is to challenge the prevailing wisdom about historical figures or events. This is perhaps unsurprising given the recent preoccupation in Spain as a whole with the idea of historical memory, 'a form of social memory in which a group constructs a selective representation of its own imagined past' (Boyd, 2008: 134). For Spaniards, this mainly relates to the need to acknowledge the horrors of the Civil War and its aftermath, and the desire to excavate mass graves to give their occupants a proper burial and their relatives some sense of closure. However, there is another aspect of historical memory in Catalonia that is more endogenous and is closely related to the evolution of Catalan nationalism. This involves attempts to demonstrate Catalonia's historical differences from the rest of Spain, to protest against historical injustices and the way in which these have been glossed over, and to legitimise discourses of sovereignty and/or secession (Keating, 2001: 29–33, 43–4). Catalan historical memory therefore has a broader sweep, concerned not only with the Civil War but with Catalonia's entire national history.

Duncan Bell argues that as far as nationalist movements are concerned, what they term historical memory is often actually myth: 'a story that simplifies, dramatizes and selectively narrates the story of a nation's past and its place in the world' (Bell, 2003: 75). The formation of such myths may be institutionally-driven or take 'multifarious subaltern forms', but it is the interaction between these myths and individual or shared memories that explains why this phenomenon has such power over our sense of national identity. Bell uses the term 'national mythscape' to describe the resulting discursive construction, which is fundamentally narrative in character and has an important 'temporal dimension' that reaches beyond the limitations of lived experience (ibid).

Analyzing cultural products and political discourses in the light of claims about historical memory allows us to pinpoint the major narratives and reveal the methods by which national mythscapes are constructed and evolve over time. As Jay Winter says, 'Collective remembrance is a matter of activity. Someone carries a message, a memory, and needs to find a way to transmit it to others' (Winter, 2006: 61). Current activity by the Catalan cultural elite very much reflects this need, which is increasingly predicated on the desire to rouse support for the idea of Catalan independence. Cultural products are a key tool in the transmission of this message because they can potentially have a 'particular resonance' within the national mythscape (Bell, 2003: 75). Also, as Bell points out, 'Myths do not simply evolve unguided, without active agency' (2003: 75). The producers of forms of culture that engage with questions of Catalan history are therefore important agents in the construction of the mythscape.

It is important to note that there are many elements that can be used to construct a national mythscape that do not in themselves presuppose a shared ethnicity. Indeed, Thomas Hylland Eriksen argues that it is possible to create a sentimental attachment to a national identity without recourse to ethnic factors at all, since in some cases aspects such as a sense of place and kinship can provide 'emotional and functional equivalents' (Eriksen, 2004: 51). These have their roots in the everyday experience of the people, but can only be operationalised if they are woven into a national ideology (Eriksen, 2004: 54, 59). Where this is done successfully, it results in 'alternative kinds of imagined communities, based not on fictional bloodlines and shared history but on shared futures and multiple pasts' (Eriksen, 2004: 61). In this chapter, I will explore some of the ways in which kinship and place are woven into the historical narrative that constructs Catalonia as a non-ethnic nation and asks all its citizens to be prepared to fight for a future state.

There are of course many case-studies that could be chosen to illustrate this, but here I am going to concentrate on the figure of the national hero. As Linas Eriksonas says, the 'concept of the national hero [is] a notion which lends the idea of nationalism a human face' (Eriksonas, 2004: 15). The virtues embodied by the figure of the national hero are exemplary in two ways: in general terms as epitomising humanity's capacity for sincerity and self-sacrifice, and specifically as a model to be emulated by other members of the nation (Eriksonas, 2004: 24, 32). This is why 'heroes become icons. Their character becomes the national character' (Reicher & Hopkins, 2001: 131). It is therefore in the interests of pro-independence groups and individuals to promote awareness of heroic figures and to paint their deeds in the best possible light.

As we will see, there have indeed been numerous ways in which Catalonia's national heroes have come to the fore over recent years, and are explicitly commended as an example to other Catalans. However, this is not just a case of engendering a fighting spirit in readiness for an attempt at secession. More subtly, these figures and their exploits are also being used to overcome a historical reluctance to the very concept of a Catalan state, and to send reassuring messages about the way such a thing would differ from the current Spanish state. This reassurance, however, masks a more painful truth: that a new Catalan state would in fact operate on the same basis as the Spanish one, requiring members 'to commit to a system of organized violence' (Marvin and Ingle, 1999: 66). To illustrate this, this chapter will explore the ways in which a particular historical event – the defeat of Catalonia at the hands of Philip V in 1714 – has provided both real and fictionalised heroes that can be used not just as models of patriotic behaviour but also as justifications for statehood. It will then consider how the framework established by the myth of 1714 can be used in the present to create contemporary heroes whose role is to convince Catalans that the kind of sacrifice made by the heroes of the past is just as necessary in the present.

L'Onze de setembre and its Historical Heroes

Catalonia's national day – 11 September – commemorates the end of the siege of Barcelona on that day in 1714. The date marks the fall of the city to the troops of Felipe de Borbón (Philip V), the preferred candidate of France and Castile to the Spanish throne after the death of Charles II. Barcelona and Mallorca were the only territories that had continued to resist after a chain of events that involved the defeat of their allies in Valencia and Aragón, the surprise installation of their preferred candidate the Archduke Charles of Austria as the new Holy Roman Emperor, and the subsequent treaties that eliminated the English, Dutch and Portuguese from the conflict. However, while this description of territorial divisions makes it sound as though there was a straightforward split of allegiances between the Crowns of Castile and Aragón,[1] this was not the case, and moreover the conflict had no separatist dimensions, since the matter at stake was who would be the best ruler for the whole of Spain (Fernández Díaz, 1993: 78–80). On the other hand, it is true that the issue of respect for the institutions, traditional rights (*fueros*) and characteristics of the different territories of Spain was the main motive in the rejection of Bourbon absolutism by many residents of the Crown of Aragón (Albertí, 2006: 44, 57–8).

The commemoration of the events surrounding the siege has been an important rallying point for Catalan resistance and remembrance since the late nineteenth century, especially during repressive regimes (Balcells, 2008: 86–161; Crexell, 1985). Despite the activities of these committed Catalanists, Francoist historical revisionism left many ignorant of these dimensions of the War of Succession, even in Catalonia itself. Furthermore, the teaching of Spanish history stressed the reign of the *Reyes Católicos* (in the late 15ᵗʰ and early 16ᵗʰ centuries) as the period in which Spain became a single nation, thus disqualifying the notion that Catalonia could have had meaningfully distinctive institutions to lose in 1714. It is therefore not surprising that Catalanists still perceive a need to put forward their own version of these events, and to stress their historical verifiability (Junqueras i Vies, 1998). Some go even further, citing the defeat of 1714 as the key cause of Catalonia's present unsatisfactory situation, and therefore part of the justification for contemporary claims to sovereignty (e.g. Pujol, 2012b). The fact that the three-hundredth anniversary of this event would fall in 2014 also led to this year becoming the focus of demands for a referendum on independence (Carod-Rovira, 2008).

The events of 1714 might seem an unlikely hunting-ground for heroes, given that they culminated in a military rout and the loss of Catalonia's autonomous insitutions. However, in his book on *Symbols of Defeat in the Construction of National Identity,* Steven J. Mock argues that there is no contradiction in finding a moment of defeat at the heart of nationalist mythology. On the contrary, it serves various crucial purposes, such as explaining the decline of the nation while at the same time mobilising its members in a project to produce a better future. 'In order for the golden age to be restored by means of a revived ethnic solidarity, it must be seen to have fallen, that solidarity destroyed' (Mock, 2012: 27). Heroes associated with national defeats not only provide role-models for this revival, but also 'the fact that the nation continues to live on in spite of the defeat to commemorate the heroic act serves as concrete proof that those who altruistically choose suffering or death on behalf of the nation do not do so in vain.' (277).

In fact, the War of Succession gave Catalonia two important national heroes: Rafael Casanova (1660–1743), who led the defence of Barcelona and survived to tell the tale, and Josep Moragues (1669–1715), a General who was executed for his continued resistance. Casanova is the 'official' hero whose actions are commemorated with a ceremony at his statue each year on 11 September. Moragues, on the other hand, has become a symbol for pro-independence groups, because his status as a martyr is more suitable for their purposes. As we have seen, it is vital that candidates for heroic status have the right qualities, since they are both icons and role-models. This is certainly apparent from the different uses that have been made of Casanova and Moragues by Catalanists, and the differing attitudes towards them of moderate and pro-independence political parties and associations.

The 'official' hero of the War of Succession, Rafael Casanova, was a lawyer and statesman. In 1713, when the siege of Barcelona had already begun, he became the head of the *Consell de Cent,* or Council of One Hundred, which was the organ of municipal government in Barcelona. This also made him responsible for the city's civilian defence force (*La Coronela*) at this crucial time. Given the small number of regular troops left in Barcelona, *La Coronela* represented the city's main defence. When the final attack came, Casanova took out onto the battlements the flag of Santa Eulàlia, in order to inspire his men.[2] This is the main reason for his heroic status, as he urged them not to give up despite the hopelessness of the situation, and was wounded as he proudly waved the flag. However, he was not actually killed during the action, but was taken to hospital, where he managed to contrive to get himself declared dead and smuggled out (disguised, they say, as a monk or priest). This enabled him to lie low until 1719, when he was able to return to public life; he later went back to work as a lawyer. In 1725 his confiscated goods were returned to him when a peace treaty was finally signed between Spain and the Holy Roman Empire. He died at the ripe old age of 83.

His survival and eventual return to a normal life is one of the reasons why he is not regarded as a suitable symbol for the pro-independence movement. He also does not appear to have had the typical disposition of a hero: Santiago Albertí describes him as 'serene and lucid', a man who preferred 'quiet, efficient activity' rather than brash acts of heroism (Albertí, 2006: 337).[3] Furthermore, he was a member of the ruling class rather than a representative of the 'ordinary' Catalans who laid down their lives during the siege, and was very firmly associated with Barcelona, rather than representing the entire people of Catalonia.

Josep Moragues has none of these drawbacks. He was an ordinary man from Sant Hilari Sacalm in the present-day province of Girona.[4] Born in 1669, he was not part of the regular army, but nevertheless was to ascend to the rank of General. His first military experience was in the small groups who would help to block the French incursions into Catalonia that were common at the time. It is thought that by the time the War of Succession started he had ascended to the rank of Captain. Moragues was instrumental in recruiting six thousand troops to support a planned conquest of Barcelona from the sea by the Archduke Charles and his English and Dutch allies. When the fleet arrived in 1705, Charles promoted Moragues to the rank of Colonel (he was later promoted to General), and together they took the city. However, once Barcelona was taken and the Catalans had turned their support to Charles, Moragues had very little to do in Barcelona, and so he returned to rural Catalonia to drum up more support for the campaign and keep fighting skirmishes against the Bourbon army.

When the English abandoned the Catalans and signed the Treaty of Utrecht in 1713, Moragues refused to lay down his weapons. His continued resistance with just a couple of hundred men meant a perilous life with them hiding in the hills, away from his family who at one point were taken hostage. Moragues was not directly involved in resisting the siege of Barcelona but had led numerous actions designed to disrupt the supply and reinforcement lines to the city. Once he was forced to surrender, he put his own life at risk to ensure that his men were given safe conduct to Barcelona as the Bourbons had agreed. After the war, Moragues was summoned to Barcelona and told that he could not leave the city and must report in each day. He and some of his companions tried to hire a boat to take them to join the on-going resistance in Mallorca, but they were betrayed and handed in to the authorities. By all accounts, it was swiftly decided that Moragues would be used as an example: he was tried and executed within just one week. The manner in which he was treated is one of the fundamental reasons for his elevation to the status of a Catalan martyr. As a General he should have been treated as a gentleman, but it was decreed that his rank should be ignored and he would be dealt with as a common criminal. He was apparently tortured for information about his co-conspirators (which he refused to give), dragged through the streets by a horse, garrotted, quartered, and then his head was displayed in a cage – for twelve years. Reprisals were also taken against his wife and family. Antoni Pladevall states that 'no other Catalan suffered similar affronts' (2007: 11).[5] Moragues can therefore be seen to have several advantages over Casanova as a Catalan hero, including the fact that his death was bloody enough for him properly to fulfil the role of sacrificial victim.

The stories of both men echoed through the centuries, with the help of contemporary written accounts of the war and nineteenth-century Romantic poetry (Castellví i Obando, 1998–2002; Crameri, 2011; Marfany, 1992). Nevertheless, it was Casanova who was chosen to be commemorated with a statue originally commissioned for the Universal Exhibition of 1888 (Balcells, 2008: 110). Later moved to a permanent home near where Casanova had been wounded, it soon became a focus of Catalan commemoration and protest (Crexell, 1985). During the Franco regime, even though the statue itself had been removed, the site continued to be a magnet for illegal Catalanist activity. It was therefore no surprise that in September 1976, when the authorities refused to sanction a gathering in Barcelona, the first mass celebration of *L'Onze de setembre* after Franco's death took place in Sant Boi de Llobregat, where Casanova is buried. In 1977 not only was the statue restored to its former position (Crexell, 1985: 131), but a demonstration on 11 September drew an estimated one million Catalans onto the streets of Barcelona to assert their Catalan identity and demand a statute of autonomy.

On the other hand, no statue had been erected to Moragues by that time, and therefore there was no focus for a commemoration of his life. Although there are local monuments in the towns of Sort and Sant Hilari Sacalm, it was not until 1999 that arrangements were made for one to be placed in Barcelona. Even then, it was regarded as 'too little too late' by many Catalanists, who criticised its location (on what is basically a large traffic island), and its contemporary, and not very imposing, design (Gallifa Martínez, 2000; Pladevall i Font, 2007: 160–161). Nevertheless, pro-independence groups carried out their own commemorative activities there each 11 September. With the anniversary of 2014 looming, finally a bronze bust (based on the 'artist's impression' used in Sort) was erected at the spot where Moragues' head had been displayed, largely thanks to the work of civil groups who sought private donations for the project.

The statue to Casanova has suffered a different fate, becoming part of the institutional ritual of Catalan political life and therefore losing the symbolism of protest that it had in the past. Each year on 11 September an official ceremony is held in which the President of the *Generalitat* lays flowers at the base of the statue. In this sense the commemoration of Casanova is perhaps too much a part of the 'banal' side of modern-day Catalanism for the independence movement to feel comfortable with it (Billig, 1995; Crameri, 2000).

It is clear from the debates around Casanova, Moragues and their monuments that the key to understanding their significance is the way in which they symbolise the Catalans' lost statehood, and the chances of regaining it. Although already a part of a wider political entity through a series of dynastic unions from the twelfth century onwards, Catalonia had retained its basic rights and governing institutions until 1714. The restoration of the *Generalitat* after the Franco dictatorship involved only a partial recovery of these, as sovereignty remained fully vested in the Spanish state. Through the institutionalised ritual of Catalonia's national day, Casanova has become a symbol of this partial recovery, whereas Moragues represents the alternative of full independence.

It is interesting therefore to look at the Catalan case in the light of Linas Eriksonas' discussion of national heroes in Scotland, Norway and Lithuania. He too finds that the main purpose of these heroes is related to the question of statehood, and not just in terms of independence. They have also been used to symbolise the strengths of nations that were constituent parts of unions: 'their national identities [. . .] furnished the unions they were part of with legitimacy and purpose' (Eriksonas, 2004: 293). For example, if we take the cases of William Wallace and Robert the Bruce in Scotland, even though their deeds were referred to in epic poetry prior to the merging of the English and Scottish crowns in 1603, it was around this time (up to the implementation of the Treaty of Union in 1707) that they became important as national heroes. '[N]ational sovereignty was the common denominator for most manifestations of the Wallace traditions. Every time the Scottish monarchy was endangered, the Wallace traditions were invoked' (Eriksonas, 2004: 85). After 1707 their names disappeared from the political discourse on Scottish identity, reappearing towards the end of the century in Romantic poetry in much the same way as Moragues and Casanova were to do during Catalonia's cultural revival in the nineteenth century (Eriksonas, 2004: 122). In the nineteenth century, when Scots were major contributors to the British Empire and reaping the benefits from it, Wallace and Bruce were even utilised as symbols of union (Edensor, 2002: 161). For example, 'When the Wallace Monument was inaugurated by the Earl of Elgin in 1856, the Earl argued that it was due to Wallace's role in the fight for independence, alongside that of Bruce, that Scotland had gained the strength to enter the Union' (Reicher & Hopkins, 2001: 135).

Eriksonas argues that the development of national heroes in the modern age was fundamentally linked to the need to legitimise the creation of the modern state.

> The traditions of the national hero were conceived amidst discussions about the nature of the nation state and its relation to other international subjects. The examination of the origins of the heroic had hinted a link between civic humanism and national identity, both of which played the constituting role in forging the traditions of national hero. In other words, the idea of a national hero was inextricably, though not causally, linked to the issue of a civil state. [. . .] The hero embodied the virtues that made people into citizens. (Eriksonas, 2004: 47–8)

The need for a new ethics that would underpin the modern state in the absence of a monarchy that had been legitimised by divine right therefore brought the figure of the national hero to the fore. Precisely because of the civic virtues of the hero, even people like Wallace, who had originally been constructed as heroes of sovereignty (in this case, Scottish sovereignty), could be re-construed as symbols of a continuing national identity within the union when this was necessary. However, in the case of Wallace, this has not prevented him being reclaimed by supporters of Scottish independence, as was evident from the Scottish National Party's reaction to Mel Gibson's film *Braveheart* (1995), which it used both to promote the idea of independence and to increase its party membership (Edensor, 2002: 150–1; Reicher & Hopkins, 2001: 133–6). This makes it clear that, as Tim Edensor says, 'the continuing significance of Wallace lies in his flexible mythic qualities' (Edensor, 2002: 168).

Why, then, does it appear that Rafael Casanova cannot also be reclaimed for the Catalan independence movement, given his significance as a symbol of Catalan rebellion against Spanish oppression throughout most of the twentieth century? The answer is that of course there is no reason why this could not happen in the future, but at the moment the nature of his particular heroism is too closely associated with Catalonia's union with the Spanish state for him to serve as a symbol of independence. The 'routine homage' (Crexell, 1985: 17)[6] that takes place around Casanova's statue each *Onze de setembre* has made it a metaphor for compromise. The history of the monument as a focus for Catalan resistance and protest, from its creation in 1886 until the beginning of the Pujol government in 1980, is not enough to counter the 'banalisation' that has taken place in the last three decades. For independentists the ritual signifies settling for second best: the institutional acceptance of Catalonia as an autonomous community within Spain.

Antoni Pladevall attributes the choice of Casanova by mainstream Catalanists to the fact that 'he was less conflictive [than Moragues], cleverer, and knew how to safeguard his life without losing his reputation' (Pladevall i Font, 2007: 153).[7] As such, he represents the stereotypical Catalan virtue of *seny* or good common sense, as well as the history of Catalan *pactisme* or willingness to find a political compromise. On the other hand, Moragues' refusal to give up fighting despite the threat to his life is a better model for independentists than Casanova's sense of self-preservation, since much of their rhetoric revolves around the assertion that the Catalans have done enough capitulating and it has got them nowhere. Pladevall comments that it is always the more radical and independentist Catalans that prefer Moragues over Casanova, especially those that are not aligned with a mainstream political party. 'Moragues has been recognised and in a certain sense "adopted" by groups of patriots who are not associated with official organisms, who have made him into a symbol of vindicatory patriotism, as contrasted with Rafael Casanova, "the official hero"' (Pladevall i Font, 2007: 12).[8]

We might therefore associate Moragues with the quality of *rauxa* – impulsive behaviour – which is said to be another characteristic of the Catalans, diametrically opposed to the common sense represented by *seny* but nevertheless responsible for the more creative side of the Catalan character. Or, using Michael Billig's terms, we could say that Moragues represents a 'hot' nationalism while Casanova has become too 'banal' (Billig, 1995). Moragues has been chosen as the human face of the independence campaign, the historical hero who tells Catalans how they should behave in the present circumstances: they should have the courage to fight for independence. If Casanova symbolised the ability of the Catalans to hold on to their identity in adverse circumstances, Moragues asks them not to accept those circumstances but to change them.

Fictionalised Heroes: Ermengol Amill and Martí Zuviría

One of the disadvantages of historical heroes is that details of their exploits are normally patchy, and there can often be little (if any) surviving record of their thoughts, impressions and motivations. While the heroes themselves can be incorporated into a mythscape that overlays their actions with particular meanings, they cannot speak to us directly, only through our interpretations of their deeds. However, certain recent works of Catalan literature seem to be attempting to overcome this problem through the fictionalisation of real participants in events such as the War of Succession. As a publishing phenomenon, this has been small in terms of number of publications but important in its impact in the best-seller lists and media coverage.

One fore-runner of this trend in its current manifestation is a trilogy by Alfred Bosch, referred to as a whole by the title *1714* (Bosch, 2008). Bosch's work will not be looked at in detail here as it uses a fictional protagonist – an Englishman, John Sinclair. However, it is an important precedent for later novels on 1714, because of its commercial success: not only did it sell well, it has also been adapted for radio by Catalunya Ràdio and, at the time of writing, was to be made into a miniseries for television. Even though Sinclair is fictional, he interacts with many of the important figures of the War of Succession, including Josep Moragues and Antonio de Villarroel (about whom more later). Bosch's scathing portrayal of Rafael Casanova –

whom Sinclair describes as a 'withered dignitary'– is particularly note-worthy (Bosch, 2008: 440).[9]

In contrast to Bosch's fictional protagonist, the two novels I propose to examine in detail use historical figures who participated in the war but about whom few facts are known. The first of these is *Lliures o morts* ('Free or Dead'), written by David de Montserrat and Jaume Clotet, and published in September 2012. The protagonist is Ermengol Amill (1665–1732), who was known to have fought in the War of Succession and to have been present at the defeat of Cardona, which took place some days after the end of the siege of Barcelona. However, he has not been identified as one of the key historical figures, and few Catalans know of his exploits. The second novel revolves around an even more shadowy figure. *Victus,* by Albert Sánchez Piñol, published just a few weeks after *Lliures o morts,* tells the story of Martí Zuviría, a military engineer who is mentioned in Francesc de Castellví's chronicle of the war but about whom very little is known, except that after the war he escaped to Vienna.[10] Both novels weave fictional versions of the lives of their protagonists around verifiable historical events and encoun-ters with real-life participants in those events.[11]

One major difference between the two novels is that *Lliures o morts* is written in Catalan whereas *Victus* was originally published in Spanish (although it was subsequently translated into Catalan). Sánchez Piñol's choice to write in Spanish despite having previously published his novels in Catalan is an interesting one and deserves some scrutiny. According to the author, even he is not sure why he ended up writing it in Spanish: 'I don't have an answer as to why I wrote it in Spanish, the creative process can involve irrational factors [. . .]. I wrote a hundred pages in Catalan but it wasn't working; when I came back to it in Spanish, the story flowed' (J.V., 2012).[12] Many other writers who have made the decision to switch from Catalan to Castilian have been harshly criticised by the Catalan literary establishment (King, 2005), but Sánchez Piñol seems to have got away remarkably unscathed. This could be partly because, as the author himself puts it, 'It's not about preaching to the converted: this novel might make Spain aware of facts of which it is ignorant' (J.V., 2012).[13] Since transla-tions from Catalan to Spanish often fare poorly (Tree, 2011: 212), writing the novel directly in Spanish might be seen as a legitimate way of reaching a broader audience.

Victus, despite coming from a clearly Catalanist perspective, is also very critical of certain elements of Catalan society, such as the Catalan ruling classes who are referred to throughout as 'los felpudos rojos' ('the red door-mats') – red because of their rich velvet garments, and 'doormats' because of their inability to make decisions for themselves. Perhaps more surprisingly, Sánchez Piñol's protagonist is highly critical of the *Miquelets*, the Catalan and Valencian militiamen that normally emerge from the story of the War of Succession as selfless heroes. Instead, Martí's initial encounters with the *Miquelets* reveal them as unprincipled and bloodthirsty mercenaries, who enjoy – for example – burning the feet of their captives and forcing them to dance (Sánchez Piñol, 2012: Kindle loc. 2434). Of course, they come good in the end, demonstrating their fearlessness in battle and their personal loyalty to Martí, who has eventually won their admiration after many encounters in which they have tried to kill him (Sánchez Piñol, 2012: Kindle loc. 9840). Even so, they are never portrayed as having any ideals that might come close to a sense of patriotism.

On the other hand, the *Miquelets* encountered by Ermengol Amill in *Lliures o morts* are much more respectable. The authors paint a picture of the *Miquelets* as humble folk – like Ermengol himself – who are fighting for a cause: 'Most of them had a patriotic spirit and knew that Catalonia's freedoms were at risk' (de Montserrat and Clotet, 2012: Kindle loc. 914).[14] Ermengol is a teacher who is forced to flee his town after protecting one of his students from being raped by a French soldier. He initially joins the *Miquelets* because he has nowhere else to go, after a chance encounter with the legendary Bac de Roda, their leader.[15] He is trained by none other than Josep Moragues, and spends his spare time teaching his illiterate colleagues to read (de Montserrat and Clotet, 2012: Kindle loc. 927). He eventually becomes the successful leader of a regiment of *Miquelets,* but unlike Martí Zuviría's experience there is never any suggestion that they are brutal and undisciplined. Ermengol himself shuns 'any practice whose aim was public ridicule through terror. Like the other fusiliers in the regiments of *Miquelets*, he was no angel, but he always followed a code of honour' (de Montserrat and Clotet, 2012: Kindle loc. 3805).[16]

This is just one example of the substantial differences in the way the two novels treat their subject, which can be attributed to the stated intentions of the authors. *Lliures o morts* was specifically conceived as a project to bring to light an unrecognised hero and to encourage present-day Catalans to emulate that heroism in a move towards independence. In an interview with *El singular digital,* Jaume Clotet states 'We believe that the collective memory of a country is constructed through its heroes';[17] David de Montserrat follows this up by saying that 'In Catalonia, in 2012 and the years to follow, Amill's spirit needs to be very much present' (Anonymous, 2012).[18] On the other hand, Sánchez Piñol deliberately set out to challenge some of the myths surrounding the War of Succession (V. F., 2012), and this is why his protagonist is something of an anti-hero. Martí spends most of his time trying to avoid the fighting and have an easy life, but consistently finds himself caught up in the war despite his best efforts to escape it.

Despite these differences, there are also similarities in the overall impression of Catalan heroism given by the two books. Both Ermengol and Martí become part of the conflict as much by accident as anything else, and in fact Martí changes sides several times during the course of the novel. The need for self-preservation that explains this lack of loyalty to a cause also gives the novel the feeling of a picaresque adventure. However, as time goes on, another element is introduced that begins to outweigh self-preservation as a motivating factor: Martí's relationship with Amelis and their adopted 'family', Nan (a dwarf) and his partner-in-crime Anfán (a child). This strange allegiance eventually leads Martí to realise not just what is important to him, but also what is driving the people of Barcelona to sacrifice themselves rather than surrender: loyalty to one another born from family ties, community and – as Martí puts it – 'the accumulation of banalities. There is nothing more significant than the sum of a million insignificancies' (Sánchez Piñol, 2012: Kindle loc. 10250).[19] Martí's words indicate that he has become caught up in their fight because, as Thomas Hylland Eriksen says, 'taken-for-granteds [. . .] create a sense of community which is linked with space rather than time; sharing the same space rather than entertaining notions of shared origins' (Eriksen, 2004: 54).

Ermengol's journey is less picaresque but, in some ways, just as unconscious, and just as driven by love and loyalty. As has been mentioned, he is forced to flee his town after defending a student from attempted rape and, in the struggle, cutting off the hand of the Frenchman responsible. Ermengol later learns that the soldier, Le Guerchois, has avenged himself by killing his wife and child. It is this loss that drives him ever deeper into the fight for the Catalan cause: 'Who knows whether perhaps he had found the way out of his suffering and would be able to convert his infinite sorrow into the military fury that the country required' (de Montserrat and Clotet, 2012: Kindle loc. 1668).[20] Le Guerchois is Ermengol's recurring adversary, popping up wherever the *Miquelet* finds himself in the course of his military exploits in different parts of Catalonia. Le Guerchois therefore becomes the embodiment of all that Ermengol is fighting, both personally – in terms of the loss of his family – and with respect to the broader conflict. When Ermengol finally kills Le Guerchois near the end of the novel there is a sense that this represents a small victory for justice despite the Catalans' defeat. The symbolism here is heavy-handed and impossible to miss, since the weapon Ermengol uses is a sickle (*falç*), in clear reference to the 'Bon cop de falç' that forms the refrain of the Catalan national anthem.[21]

Unlike Martí who loses all his 'family', Ermengol regains contact at the end of his life with the son he engendered during the conflict. This suggests a certain continuity, which is reinforced by another symbol: the black flag he raises over the castle in Crotona (Italy) of which he is the governor. The flag was taken from the ruins of the church of Santa Maria del Mar, where it had been flying proudly on the bell tower as a proclamation of the Catalans' refusal to surrender. As Ermengol himself puts it at the very end of the novel, 'he had not lost everything. He had a son and a flag. "Maybe we're not free, but we're certainly not dead either"' (de Montserrat and Clotet, 2012: Kindle loc. 6183).[22] The use of 'we' here – and the present tense – clearly implicates the Catalan reader, inviting twenty-first century Catalans to play their own heroic role in what has turned out to be an on-going fight for freedom.

Both Ermengol and Martí survive for many years after the conflict and live to pass on their stories to others, and it is interesting to note that *Victus* also ends on a clear note of continuity. At the moment when Martí takes a cannon blast in the face, he experiences a moment of realisation that leads to these final words of the novel: 'the darker our dusk, the happier the dawn of those who are yet to come' (Sánchez Piñol, 2012; Kindle loc. 10652).[23] Nevertheless, Martí remains the anti-hero, and it is left to another character to embody the kind of heroism normally associated with key national figures: Antonio de Villarroel.

Villarroel was the military commander in charge of the defence of Barcelona. Ironically, he was not a Catalan and had originally fought for Philip V before switching sides. Furthermore, he resigned his post just a few days before the end of the siege of Barcelona in disagreement with the decision to fight on, fearing that this would turn out to be a senseless waste of life. Nevertheless, his heroism is never in doubt. Firstly, Martí makes very clear to the reader his admiration for Villarroel and his own estimation of him as the war's unsung hero. Weighing up some of the pivotal figures on the Catalan side, he says

> More than anyone else, I think of don Antonio, don Antonio de Villarroel Peláez, renouncing glory and honour, his family and his life, and all because of a foolish loyalty towards nameless men. I think of him, a son of Castile, with all the goodness of that harsh land, sacrificing himself for the defence of Barcelona itself. And what was his reward? To suffer infinite pain, and to be eternally forgotten.[24] (Sánchez Piñol, 2012: Kindle loc. 10566)

Secondly, one of the main reasons for this admiration is that Villarroel actually decided to lead his men into the final battle despite having resigned his command. According to Martí, Villarroel understood much better than Rafael Casanova that 'if you want your country to love you, you have to be prepared to sacrifice yourself for it' (Sánchez Piñol, 2012: Kindle loc. 10335).[25] Villarroel, as the great leader, is also the figure that glues together the heroism of ordinary Catalans (Sánchez Piñol, 2012: Kindle loc. 10597): he is its ultimate embodiment but not by any means its only representative, as is clear from Martí's own self-sacrifice. As far as *Lliures o morts* is concerned, the subject of heroism is explicitly addressed in much the same way that it is in *Victus*. The third-person narration contains various comments on heroism, especially when referring to Bac de Roda, Moragues, the *Miquelets* or the combined actions of the people of Barcelona. Ermengol himself denies that heroes really exist, describing them as nothing more than 'children's stories' (de Montserrat and Clotet, 2012: Kindle loc. 2760).[26] However, this is of course the type of modesty that befits a national hero. As with *Victus,* no one person has the monopoly on heroic acts, which is not surprising. As Steven Mock says, 'The heroic element of myth does not always find expression in a single figure. Indeed, because it represents a mode of sacrifice accessible to and demanded of the group as a whole, it is often far easier to portray this element through the depiction of heroic common and collective sacrifice.' (Mock, 2012: 175). In this case, the fact that neither Ermengol nor Martí are killed in combat also has to be mitigated by reference to others who did fulfil this sacrificial function.

Lliures o morts makes no bones about its attempt to elevate Ermengol Amill to heroic status, and the same could be said of *Victus*' perspective on Antonio de Villarroel. There is, however, a key difference in the sense that while Ermengol is clearly presented as a *national* hero, the heroism of Villarroel, Martí Zuviría and the other protagonists of *Victus* resists attempts to classify it as national or even patriotic. Sánchez Piñol suggests that his novel could therefore be seen as an attempt to lift the veil of myth from the events of 1714 because 'to explain reality is to demystify' (V. F., 2012).[27] However, he also states elsewhere that 'What is clear about the book is that we Catalans have survived until today thanks to the symbolic value of the resistance to the siege of 1714, because it involved a behaviour that brought out all the *rauxa* of the people' (J.V., 2012).[28] The myth of the single national hero is therefore dismissed in favour of a community heroism epitomised by the will to stick together against injustice. Those who are singled out as performing heroic acts are praised for their sense of ethical responsibility towards the people they lead, rather than to any national ideal. This 'reality', according to Sánchez Piñol's interpretation, then becomes operationalised as part of the national mythscape because of its symbolic value.

Both *Lliures o morts* and *Victus* therefore tell us something similar about heroes despite their differences in approach, but what do they also tell us about Catalonia's claim to statehood? If Eriksonas is right and 'the idea of a national hero' is 'inextricably [. . .] linked to the issue of a civil state' (2004: 48), then surely this will also be reflected in these fictional portrayals?

There are of course elements in both novels that reflect negative aspects of the kind of Spanish state represented by Bourbon absolutism. *Lliures o morts* makes specific reference to Louis XIV's scorn for the Catalan language, and to Philip V's disdain for Catalonia's Constitutions and the principle of free trade (de Montserrat and Clotet, 2012: Kindle locs 437, 473, 918). In contrast, the Catalans are pictured as fighting for their rights, Constitutions, and the means to ensure the region's economic prosperity: these are clearly elements of a modern civil state rather than of either absolutism or ethnic traditionalism. Similar motifs occur in *Victus*, always with Sánchez Piñol's particular ironic spin: the best King as far as the Catalans were concerned was one who ignored them and allowed them to get on with things in their own way, which is why the authoritarian Bourbons were so despised (Sánchez Piñol, 2012: Kindle loc. 1995). Moreover, the Castilians are painted as instinctively supportive of state intervention and authoritarianism, since the harsh Castilian landscape had engendered a set of tyrannical overlords, and the average *hidalgo* was incapable of doing anything constructive for himself (Sánchez Piñol, 2012: Kindle locs 2033, 2075). The Catalans, on the other hand, were fighting for 'Catalan liberties, which were perfectly tangible, the opposite kind of regime to the horror that was heading their way' (Sánchez Piñol, 2012: Kindle loc. 2137).[29]

However, we also need to look beyond these obvious statements, and to do so we can go back to Steven Mock's work on symbols of defeat. Basing himself on the modernist theories of nationalism of Gellner, Anderson, and others, Mock notes that one of the key premises of the modern state is an assumption of 'baseline equality of all members, common rights and responsibilities, homogeneity of culture, and a horizontal rather than hierarchical structure of authority' (Mock, 2012: 85). A key attraction of symbols of defeat for nationalist ideologies is that they stress the continuity of the nation while also allowing for its repositioning within this modern framework. As Mock puts it:

> The nation, to give structure and meaning to its symbol system, collectively chooses totemic symbols in the form of images from its cultural heritage, and this totem, in encapsulating and representing the unique

cultural values of the nation, is sanctified and worshipped by the group. However – and here is my key point – the totem must also be seen to die if the nation, as a horizontally structured brotherhood of equals, is to come into being. This necessary ambivalence, addressed in totemic society through rites of sacrifice, is resolved by the myths, symbols, and political rituals of the modern nation. (ibid.)

The hero's sacrifice, and that of the defeated nation itself, is therefore not just in the name of the original cause for which they were fighting, but also allows the resurrection of a different kind of nation.

The stress on Catalan egalitarianism in both *Lliures o morts* and *Victus* certainly points forward to a present-day nation with these characteristics, but as Eriksonas has argued, the national hero has something specific to tell us about the state rather than just the nation. Mock also takes up this point with reference to Weber's definition of the state as having a legitimate claim to the use of force, which means it needs to channel the individual citizen's potential for violence into the service of the state (Mock, 2012: 82). Heroic sacrifice therefore speaks to the need for each member of a society to 'surrender[s] his own capacity for violence to the will of the group' (Mock, 2012: 91). Such a surrender must be both voluntary and 'sentimental' (Mock, 2012: 73; see also Marvin and Ingle, 1999: 11). Moreover, the symbolic death of the nation at the moment of defeat, as well as coming to represent the founding of the egalitarian nation, also allows the birth of the modern state and legitimises its control of individual violence.

Yet Catalonia does not possess a state, and Catalan nationalism has traditionally been reluctant to claim one. In *Notícia de Catalunya* (1960), Jaume Vicens Vives traced this reluctance through Catalonia's history, using the metaphor of the Minotaur both to represent power (in the abstract) and the state as the instrument through which power is exercised. Never having learnt how to handle the Minotaur, Catalans ended up considering the state 'an alien phenomenon', and therefore not something to which Catalonia should aspire (Vicens Vives, 1992: 97–8, 105). This idea in itself has become one of the ways in which Catalans construct themselves as different from other Spaniards. Nevertheless, a fundamental question about the recent rise in support for independence is the extent to which people really have now accepted the idea of a Catalan state, as opposed simply to taking pro-independence positions in opposition to the Spanish state. In other words, does the rhetoric of the 'right to decide' actually conceal the same lack of commitment to the idea of the state that Vicens Vives identified as a constant characteristic of the Catalan nation?

The Catalans' participation in the War of Succession was never predicated on a bid for separate statehood. Nevertheless, I would argue that both *Lliures o morts* and *Victus* do speak indirectly of a Catalan state – and not just the will to fight against Castile – to their twenty-first century audience. In fact, both novels make specific reference to a rejection by the Archduke Charles of a compromise whereby he would take the Crown of Aragon and Philip the Crown of Castile, as if wistfully indicating what might have been if circumstances had been different (de Montserrat and Clotet, 2012: Kindle loc. 2731; Sánchez Piñol, 2012: Kindle loc. 5406). Clotet and De Montserrat certainly made no secret of their desire to influence readers' ideas about the necessity of a Catalan state (Anonymous, 2012). Even Sánchez Piñol – while denying that the timing of the release of the novel was anything more than a coincidence – has drawn his own parallels with the current situation: '1714 is the great turning point in the narrative of the history of Catalonia', 'now, precisely, we are about to arrive at the second turning point in the narrative [. . .] and I hope it turns out well this time' (Solà, 2012).[30]

Both novels narrate a process by which individual violence becomes channelled into the service of society, as if in preparation for creating the state that never was. Ermengol and Martí are 'loose cannons' – Ermengol because of his initial directionlessness and his desire to avenge the death of his wife and son, and Martí because of his picaresque journey through the vicissitudes of war. Yet both eventually end up devoting their capacity for violence to the good of a specific community. In this sense, Ermengol's killing of Le Guerchois, mentioned above, is significant because it is firmly legitimated by the overarching conflict and not just an act of personal revenge. The sickle with which he finishes off Le Guerchois is therefore not just a symbol of the Catalan nation but of Ermengol's acceptance that he commits the act on its behalf. Villarroel's command to Martí, 'dese' ('give yourself'), also suggests a subjugation of the individual to the greater good, giving Martí's eventual willing sacrifice the necessary hallmarks of heroism in the service of both the nation that must die and the nation-state to come.

The *Miquelets'* incorporation into the military structures of Barcelona's defence force is another obvious example of the necessary constraint of violence. Martí even comments on the irony of their leader, Ballester, behaving in a way that befits 'a responsible government official' at a moment when Martí forgets his own sense of discipline and hurls insults at the Bourbon attackers.[31] There is also an interesting moment in *Lliures o morts* in which news reaches Ermengol and his fellow exiles in Milan that the defeated Barcelonans have had their weapons confiscated. One of them protests that 'an unarmed Catalan is half a Catalan', and another confirms that 'the link between Catalans and their arms had an almost spiritual meaning, linked with belonging to a free people with its own Constitutions and laws' (de Montserrat and Clotet, 2012: Kindle loc. 5942).[32] This defence of the right to bear arms suggests that the embryonic state that would have sanctioned the use of these weapons has been rudely emasculated.

Victus provides us with another example of this subtext of statehood, and to examine this we need to return once again to the concept of heroic sacrifice. Sánchez Piñol has highlighted in interviews his criticisms of the Catalan ruling classes – the 'felpudos rojos' – and has claimed that this is one of the ways he questions the prevailing myth of 1714. For example, in an interview with the Spanish news agency EFE 'he makes it very clear that the role of "the Catalan ruling classes was very unfortunate, including actions that might almost be seen as treason"' (EFE, 2012).[33] However, according to Mock, the archetypal myth of defeat benefits from an act of treason, because it then has greater parallels with what for Christian communities is the ultimate act of sacrifice: that of Christ on the cross (Mock, 2012: 193–223). If we return for a moment to the story of Josep Moragues, we can see that his betrayal by the boatman who was supposed to carry him to safety nicely completes the parallels of his sacrifice with Christ's: he was betrayed, tortured, humiliated, and executed as a common criminal, only to 'rise again' – in Moragues' case as a secular national hero.[34]

However, not only does the presence of a traitor complete these sacred parallels, it is also a pointer to the need for a modern civic nation in contrast to a previous reliance on shared ethnicity. If blood ties alone are not enough to ensure loyalty (and that the capacity for violence of the individual is directed towards legitimate goals), then something else must take their place. As Mock puts it

> this narrative motif depends on a decidedly civic framework of national identity, whereby individuals who might otherwise share all of the ethnic signifiers of language, culture, religion, or descent are nonetheless expelled as outsiders for their failure to identify with the nation. (Mock, 2012: 215–16)

It is this that we see in *Victus* – in the shape of the thoroughly Catalan 'felpudos rojos' and 'their false and vacuous patriotism' – rather than one individual who betrays another (Sánchez Piñol, 2012: Kindle loc. 7499).[35]

In fact, the 'felpudos rojos' come in for just as much direct criticism as the 'botifleros' – those Catalans who openly supported Philip V – because of their hypocrisy and weakness. Martí forcefully condemns the dysfunctionality of Catalonia's institutions and bemoans the lack of willingness to do anything about this (Sánchez Piñol, 2012: Kindle loc. 2099). He is also scathing about the authorities' treatment of the enemy military engineer Verboom, whom they looked after so well after his capture that his life was much more comfortable than ordinary Catalans', and who was able to stroll around the city under guard surreptitiously examining Barcelona's defences – knowledge which he put to good use on his release. The imagery used here is worth noting: 'we brought the serpent's egg into the house and cosseted it until the viper was born' (Sánchez Piñol, 2012: Kindle loc. 5317).[36] The treachery of the 'felpudos rojos' therefore resides in their incapacity for leadership, but the gap this leaves is later filled by the ordinary people of Catalonia.

The key scene here is Sánchez Piñol's extended description of the debates that eventually led to the decision that Catalonia should fight on after the withdrawal of Austrian and English support. The 'felpudos rojos', unable to make a decision, call a meeting of parliament to discuss the two options: fight or surrender. Initially, the nobility and clergy are firmly in favour of surrender, however one nobleman (Emmanuel Ferrer) distinguishes himself from the rest by speaking in favour of continuing the fight (although on the false premise that their former allies could not ignore their plight and would come their aid) (Sánchez Piñol, 2012: Kindle loc. 5618). However, the vote of both the clergy and the nobles goes in favour of surrender, leaving the commoners to make their decision the next day. Many of the ordinary people who have been in the square outside awaiting the news are so shocked by the outcome of the vote that they stay there all night, and Martí remarks that this and Ferrer's speech are the two actions that swung the popular vote in favour of continuing the fight: 'Not an act of rebellion, but a deaf refusal to comply' (Kindle loc. 5658).[37] When the commoners' vote is announced, the public commotion and support is so great that many of the 'felpudos rojos' change their minds, forcing a continuation of the debate. Again, a lone voice of the nobility plays a key role here, Carles de Fivaller, as well as an unintended intervention from Martí himself, in which a demand that his own needs be attended to is misinterpreted as a plea for resistance (Kindle loc. 5729). Ferrer then dictates the *Crida* – the official call to arms that legitimates the use of violence on behalf of the nation (Kindle loc. 5560) – and the decision is made.

The crucial role of the ordinary people in this episode is designed to highlight what Sánchez Piñol describes as 'the great protagonism of the popular classes in the defence of Barcelona, which has always been tiptoed around' (EFE, 2012).[38] However, it also points to the weakness of the elite Catalan institutions of the time and the need to replace them with modern, democratic forms of government. As Mock says,

The ultimate nationalist sin is disunity. The defeat and the negative state of affairs following from it are depicted as having been caused by the failure of the community to achieve the ideal of unity and horizontal loyalty under the signifiers of the common culture. And these failures are seen as having been built into or, at the very least, allowed for by the very fabric of the society that is consequently destroyed. (Mock, 2012: 203)

This is also seen in Martí's own ambivalence towards the 'felpudos rojos'. He concedes that many had perfectly honourable motives for advocating surrender, and makes it clear that in many cases it was the constraints imposed by their social status and the institutions within which they operated that were the cause of their personal ineffectiveness. In this respect, they conform almost perfectly to this description of the mythical traitor by Steven Mock:

The Traitor in the national mythology rarely acts as an instrument of divine judgment, but neither is he dismissed as driven by a motiveless, diabolical evil. The circumstances that place him in a position to act against the common interests of the national community, and the motivation that drives him to do so, are frequently attributed to the flawed structure of the society itself. His actions, although dishonorable in their selfishness, are portrayed as entirely sensible in their social context, merely perpetuating the social stratification and factional in-fighting already prevalent in the ambivalent Golden Age that prevented it from being a vehicle for true national fulfillment. He is simply following the imperatives of his role rather than transcending and violating those imperatives in the interests of national solidarity. (Mock, 2012: 216)

Sánchez Piñol's treatment of the 'felpudos rojos' therefore actually affirms the myth of 1714 rather than substantially challenging it.

Both *Lliures o morts* and *Victus* paint pictures of heroes who come from the ordinary people or sacrifice themselves willingly to the cause of these people because of a sentimental attachment to them. In the ultimate endorsement of civic nationalism, the Castilian Villarroel becomes for Martí the greatest hero of the War of Succession: his ethnic origins are irrelevant to the kind of nation-state envisaged for a future Catalonia. These heroes speak of a modern Catalan state that has never existed but that is known with certainty to be radically different from a Castilian state: democratic, egalitarian, based on clear rights and responsibilities that are vested in the people rather than the ruler, and with a legitimate mission to which the individual can willingly surrender control of his capacity for violence.

The Strange Case of Èric Bertran

As Mock says, it is important that nations have at their disposal myths of defeat that exist at a sufficient historical remove, before the creation of the modern nation-state and its concomitant nationalism, in order to make the case for the civic nation-state rather than the ethnic nation (Mock, 2012: 88). However, to end this chapter I propose to examine a specific example of how heroic themes from the past also find their echoes in the creation of modern-day national mythscapes of unfulfilled statehood: the strange case of Èric Bertran.

Èric was a fourteen year-old schoolboy living in Lloret de Mar when, in the autumn of 2004, the anti-terrorist squad of the Civil Guard arrived at his house late at night with a search warrant. Èric was accused of sending a threatening email to two supermarket chains and the milk producer *Leche Pascual,* demanding that they label all their products in Catalan. The email was sent under the alias 'Fènix 1123' and demanded a reply by a certain date:

> If I don't receive anything before 1 October 2004 I'll think you are ignoring me. In that case, I won't ask nicely again, my whole organisation will come and ask you to translate it and I don't think they'll be very nice about it.[39] (Bertran, 2006: Kindle loc. 156)

The 'organisation' referred to in the email was 'The Order of the Phoenix', a small group of pro-independence youngsters who were concerned for the future of the Catalan language. The fact that they had taken their name from a fictional group of young witches and wizards in the Harry Potter series perhaps should have alerted the Civil Guard to their age and the likely level of threat they posed. Nevertheless, Èric's house was searched, computers and other items were removed, and Èric was asked to give a statement the next day. His parents and lawyer hoped that was the end of it, but the case was pursued further. Èric was asked to go to Madrid to appear before the *Audiencia Nacional*, the special court that deals with international matters and terrorism. By that time, the case had attracted a large amount of publicity and Èric had received support both from the public – in the form of a petition – and from politicians representing ERC, CiU and ICV, who accompanied him during the hearing in Madrid.

Èric subsequently wrote a book about his experiences, *Èric i l'Exèrcit del Fènix. Acusat de voler viure en català* ('Eric and the Order of the Phoenix. Accused of Wanting to Live in Catalan') (Bertran, 2006), in which he detailed some of the more absurd aspects of the episode. At the centre of these is the hearing in the *Audiencia Nacional*, at which Èric insisted on speaking in Catalan, thus requiring the prosecutor to use a translator. Referred to in the book as 'Blanca', the prosecutor first tried to get Èric to confess to sending a threatening email, but when challenged to produce a copy she unwittingly revealed that she had never read it: she claimed not to understand the email because it was in Catalan, when in fact it had been written in Spanish. When a copy was finally located and Èric continued to deny that he had made any kind of threat, the questioning moved on to other matters: a picture of a burning Spanish flag found on his website, a copy of a chat session in which Èric talked about 'bombarding' the companies with emails, and another in which he responded to a threat from local right-wing boys by saying he would send his friends from ETA round to bomb them.

According to Èric's account, the prosecutor's frustrations boiled over when he refused to recognise the gravity of the act of flag-burning, saying that the Spanish flag was not his flag (Bertran, 2006: Kindle loc. 850). Tired of trying to convince him that it was indeed his flag, that burning it was a serious crime, and that he was Spanish as well as Catalan, the prosecutor is reduced to saying 'Say you're Spanish or I'll lock you up!' (Bertran, 2006: Kindle loc. 860).[40] This becomes the pivotal episode of the book: Èric is eventually forced to stammer a reply ('Politically, unfortunately, I am . . .' (Kindle loc. 862)),[41] but the absurdity of the threat stands out as the culmination of the absurdity of the whole situation. Eventually the case is dropped, but not before Èric undergoes an intrusive psychological assessment that, in his own words, concludes that 'I'm a very violent boy because we speak Catalan at home and I watch TV3 [Catalan television]' (Kindle loc. 1070).[42]

Èric's story might have been forgotten had it not been for the determination of a number of individuals to keep it in the public eye. The same year Èric published his book, Xevi Mató made a web documentary about the episode, which was later subtitled in English and at the time of writing is still available on YouTube, having received over a million hits (Mató, 2007). This was followed by a play written by Víctor Alexandre that was first staged in Barcelona in 2007 and later published (Alexandre, 2007). Most importantly, the actor Joel Joan latched on to the story and started to make plans for a film based on Èric's book. Funding the film proved a challenge, but it was eventually made with the support of various institutions – including *Televisió de Catalunya* (Catalunya Television) – and some crowd funding. It premièred in November 2012 just before the Catalan elections. (Bertran says this timing was a coincidence, given the length of time the project had been in the pipeline (A. D., 2012)). The film is based on Èric's book, although it leaves out some of the episodes, including the psychological assessment and an incident in which Èric's father has his Catalan credit card refused while eating in a restaurant during their enforced stay in Madrid. It also takes one significant liberty, showing Èric remaining silent when asked to say he is Spanish rather than giving the response recorded in the book.

All these various representations of Èric's story, especially the film, have made him something of a living myth. Joel Joan – who had previously wanted to make a film about Josep Moragues that would be the Catalan equivalent of Mel Gibson's *Braveheart* – went as far as to call Èric 'our Kunta Kinte' (Serra, 2012), in reference to the young protagonist of the ground-breaking television series *Roots,* about African slaves in America. In saying this, he appears to be making a parallel with Kunta Kinte's refusal to give up his African identity despite the torture he undergoes at the hands of his owners. However, Joan also describes Èric Bertran as – like Kunta Kinte – 'the first free man',[43] perhaps intending to indicate a freedom of spirit that can serve as a model for others, who in the future will also be physically 'free', i.e. independent (Serra, 2012).

The hyperbole of this comparison with an African slave should not divert our attention from the ways in which Èric's story corresponds to already-established patterns of Catalan heroism derived largely from the mythical figures of 1714. (In analysing this correspondence I will draw examples from the 2012 film, given that it is the most recent version of the story and likely to have the widest audience in the long run.) Firstly, Èric is an ordinary Catalan and not a figure of power, and is all the more vulnerable in this case for being a child. The film makes this vulnerability clear in its casting of the small and fragile-looking Nil Cardoner as Èric, in contrast with his larger classmates, especially the skinhead bullies who physically attack him for his views, who look older as well as larger. This fragility is also highlighted in the final scene, when Èric is invited to speak at a gathering of the *Plataforma per la llengua:* a tiny-looking Èric steps onto a dark, empty stage to be greeted by a sea of faces in the crowd, the height and size of the microphone further emphasising his diminutive stature.

The twenty or more civil guards who stream into Èric's house late in the evening therefore represent a ridiculous level of force. The Spanish-speaking mob turn the house upside down, even confiscating Èric's brother's computer containing his university assignments. The trope of 'unreasonable Castilian force' that forms part of the myths of 1714 (and the memory of the Franco regime) is therefore reproduced here, as is the figure of the despotic ruler – this time personified in the female prosecutor. Her insistence that Èric should admit he is Spanish would be purely comic if it was not for the groundwork done in the film to make her threats credible. In one scene, Èric's mother is visited by the mother of a young woman who was arrested and imprisoned for terrorist activities. She insists her daughter is innocent and has been gathering evidence of police brutality against terror suspects, including – most importantly – during the period in which they are allowed to be held for questioning without access to a lawyer or other support. She shows Èric's mother – and us – photographs and other evidence of this ill-treatment, and warns her not to think this could not happen to her son. The prosecutor's threats, and the possibility that Èric might actually be arrested, are therefore presented as perfectly plausible despite the ridiculous nature of the situation.

The nature of Èric's 'crime' also mirrors the actions of the heroes of 1714, who, as we have already discussed, are shown fighting to protect their family, traditional rights and way of life rather than being motivated by power. Èric is portrayed in the film as very politically aware for someone his age and most definitely in favour of Catalan independence, but his 'crime' relates to a simple demand that products should be labelled in Catalan. It is worth noting here that the film pushes the pro-independence angle more strongly than Èric's own account, which ends with statements related to the question of product labelling in Catalan rather than anything more radical. Víctor Alexandre's prologue to the book also concentrates firmly on the question of linguistic rights. Although the film takes on more of the pro-independence mood of 2011/12, it also makes it clear that Èric and his friends had no intention of acting violently in support of their views. The only violent acts are those of the Spanish state (the search of the house by the Civil Guard, the accusations of torture of terror suspects, and the 'legitimate' violence that underpins the power of the prosecutor) and its 'affiliative groups' (the right-wing bullies at school) (Marvin and Ingle, 1999: 172–80).

Opposed to this violence is the power of family and community. Despite some divisions caused by the stress of the situation in which they find themselves, Èric's family is shown as loving and supportive, as is his girlfriend Mirella (despite her mother's disapproval). Other community support comes in the shape of the petition which gathers two thousand signatures by the time Èric goes to Madrid, and the Catalan politicians who help him while he is there. This sense of Catalan unity in response to the threat to Èric comes through most strongly in the final scene of his speech to the *Plataforma*, where he is greeted with a sea of pro-independence flags and a standing ovation. In the end, it does not matter that Èric was not imprisoned or tortured – i.e. that the full sacrificial ritual was not enacted – because we know he was prepared to stick to his beliefs even in the face of these threats. The message is that all Catalans should have the courage to do the same.

The speed with which Èric Betran has become part of Catalan mythology corresponds in large measure to the way the story fits with a pre-existing schema, but there are of course other factors. Modern communications allow the story to reach a mass audience quickly and cheaply using various kinds of media and cultural products: a book, a play, a web documentary, a feature film; newspaper, television and radio interviews; webpages, news reports. It also would have been unlikely that the tale would have spread so quickly or so far at a time when there seemed to be less at stake for Catalan identity, and without the help of certain key individuals such as Víctor Alexandre, Xevi Mató, Joel Joan and the ERC politician Joan Puig (who appears in the documentary). Also vital has been the endorsement of Noam Chomsky, who apparently declared after seeing Mató's documentary that the world should know Èric's story. This quotation appears on the cover of the DVD of the 2012 film.

Of course, the film has not gone unnoticed in the rest of Spain. Seen as pure Catalanist propaganda by a number of critics, one of the specific criticisms it has attracted is that it was funded by public money given by institutions attached to the *Generalitat*. This is not surprising since, as we will see in the next chapter, such criticism of the way Catalonia's film and television industries are supported to produce pro-independence material was commonplace by the time *Fènix 11*23* was made. For example, a video report from *Intereconomía* complains that Joel Joan lives off subventions from the *Acadèmia del Cinema Català* (Catalan Cinema Academy), and that the film makes Èric 'a martyr of Catalan nationalism' and 'exalts the independentist struggle' (Intereconomía, 2012).[44] However, it also tries to cast doubt on the reliability and authenticity of the film, with three points: (1) Èric was not as brave as he was made out to be because the emails he sent were anonymous, something which the film glosses over; (2) Bertran is now a member of CDC with responsibilities in its Foundation for New Catalans; (3) 'Èric Bertran himself does not have his origins in Catalonia' – presumably implying that his heroic status within the independence movement is based on some kind of false claim to Catalan identity.[45] These arguments are largely spurious: the film does show Èric typing the email, in which he writes that he is sending it anonymously; his later decision to join CDC has no bearing on the events portrayed in the film; and Catalans of course do not care whether his parentage was Catalan or not, indeed he is a prime example of the non-ethnic nature of the Catalan nation. However, they are yet another illustration of the particular terms in which Spanish nationalist criticisms of Catalan nationalism are couched, especially the assumption that it is based on ethnic criteria. It is also significant that *Intereconomía* should dedicate such a report to the film at all, rather than simply ignoring it.

The case of Èric Bertran demonstrates that new myths useful to the Catalan independence movement can be created and propagated quickly if their underlying schema corresponds with recognisable patterns. This shortcut is complemented by twenty-first century processes of dissemination through multiple channels. Taken together, they condense the myth-making process into just a few years, rather than the decades or even centuries needed to create heroes such as Casanova and Moragues. While myths of past heroes serve to remind Catalans that they belong to an enduring nation whose defeat can be redeemed by struggle in the present, contemporary heroes are just as necessary because they show that the arguments for struggle are not only located in past injustices. As Marvin and Ingle put it, 'where blood is not at stake, groups are not enduring' (Marvin and Ingle, 1999: 315). Accounts of the over-zealous pursuit of Èric Bertran and the possibility that this might have escalated into something much worse encourage Catalans to see that blood is indeed at stake.

It has been argued in this chapter that Catalonia's heroes – whether in their real or fictionalised guises, and whether historical or contemporary – do not only fulfil the obvious function of providing models of self-sacrifice that underpin the current push to win support for independence. They also speak to Catalans specifically of a future non-ethnic Catalan state to which they already owe their allegiance. Cultural products are vital in this process not just because of their ability to disseminate the myth but also because of the way they speak to sentiment, in a way that history on its own cannot. Nevertheless, this appeal to sentiment cannot entirely eradicate the ambivalence about a Catalan state highlighted decades ago by Vicens Vives. A Catalan state based on civic values rather than ethnic exclusivism is still a state, with its attendant expectations of individual submission to organised violence. Trying to legitimate such violence in terms of loyalty to a community masks the fact that only the state, rather than the nation, actually has the legitimate right to demand this sacrifice: a power that the Catalan state would necessarily have to exercise were it to come into being.

Chapter 5

Stimulating Affect
Catalan Television and the Independence Debate

As we saw in the previous chapter, one of the main criticisms of the film *Fènix 11*23* from outside Catalonia was that it had been supported by public money in the form of grants from institutions controlled by the *Generalitat*. This is a symptom of a much wider debate on the extent to which Catalonia should control its own audio-visual space (Gifreu, 2003), and whether it is acceptable for this to be used not just for the promotion of Catalan language and culture, but also as a vehicle for nationalist and secessionist views. For example, concerns about the influence of such views in the Catalan media explain why the psychological evaluation of Èric Bertran made so much of the apparently innocuous fact that he watched Catalan television.

The main 'culprit' here is TV3, the television channel created by the *Generalitat* under the new legislation on regional broadcasting brought in by the PSOE in 1983. TV3 – the first channel operated by *Televisió de Catalunya* (TVC) – was initially conceived mainly as a way of promoting and disseminating the Catalan language, while also improving Catalans' awareness of belonging to a distinct cultural community. The debates that surrounded its function in the 80s and 90s primarily concerned the exact nature of the language and culture it should be attempting to reflect and shape (Crameri, 2008: 109–14). However, as discontent with Catalonia's political autonomy grew, so did TV3's role in stimulating debate about possible alternative relationships with the Spanish state.

As Manuel Castells reminds us, 'media industries built around cultural and political identities can grow in quasi-parallel networks' (Castells, 2009: 91). This is certainly the case in Spain, where regional channels operate on a similar organisational basis to the state-run *Televisión Española,* but within a particular territory. The channels run by the Autonomous Communities of Galicia, the Basque Country, Catalonia and Andalusia are good examples of such quasi-parallel networks, especially in their potential for political influence over their regular viewers and their role in 'the construction of difference' (Lash and Lury, 2007: 5; cited in Castells, 2009: 117; see also pp. 116–21). The debate on the legitimacy and function of these autonomous channels therefore reflects the two perspectives on processes of power-making described by Manuel Castells:

> on one hand, these processes can enforce existing domination or seize structural positions of domination; on the other hand, there also exist countervailing processes that resist established domination on behalf of the interests, values, and projects that are excluded or under-represented in the programs and composition of the networks. (Castells, 2009: 47)

Since the Spanish and Catalan institutionally-controlled media networks are quasi-parallel, the Catalan media can either resist the cultural domination represented by the Spanish media and try to represent values that it ignores, or it can attempt to seize a position of domination for itself within its own more limited territory, or a mixture of both. As Castells points out, both processes 'operate on the same logic' (ibid.), and are distinct but not contradictory.

Criticisms of the Catalan media relate to a perception that it is exceeding its remit to represent the cultural interests of Catalans and straying into political power-making in a way that is fundamentally unethical. This has especially been the case since the stakes in this power-making game have been raised by the increased public support for independence. This chapter will look at two different kinds of contributions by TV3 to the independence debate: documentaries and political satire. Its purpose is to analyse specific examples of these contributions, in order to explore the ways in which they attempt to exert some kind of influence on their viewers, whether via appeals to Catalanist sentiment, to rational argument, or both.

Documentary or Propaganda?

Televisió de Catalunya's role in producing and broadcasting documentaries that tackle the topic of Catalonia's constitutional relationship with Spain has become the target of much outrage from the Spanish media and politicians. At the heart of their criticisms is the notion that TVC is abusing its power by feeding biased opinions and distorted facts to its viewers, and deliberately pushing a pro-independence agenda. This criticism draws heavily on an apparently 'common sense' view of documentary as a form of neutral or objective filmmaking. However, as Paul Ward points out, in fact the idea of objectivity in documentary-making is highly problematic:

> The confusion here is between a supposedly 'objective' position that the documentarist takes in relation to their subject, and the idea that this somehow equals 'neutrality' or 'impartiality'. [. . .] First of all, there is no such thing as 'an objective position' in the sense that it is often meant: that is, as a position that is somehow magically 'outside' the socio-historical context that it is depicting. Secondly, the assumption [. . .] appears to be that 'neutrality' should be the necessary aim of all documentarists and, furthermore, that by being perceived to be 'neutral' or 'impartial' [. . .] one somehow automatically achieves 'objectivity'. (Ward 2005: 60)

In fact, documentary makers will always be able to present only their own version of 'the truth' (Estrada, 2010: 193). It is therefore unfair to criticise TV3 just because it shows documentaries that take a particular stance on their subject.

Nevertheless, filmmakers still have an ethical responsibility for the way in which this 'truth' is presented to the audience (Sanders, 2010: 45–46). As Garnet Butchart explains, the assumption that they will discharge this responsibility properly is 'based largely on a kind of faith', including 'faith that what we see in the documentary image will be a fair and reasonably accurate account of events' (Butchart, 2006: 430). When documentaries are perceived to have broken this faith, whether intentionally or as the result of sloppy practices, viewers may become upset or angry. This is especially the case if they feel themselves to belong to a particular group that has been unfairly represented on screen. However, as Butchart says, 'A given documentary is but a depiction, a work reflective of the intentions of the filmmaker rather than of an available real' (Butchart, 2006: 443). Therefore, the essentially subjective nature of the truth claims presented in any documentary make it difficult to draw a strict line between responsible and irresponsible filmmaking.

It is also true, as Paul Ward points out, that it can sometimes be ethically acceptable to present a one-sided argument, because 'to remain stubbornly "impartial" and "balanced" in the face of clear *imbalances* in the real world is to actually misrepresent that world, and the power struggles that go on within it' (Ward, 2005: 61). As we will see later, one of the arguments used to counter Spanish criticisms is that the issues are not being properly aired elsewhere and anti-independence arguments have their own champions in the more widely-disseminated Spanish media, creating an imbalance of power. Balance can therefore be achieved – in theory – by viewers having access to a suite of products that take different stances. In practice, of course, *Televisió de Catalunya*'s products have a limited territorial reach, affecting its capacity to influence viewers elsewhere. Furthermore, as a former head of Catalonia's Professional Audio-visual College pointed out, while Catalan viewers have access to Spanish media, no Spanish television channel was ever going to show a Catalan pro-independence documentary at prime time (Condeminas, 2010).

The intention in this section is to examine the techniques with which Catalan documentary-makers have used the resources of television in order to contribute to the debate on independence. In doing so, we need to bear in mind not only the thin line between ethical and unethical practices in documentary filmmaking, but also the prevailing conditions of production and distribution. The discussion will concentrate on three documentaries shown on TV3 between 2010 and 2013: *Adéu, Espanya?* ('Goodbye, Spain?'), *El Laberint* ('The Labyrinth'), and *Hola, Europa!* ('Hello, Europe!'), each of which tackled the question of Catalonia's constitutional relationship with Spain. While each documentary has a specific approach to this subject, there are also several things that they have in common. The most obvious of these are: (1) their reliance on 'talking heads' interviews, in which the questioner is not heard and the viewer is therefore unaware of the way in which the interviewee has been directed towards a particular answer; (2) the type of participant, usually a politician, academic, businessperson or journalist and therefore an 'expert', in some sense or other, rather than a member of the general public; (3) the major questions that are addressed, which very much reflect the debates raging in Catalanist circles and the media at the time the documentaries were made.

The first of these documentaries to appear was *Adéu, Espanya?* shown on TV3 on 3 June 2010 as part of an on-going series of topical films called *Sense ficció* (literally, 'without fiction'). Directed by Maria Dolors Genovès, the film compared four different stateless nations – Greenland, Scotland, Quebec and Catalonia – with the aim of demonstrating that the first three of these enjoy advantages within their respective nation-states (including some form of recognition of their right to self-determination) that Catalonia does not. Not surprisingly, given its focus, *Adéu, Espanya?* boasts the most international list of interviewees, including Scotland's First Minister Alex Salmond. *Adéu, Espanya?* was followed just a week later (10 June 2010) by another documentary in the same series entitled *El Laberint*, directed by Jordi Mercader. Unlike *Adéu, Espanya?*, *El Laberint* acknowledges the complexities of Catalonia's relationship with Spain since the creation of the *Estado de las Autonomías* without projecting an overriding assumption that independence is the best solution to these problems. *El Laberint* boasts the most heavyweight political contributions: from two former Presidents of the *Generalitat de Catalunya* (Jordi Pujol and Pasqual Maragall), a former *Lehendakari* (Xabier Arzalluz)[1] and former Spanish Prime Minister José María Aznar. Our final film from the *Sense ficció* stable is *Hola, Europa!*, screened on TV3 on 7 May 2013, which was directed by Genovès as a follow-up to *Adéu, Espanya?* It consists of a series of interviews with 31 Catalans, and is structured around ten themes that are often used to make Catalans wary of the negative consequences of independence, relating to language, culture, pensions, power generation, boycotts of Catalan products, cost, telecommunications, financial security and the euro, debt, and water supplies. The interviewees' job is to present counter-arguments to this 'discourse of fear' (*Sense ficció*, 2013), which makes *Hola, Europa!* the most obviously one-sided of the three documentaries.

Before we turn to these three films we need to mention an important precedent: *Cataluña-Espanya* (Catalonia-Spain),[2] directed by Isona Passola. Made for cinema rather than television, it was first screened in 2009 on the symbolic date of 23 April, the day of Catalonia's patron saint (Sant Jordi). However, it was co-produced with *Televisió de Catalunya,* and later shown on TV3 on the equally symbolic date of 11 September 2010, when it managed a respectable 327,000 viewers (directe!cat, 2010). The film was deliberately conceived as a Catalan version of Julio Medem's *La pelota vasca* ('Basque Ball', 2003), which had attempted to face head-on the complexities of the political violence in Euskadi (VilaWeb, 2009). It is therefore interesting to note the similarities in their methods, apparently allowing participants to speak for themselves without intervention while actually shaping an overall argument through careful editing. Like *La pelota vasca, Cataluña-Espanya* does not use a voice-over and instead constructs a coherent narrative entirely through the juxtaposition of different contributions from the interviewees.

Cabeza San Deogracias and Paz Rebollo have carried out a detailed examination of the use of this method in *La pelota vasca* (Cabeza San Deogracias and Paz Rebollo, 2011). Their basic unit of analysis was each interview fragment rather than the sum of the contributions by a particular interviewee, since it is impossible to know in what order the fragments appeared in the original interview(s), and what might have been said that was eventually omitted (4–5). Nevertheless, these fragments cannot be analysed in isolation, because without a specific placement in the documentary by the director/editor they could not be used to create a cumulative argument that remains with the viewer after the film has finished. The fragment's placement within the film establishes 'relationships' between the participants which either add or remove legitimacy from their views (6). Thus, particular roles are assigned to participants by the director, regardless of their original intentions when speaking. Having carried out both a quantitative and a qualitative analysis of the interventions in the film, the authors conclude that

> Definitively, *La pelota vasca* is a documentary in which the nationalist point of view dominates over any other, more because of the stress on the themes, conflicts and concerns of the nationalists than because of a clearly greater percentage of interviewees who come from or adhere to that ideology. [. . .] the important thing is not what enters the editing suite but what comes out of it; the creation of sense out of the material that forms the montage.[3] (27)

The same is quite clearly true of *Cataluña-Espanya,* if not more so. For instance, dissenting voices are sometimes omitted from sections where they would confuse the attempt to create a coherent argument from the different fragments (for an example, see Crameri, 2012: 47–8). Not only this, but many of the comments that oppose Catalonia's demand for greater self-determination are included in specific sections where the effect is to demonstrate the unreasonableness of such opinions. One example of this careful framing relates to a sequence in which first the former Prime Minister of Spain José María Aznar, and then his successor as leader of the PP Mariano Rajoy, are shown affirming that Spain is a single nation. The clip of Aznar is sandwiched between two contributions from Herrero Rodríguez de Miñón – one of the small team that drafted the Spanish Constitution –, who first states that Catalonia's demand for recognition is a matter of identity, not of the transfer of political competencies. He then affirms that Catalonia's status as a nation is fully compatible with the idea of a 'big Spain' and says that others should be helped to recognised this.[4] Aznar's insistence that there is no obligation to recognise the multinational nature of Spain because there is no reference to this in the text of the Constitution therefore comes across as petty and legalistic.

Passola did not try to hide the proselytising mission of *Cataluña-Espanya,* commenting that she acknowledged that the film's message was radical but she was trying to broaden the circle of those who accept the viability of such arguments (VilaWeb, 2009). She also said that her film 'aims at the brain, not the heart' (VilaWeb, 2009),[5] presumably meaning that it was designed primarily to make people think about the subject in new ways, although it also appears to be a reference to what Carod-Rovira called Catalanism of 'the head or the pocket', as opposed to that of the 'stomach' or the 'heart' (Carod-Rovira, 2008: 27). Even if Passola's claim is true, the film very much plays on the target audience's emotions, encouraging them to feel anger at the numerous clips containing anti-Catalan comments. The opening sequence, for example, is a recording of a radio broadcast by César Vidal in 2007 in which he accuses the Catalans of 'insatiable greed', 'a selfish lack of solidarity' and 'persecuting Castilian Spanish' (Passola, 2009).[6] Vidal, and other contributors to the radio station *La COPE*, are well known for their inflammatory anti-Catalan comments. Using his words to open the documentary can therefore only be an invitation for Catalans to react against his opinions, and against other similar statements to follow.

This means that the type of 'angry Catalan' regarded by Carod-Rovira as an obsolete prototype of the Catalan independentist is directly addressed in particular sequences of the film (Carod-Rovira, 2008: 27). This potentially has consequences for viewers' reactions to the arguments presented, since research has shown that angry people are quicker to jump to conclusions based on stereotyping and their own preconceptions (Huddy et al., 2007: 208–9). Viewers who react angrily to the anti-Catalan comments are therefore likely to spend less time weighing up the different arguments presented and to base their approval or disapproval of these on pre-existing opinions. More importantly, 'lower levels of perceived risk among angry people are likely to facilitate steps towards potentially risky action' (Huddy et al., 2007: 228). This means they are also likely to underestimate the risks of opting for a move towards independence, perhaps becoming more convinced than they already were that this is the right option.

The inseparability of emotion and reason (or – using Carod-Rovira's terms – of heart/stomach and head/pocket) must necessarily have a bearing on our discussion of the ethical questions surrounding such documentaries. Of course it is legitimate for documentaries to 'invite and orchestrate spectator affect' (Marquis, 2012: 439): indeed it is often the mark of a good documentary that it does so effectively. The manipulation of emotion by the documentary-maker is not in itself unethical, but rather an accepted feature of the genre. Nor is it helpful to define ethicality in terms of the difference between overt and covert manipulation, since spectators will vary both in their ability to perceive manipulation and their rational/emotional response to the knowledge that they are being manipulated.

On the other hand, viewers who already have entrenched views about a subject that differ from those being presented are likely not only to dismiss the documentary as 'bad' or 'unethical', but to experience negative emotions such as anger and frustration in response to it. Elizabeth Marquis suggests that 'text-directed outrage [. . .] makes it more likely that affected viewers will engage in action designed to redress the film's perceived imbalance or to otherwise punish those responsible for its making' (Marquis, 2012: 437–8). Not only do emotionally-charged documentaries about Catalonia therefore polarise opinion, as common sense would suggest, they may also have the effect of increasing the likelihood of people on both sides of the debate being willing to act on their convictions. The question of the ethics of this kind of documentary therefore revolves around its role in constructing not just difference but conflict. The following discussion of the three television documentaries that came hot on the heels of *Cataluña-Espanya* will shed further light on this assertion.

Adéu, Espanya?, *El Laberint* and *Hola, Europa!*

Adéu, Espanya? begins with a quotation from the last verse of the poem by Joan Maragall (written in 1898) from which its title is taken:

> Where are you, Spain? I can't see you anywhere.
> Don't you hear my voice resounding?
> Don't you grasp the speech I use at risk?
> Have you unlearned your children's words?
> *Adéu, Espanya!*[7]

The poem is of course charged with emotion, which is expressed through the metaphor describing Catalan speakers as Spain's abandoned children. As Ronald Puppo puts it, 'The choreography of the final farewell is one in which the poet and the peripheral culture he represents are standing in place – it is Spain that walks away' (Puppo, 2011: 223). Maragall was therefore engaging in a plea for dialogue and recognition rather than threatening that Catalonia would itself initiate separation. More than a century later, Genovès' documentary places a question mark in its title rather than using Maragall's plaintive exclamation mark, indicating that there is room for debate, but also perhaps suggesting that it is less clear who might walk away from whom.

If the opening sequence of *Adéu, Espanya?* is framed around a question, its closing words represent a clear call to action. Here, the female narrator portentously relates an anecdote about the independence of Norway. When Santiago Ramón y Cajal went to Stockholm in 1906 to collect his Nobel prize for medicine, he was prompted to ask how it was possible that the Swedes had just allowed Norway its independence. The answer, and the final word of the film, is 'that's what the Norwegians wanted' (Genovès, 2010).[8] Not only does this anecdote reinforce the documentary's message that self-determination is a fundamental democratic right, it is also used to suggest that Catalonia should strive to attain this right. This is done by placing the presenter's words over slow-motion footage of *castellers* (groups of men, women and children who form human towers in competition with one another). *Castells,* like the national dance the *sardana*, are a well-known metaphor for Catalan cooperation, inclusivity and willingness to engage in a common project (Crespi-Vallbona and Richards, 2007: 113). The footage, when coupled with the anecdote, therefore challenges Catalans to work together to achieve the same outcome as the Norwegians.

Of the three *Sense ficció* documentaries, *Adéu, Espanya?* is furthest in technique from *Cataluña-Espanya* (and *La pelota vasca*) because of its more limited use of interview footage and its greater reliance on voice-over. This means, in turn, that it is more dependent on images other than those of the people being interviewed. These take two main forms: beauty shots and b-roll. 'Beauty shots [. . .] convey a sense of time or place', and mainly consist of 'event re-creations that illustrate events for which there was no field video and poetic images that convey a sense of abstract ideas' (Hewitt and Vazquez, 2011: 30). Since the documentary compares Catalonia with three other stateless nations with which viewers may not be familiar, a lot of these beauty shots provide necessary context for the audience. They include both rural and urban landscapes, inside and outside shots of important institutions such as parliament buildings, and everyday scenes of people walking, shopping, eating etc. B-roll footage on the other hand is directly connected to the voice-over commentary and is used either to illustrate or expand upon what is being said (Hewitt and Vazquez 2010: 30). The footage of *castellers* mentioned above is an example of b-roll footage that does not just reinforce the point made in the narration but subtly alters the way the viewer relates to it.

Adéu, Espanya? also uses animated sequences to illustrate historical events. Even though the director felt this was the most effective way to represent these key moments succinctly (Cassadó, 2010), the decision to use Playmobil figures – rather than, say, a series of still images of paintings, historical documents and relevant locations – does have some potentially negative consequences. As Paul Ward says of animated documentary in general, 'the ontological status of the images [. . .] means that the perceptions of "animatedness" and "documentariness" are in conflict to a large degree' (Ward, 2005: 89). Although he points out that this may not necessarily be a problem, in the particular case of *Adéu, Espanya?* the idea of using toys might give the impression of trivialising important events (the execution of Charles I of England and Scotland, for example, which becomes somewhat humorous when it involves one Playmobil figure beheading another). Whether or not the viewer has this reaction, all the forms of visual material used in the documentary draw attention to *Adéu, Espanya?*'s status as a constructed artefact in a way that is not true of *Cataluña-Espanya, El Laberint* and *Hola, Europa!*, with their greater reliance on talking heads.

El Laberint specifically sets out to examine the relationship between Catalonia and Spain since the transition to democracy. It locates current issues firmly within the framework set up by the Spanish Constitution of 1978 and the subsequent processes associated with the creation of the *Estado de las Autonomías*, especially in the 1980s. This is the most balanced of the documentaries, portraying different opinions in ways that indicate that they are to be taken equally seriously. For example, José María Aznar is a willing contributor to the discussion, and the director has also remarked that he would have very much liked Felipe González to take part (Europa Press, 2010a). Aznar appears in the first and last sequences, and also has an important intervention half-way through in which he claims that the *Estado de las Autonomías* weakens the state and is unsustainable from a financial perspective. Rather than being instantly refuted, his argument is then backed up by contributions from two different businesspeople. Aznar's opinions, although of course controversial, are therefore framed within a debate that is much more nuanced and intellectually complex than the other documentaries.

Nevertheless, there are other strong voices that tip the overall balance of power towards representatives of the Autonomous Communities, in some cases specifically because of their recognised authority to speak about the events of the 1970s and 80s. These include Xabier Arzalluz (who was a member of parliament representing the *Partido Nacionalista Vasco* at the time the Constitution was drafted, and subsequently its leader) and Jordi Pujol (President of the *Generalitat* from 1980–2003 and therefore – like Arzalluz – intimately involved in key stages of development of the *Estado de las Autonomías*). Pujol and Arzalluz dominate the discussion: Arzalluz is the first 'talking head' to appear and Pujol has the last word; both have significant exposure throughout the documentary. Arzalluz's first contribution relates directly to the documentary's title, which is a reference to *The Spanish Labyrinth* by Gerald Brenan (1960): 'Spain has always been a labyrinth, whether with Moors or Christians, and I very much doubt it can get out of that labyrinth' (Mercader, 2010).[9] Pujol's final contribution, on the other hand, exhorts Catalans not to give up the struggle and to construct the Catalonia they want to see, using whatever means they have to hand. This exhortation is expressed in very idiomatic Catalan: 'Amunt i crits!' – which roughly translates as 'soldier on!'. The strongest argument to emerge is therefore the view that current arrangements for autonomy in the 'historic nations' are inadequate and this needs to be addressed. Nevertheless, the documentary makes no direct appeal to emotion and spends little time on questions of identity politics, concentrating instead on the rational arguments representing different political points of view on the spectrum centralisation – autonomy – federalism – independence.

Hola, Europa! takes a very different approach, since it unashamedly gives only the pro-independence case, with its interviewees selected for their authority to refute common anti-independence arguments. In his article 'On Ethics and Documentary', Garnet Butchart says that 'truth in documentary must be pursued without advance knowledge of what it will look like' (Butchart, 2006: 442), but it is clear that this is not the case with *Hola, Europa!* Apart from this deliberate one-sidedness, another element of the documentary that is particularly striking is its use of 'beauty shots': 'the stunning sunrises, sunsets, pastoral landscapes, or frantic urban chaos that add texture or chronology' (Hewitt and Vazquez, 2010: 34). In this case, more than simply 'texture', the shots of Catalonia's landscape, cities and people that precede each group of interviews seem designed to prime the viewer to have positive feelings towards the pro-independence arguments to follow. For example, the montages include 'portraits' of fifteen anonymous Catalans who simply look at the camera and say nothing. The implication is that viewers are supposed to identify themselves in the faces of these people, thus increasing the level of affective response.

These constant images of people and places the viewer is likely to find familiar could be seen as performing what Sara Ahmed calls 'the repetition or reiteration of signs of "fellowship"' (Ahmed, 2004: 74). Ahmed argues that when we collectively turn away from an 'object of fear' we instinctively turn 'towards home' (ibid), and although this comment was made in the context of the threat of terrorism after September 11, her phrasing seems apt here too. If the rational arguments in *Hola, Europa!* are designed to counteract a 'discourse of fear' from those who are opposed to Catalan independence, the images that frame these arguments prompt the viewer to turn towards the 'fellow feeling' found at home (ibid). Even the joy and pride elicited by the simple beauty of the landscape shots can perform this function, since 'emotions directed at the geographical features of a nation are ways of channeling emotions towards its key commitments' (Nussbaum, 2013: 2). By interposing montages of the most beautiful or familiar parts of Catalonia throughout the documentary, this response is constantly re-activated.

As we know from affective intelligence theory, the emotions that Catalans feel about their homeland and fellow citizens can have a direct effect on their political decision-making (Cassino and Lodge, 2007).

However, affective priming does not condition our attitudes so much as the way in which they are operationalised in a given situation (Mackuen et al., 2007). In experiments where words (or pictures (Hermans et al., 1994)) with positive affective connotations are shown to subjects, they are likely to have carried out only a cursory evaluation of any subsequent stimulus that is also then judged to be positive (Cassino and Lodge, 2007: 103). In contrast, a longer time will elapse if the subject evaluates the stimulus as negative. This is because the memory of the positive stimulus pre-conditions a positive response, allowing this to be made automatically. Where the response is negative, a more rational process has been necessary to counteract the effect of the positive priming. For those who have a strong attachment to Catalonia and are already in favour of independence, there is no need to evaluate closely the arguments presented in *Hola, Europa!* as they are automatically accepted in accordance with their predispositions, even if this carries the risk of ignoring important information and committing an error of judgement (Cassino and Lodge, 2007: 105, 119). Affective priming reinforces the rapidity of the response, making it difficult to engage with the topic rationally. However, for those who are not yet sure whether independence is the best option, the process is more complex.

Viewers who are anxious about the possibility of independence will tend to seek out more information and process it more carefully, since, as Castells reports, 'anxiety is connected to avoidance and induces a higher level of threat evaluation, a higher concern about risks involved, and a cautious assessment of information' (Castells, 2009: 147). For these viewers, the arguments put forward in *Hola, Europa!* will be vital and they are likely to weigh them carefully, regardless of the priming beauty shots. In this case, the construction of the documentary around ten questions relating to 'the discourse of fear' is ideal,[10] since the anxious spectator will be seeking just the kind of information being offered (*Sense ficció*, 2013), and although this does not necessarily mean they will find it convincing, there is a better chance that they will be open to persuasion. On the other hand, viewers who are neither particularly anxious about the topic nor much affected by strong patriotic emotions aroused by the beauty shots will tend to respond to these arguments in accordance with their prior attitudes, whatever they may be (Cassino and Lodge, 2007: 101). It is therefore the viewer who is most anxious about the possible consequences of a push for independence who is most likely to shift their position as a result of the information presented in the documentary, because 'when citizens become anxious they are more likely to abandon partisanship and ideology as ironclad guides to political behavior' (Mackuen et al., 2007: 139–40). *Hola, Europa!* therefore works on two levels, further cementing the unquestioning opinions of those in favour of independence while potentially swaying a small minority of viewers who might have turned on the television precisely because of their anxiety about the topic to be addressed.

Like *Adéu, Espanya?* and *El Laberint, Hola, Europa!* ends with a call to action, although in this case a rather subtle one. The chief academic adviser for the film was Professor Montserrat Guibernau of Queen Mary, University of London (she had also been consulted for, and appeared in, *Adéu, Espanya?*). Guibernau is Catalan, and not only an expert on Catalan nationalism but on theories of nationalism and ethnicity more generally. In *Hola, Europa!* she is given the last word, calling for a referendum so that the Catalan nation can express its ideas about 'what kind of political future it wants', and if it wants independence, 'then why?' (Genovès, 2013). This question at the end sounds rather tentative, but it does not appear to mean that Guibernau is querying the desire for independence, rather she is asking Catalans to refine their arguments for wanting it. The final shot of the film shows a smiling Guibernau getting off the high stool on which she had been sitting for the interview, as if in a symbolic invitation to Catalans to 'get off their backsides' and make something happen.

All three filmmakers have been interviewed both on television and in the press about the motivations behind their documentary, the process of making it, and in some cases its reception. As is customary in the *Sense ficció* series, each director took part in a studio interview that began before the film was screened and was continued afterwards. This means that viewers of the documentary were made aware of some of the motivations of the filmmaker prior to or just after watching the film. Naturally, one of the common themes in their comments is the need to open up debate and invite people to reflect on the issues. Mercader does so only implicitly, by referring to the fact that some Catalans have become so accustomed to living in the 'Spanish labyrinth' that the fear of change stops them from seeking other options (Salvat, 2010a). On the other hand Genovès was clear that her primary aim was that her films should make people think: she says of *Adéu, Espanya?* ' what it does [. . .] is to make people reflect on the subject [. . . .] and stop them being so afraid' (Salvat, 2010b).[11] For Genovès this explicitly includes an invitation to reflect on independence as one of the possible solutions, although she says that it will be up to the people of Catalonia to decide which of these is the correct one (Salvat, 2010b). Genovès felt an imperative to bring to the screen something that had not been given sufficient air time up to that point, thereby redressing the overall balance. She argues that there are plenty of people publicly expressing reasons why Catalonia should <u>not</u> be independent, so what is needed is something that puts forward the opposite view in a calm, rigorous and rational way (Europa Press, 2010b; Salvat, 2013).

As was to be expected, these stances led to criticism in the Spanish media, especially of *Adéu, Espanya?* and *Hola, Europa!*, for their one-sided treatment of the issues. For example, the politician Jorge Fernández of the PP lambasted TV3 for showing *Adéu, Espanya?*, stating that as a public broadcaster it had a duty to respect a plurality of views rather than putting forward an image of the relationship between Catalonia and Spain 'which only exists in the minds of separatists' (Europa Press, 2010a).[12] The director of TV3 Mònica Terribas was forced to defend the channel's position and to insist (whether naively or disingenuously) that the documentary 'isn't trying to convince anyone of anything' (Pelayo, 2010).[13] Opponents of the documentary were unconvinced by this argument and warned Terribas that she should not use the publicly-funded TV3 as a 'toy' that can be manipulated in favour of Catalan separatists (Europa Press, 2010b). In the case of *Hola, Europa!*, its blatant refusal to attempt any kind of balance led to it being branded a form of indoctrination, which supposedly broke Catalonia's own media laws on reflecting the plurality of its population's views (Sala, 2013).

Whatever we may think about these specific criticisms, questions remain about the implications of the filmmakers' power not only to influence viewers' rational judgements, but also to manipulate their emotions. As we have seen, the main issue is whether viewers can be prompted to act in a particular way, for example by participating in a demonstration, writing a letter to a newspaper, or changing their intended vote in the event of a referendum. Since it is anger that most effectively spurs viewers into action (Marquis, 2012: 437–8), our documentary makers might have been hoping that one of the reactions of their audience might be a sense of injustice at the 'wrongs' they highlight: e.g. Spain's refusal to recognise Catalonia as a sovereign nation (*Adéu, Espanya?*), the misguided watering-down of autonomy for the 'historic nations' (*El Laberint*), and attempts to dissuade Catalonia from seeking independence through scare-mongering about its consequences (*Hola, Europa!*). Crucially, as Elizabeth Marquis puts it, 'should the perception of injustice be accompanied by an attribution of blame for that injustice, [. . .] anger and indignation are likely to follow' (Marquis, 2012: 430–1). Moreover, anger 'entails a shift of attention from the victim to the perpetrator', (Marquis, 2012: 430) meaning that wherever 'Spain' can be blamed for such injustices, the viewer's emotion shifts from passive sympathy for the victim (Catalonia/Catalans) to anger directed at the perpetrator (Spain/Spaniards), which is a much more productive emotion in terms of motivating action.

Our documentary-makers could therefore be accused of increasing the potential for conflict by deliberately seeking angry reactions to the material they present. However, the Catalans are by no means the only culprits here. As we saw in the case of Èric Bertran, *Intereconomía Televisión* has often produced news reports whose sole purpose is to condemn what they portray as outrageous or hypocritical aspects of Catalan nationalism. *Telemadrid*, which serves the Autonomous Community of Madrid, has also been guilty of setting out to discredit Catalan nationalism in such documentaries as *Ciudadanos de segunda* ('Second-Class Citizens') (Wieting, 2007), whose target was the policy of Catalan language immersion in schools, and *Cataluña: Violencia Callejera* ('Catalonia: Street Violence'), which attempted to link an increase in street violence to Catalan separatism (Cerdán, 2011). Both films play on Spanish fears in order to demonise the Catalan independence movement by refuting the idea that Catalan nationalism is peaceful, democratic, inclusive, and civic rather than ethnic. In this case, anger at the perceived injustice of Spanish-speaking children being forced to learn in a Catalan-speaking environment – for example – is being used to motivate support for anti-Catalan political agendas, especially that of the PP.

Telemadrid and *Televisió de Catalunya* address both geographically and ideologically distinct audiences; the PP has won a majority of votes in the Autonomous Community of Madrid since 1991 and *Telemadrid* has a right-leaning editorial stance. Filmmakers airing their products on *Telemadrid* and *TV3* do so in full knowledge of the predominant perspectives on Catalan nationalism of each of these channels. However, the free availability of their documentaries on the internet means that their distribution is not limited by territorial boundaries. Press coverage of these controversial programmes also has the result of directing attention to them, potentially prompting people to seek them out precisely in order to confirm their disapproval. This then incites a different kind of anger, not the anger related to sympathy for the victims of the injustices portrayed in the film, but anger at the filmmaker and the ideology and institutions s/he is assumed to represent. Comments left on YouTube and other video-sharing sites are testament to the existence of this kind of viewer, and to the satisfied fury they feel as their expectations of disapproval are confirmed. Furthermore, internet availability increases the shelf-life of these products, which can enjoy renewed bursts of popularity whenever something happens to draw attention to them once again. The 'gradual decoupling of contiguity and time-sharing' that is facilitated by new media therefore has some very specific effects in the case of documentaries on Catalan independence (Castells, 2009: 47), increasing the likelihood that they will reach the audience who will react most negatively to them, and thereby heightening the potential for conflict as expressed either in words or deeds.

Polònia: Harmless Infotainment or Pro-Independence Misinformation?

The questions relating to affect and ethics that have been discussed above are equally relevant, although in different ways, to our next object of study: political satire. If documentaries on Catalan independence have the potential to enhance their viewers' disposition to act in particular ways through tapping into their anger, frustration or anxiety, what of programmes that tackle the same subject in a way that is primarily designed to make their audience laugh? Do their makers still have an ethical responsibility to achieve some kind of balance in their treatment of political targets, or is the influence of television comedy too limited for this to be an issue?

A slight digression here will help to set the scene for the discussion to follow. In the run-up to the Scottish referendum on independence, an interesting debate emerged about the lack of political satire being produced on this subject, whether in Scotland or in the UK as a whole. One of the main participants in the debate was impressionist and comedian Rory Bremner, who devised a one-off television programme exploring the reasons for this lacuna which was shown by BBC Scotland in June 2013. The cameras followed him as he prepared and then performed in Edinburgh a one-man show on the topic of Scottish independence. During the programme, entitled *Rory Goes to Holyrood*, he explained that he was puzzled by the lack of comedy dealing with Scottish politics in general and the referendum in particular, and made several arguments in favour of satire as a necessary part of any political system. One of his key points was that even Scots – let alone the rest of the UK – were quite ignorant about their leaders and were largely unable to recognise more than two or three of the main figures. Only the Scottish First Minister Alex Salmond was instantly recognisable to all. This led to a 'chicken and egg' situation in which any attempt at satire had to be relatively superficial because audiences would not have enough knowledge to understand the joke, but the lack of satire itself was denying them access to a medium that could help them get to know their politicians better. As Bremner himself puts it during the programme, 'When there's nothing like that only the politically-minded get to see the politicians and watch them, and I think politics is far too dangerous to be left just to the politically-minded' (Hart, 2013).

Bremner was not the only Scottish comedian lamenting the lack of willingness to lampoon Scotland's politicians and the arguments of the 'Yes' and 'No' campaigns. Susan Calman was the target of abusive messages from fellow Scots after daring to joke about the subject on BBC Radio. Responding to their comments, she wrote on her blog that 'Comedy plays a vital role in informing and lightening the mood somewhat. We are over a year away from the vote. If we don't start laughing soon it's going to go horribly wrong'.[14] She was also one of a group of comedians who were reported by Scottish newspaper *The Herald* as saying that 'broadcasters are failing the country by letting politicians escape the scrutiny that a regular public mocking provides' (Anonymous, 2013b). Calman herself remarked that she had pitched several ideas for shows on the topic but had found it hard to generate any enthusiasm for them.

Comedians themselves, then, assume that satire is a healthy part of the political process because it brings the personalities and issues to the people in ways that can positively affect their level of political participation and help them to hold their elected representatives to account. By this measure, Catalonia enjoys a much healthier situation than Scotland because political satire is a constant presence on both television and radio. One of its main vehicles is the weekly show *Polònia*, in which actors impersonate politicians and personalities from the world of media and culture in short sketches or 'gags'.[15] The sketches often involve parodies of other television programmes and genres, or forms of popular and traditional culture. Launched in 2006 and still running at the time of writing, the show is one of the major successes of TV3, with consistently high audience figures and a handful of awards. *Polònia* – named after the pejorative classification of Catalans by other Spaniards as 'Poles' – will provide examples for our analysis of the role of comedy/satire in the independence debate. However, before we turn to specific sketches from the show, we first need to think about the distinctions between satire and parody, the specific forms given to them within television comedy, and their capacity to inform, influence and entertain.

Although satire and parody often accompany one another, they do not always do so and are treated by theorists as distinct phenomena. For Matthew Hodgart, the key distinction is the intent of the parodist or satirist, since satire is often aggressive, humiliating and contemptuous whereas 'parody is not always used with malicious intent, for it may spring from the sheer joy of travesty' (Hodgart, 2010: 10–11, 122). In general, satire is viewed as more serious and provocative while parody is playful and funny, although of course one form can make use of, or slide into, to the other at any given moment (Simpson, 2003: 119). When the overall intention is to entertain, as is the case with comedy, the scope for true satire is very much reduced. As Hodgart puts it, 'Comedy accepts the rules of the social game, satire does not: it is a protest against the rules as well as against the players, and it is much more profoundly subversive than comedy can afford to be' (Hodgart, 2010: 189). As a form of entertainment whose purpose is to generate laughter, then, *Polònia* has only a limited capacity to be aggressively satirical, but it can make use of all of the possibilities of parody, which still has the potential to be 'polemical' (Dentith, 2000: 9).

Polònia and other such shows are often labelled 'infotainment', a format that feeds off newsworthy events but whose primary aim is to entertain (Ferré-Pavia and Gayà-Morlà, 2011). The rise of infotainment represents a blurring of boundaries between news and entertainment that works both ways, since not only do shows whose primary purpose is to entertain generate this entertainment from real news stories, but news and current affairs programmes also feel increasing pressure to keep their audience entertained as well as informing them. In both cases, critics fear that the genre trivialises important issues and potentially increases political apathy through its tendency to belittle our political representatives. As with parody (Dentith, 2000: 20), there is also a suspicion that infotainment may work as a conservative rather than a subversive force, since it concentrates its criticisms on the representatives of democratic institutions rather than revealing the shortcomings of the institutions themselves.

With its use of satire limited by the need to be funny, *Polònia* therefore runs the risk of appearing to be subversive while really upholding the status quo. But to what extent does it actually have a mission to inform its audience, and the power to affect their opinions and behaviours? The Scottish satirists' comments suggest that the role of such 'parodic info-satire' (Sampedro Blanco and Valhondo Crego, 2012: 44) is limited to generating an interest in politics and improving awareness of the key figures and their policies – which might in turn lead people to take a more active role in the democratic mechanisms which hold them to account. If so, then *Polònia*'s interventions in the debate on independence would have positive effects. However, this relies on it maintaining a degree of neutrality regarding the independence debate itself (something which Rory Bremner, for example, scrupulously upheld in *Rory Goes to Holyrood*). As we have already seen, many critics believe TV3 itself is biased in favour of independence, and although *Polònia* is made by an independent production company, one of its owners – and the show's director – is Toni Soler, a strident supporter of Catalonia's 'right to decide'. Might it therefore be attempting to influence viewers' opinions in a specific direction?

To answer this question we will look in detail at some specific aspects of *Polònia*, using examples of sketches taken from shows aired between September and November 2012. This period has been chosen because it spans the demonstrations of 11 September and the elections of 20 November, when independence was very much a live topic. Since the main force of 'parodic info-satire' lies in characterisation, the way in which political figures and others are portrayed is central to this analysis, but in broader terms *Polònia*'s parodies of cultural and linguistic forms not specifically related to a particular character are also crucial. As we will see, these are vital in ensuring the complicity of the audience, who are drawn into an active community of viewers sharing both knowledge and a particular set of values, whatever their views on a particular party or ideology.

Characterisation

Polònia operates with an ever-changing set of core characters depending on who is in power or most newsworthy at the time. During our sample period from September to November 2012, core political characters included Artur Mas, Oriol Pujol, Oriol Junqueras, Alicia Sánchez Camacho, Mariano Rajoy, Josep Antoni Duran i Lleida, Pere Navarro and Josep-Lluís Carod Rovira. Each is impersonated by one of the cast, who may contribute several different characters in a given episode. They are made up to look as far as possible like the person they are impersonating, sometimes exaggerating particular features, although not to the point of becoming a 'Spitting Image'-like caricature. Linguistic tics are more deliberately parodied than physical attributes, with particular accents, speech impediments and pet phrases used as a characterisational shorthand (Ugarte Ballester, 2011). Characters speak Catalan or Spanish in the same way they would in similar real-life situations.

As has already been noted, satire normally relies on an aggressively critical portrayal that is designed to humiliate its target, although a distinction is sometimes made in this respect between the horatian and juvenalian traditions: the 'bitter and harsh' tone of Juvenal's satire being contrasted with the 'light and witty' horatian form (Holbert et al., 2013: 172). Indeed, Holbert et al. have shown that while both forms of satire are perceived as intending to sway the audience towards a particular viewpoint, the young Americans that were the subjects of their experiments 'identified the horatian satirical messages as retaining decidedly weak message strength and lower levels of perceived influence on oneself' (Holbert et al., 2013: 182). In common with many of the American shows they cite, *Polònia* owes more to Horace than to Juvenal, as is evidenced by the light-hearted characterisation of most of its targets: we may laugh at them, but we are only occasionally invited to despise them.

One of the reasons for this general lack of 'bite' is the way the show concentrates on the relationships between characters and – crucially – their own inner emotions. It is true that emotion has begun to enter politics in a way that would previously have been unthinkable (6 et al., 2007: 1–2), but normally politicians save their emotional speeches for specific and well-orchestrated occasions on which they need to represent the collective feeling of the nation. We are very rarely party to their inner needs, desires and frustrations, but this is exactly what *Polònia* imagines for us. As Marçal Sintes puts it:

> TV3's programme allows the public to penetrate – as a voyeur – the personality and motives behind the actions of very famous people that, given the theatricality and rhetoric characteristic of mediatised politics, they have the vivid sensation of not knowing, of not really having much information about them. They have the sensation that their access is vetoed, that they are forced to stay on the other side of the door. *Polònia* flings that door wide open. [. . .] *Polònia* unmasks politics by means of the mask [. . .]. It opens up to the audience the hidden spaces of politics. (Sintes i Olivella, 2010: 50, 52)[16]

Thus we are privy to the politicians' fear, disappointment, elation and ambitions, and – as they interact with others – their complicity, hypocrisy, stubbornness, uncertainty and vulnerability. This has the paradoxical effect of humanising the Catalan political class by 'revealing' the intimate thoughts of its main representatives (Ferré-Pavia and Gayà-Morlà, 2011: 47). A good example of this is *Polònia*'s treatment of Artur Mas during the autumn of 2012. As the independence movement gains momentum, we see the shift in Mas's own position, and especially his language. Unable to pronounce the word 'independence' in public, he nevertheless dreams in private of an independent Catalonia, with himself as the 'Messiah' who makes this possible. In the episode broadcast two days after the 11 September demonstrations, Mas is shown sneaking down to join the march *incognito* but only being able to chant the words 'pacte fiscal'. Later in his office he waits for an expected call from Rajoy (which never comes), draped in an *estelada,* and dreaming that independence will now magically happen. It is Oriol Pujol who brings him down to earth by telling him it is his job to make it happen: something which Mas is patently afraid to do. A couple of episodes later he is seen in the parliament announcing elections, but he is barely able even to pronounce the word 'self-determination'. The next week, he is taunted by journalists trying to get him to say 'independence', but all he can manage is 'right to decide'. One of the most popular sketches of the period occurs in the following episode, with Mas rapping and dancing 'Mas Style' in a parody of the contemporary hit 'Gangnam Style'. The lyrics are changed so that they become a plea for votes at the upcoming election, based on the promise that Mas had changed and adopted a 'new style' – pointing to a new policy on independence. However, when Oriol Pujol contributes the line 'we want to be independent', Mas stops the song to chastise him: 'Oriol, we said we wouldn't say that!'.[17] Mas himself only uses the term 'Estat Propi'.

While this running gag is clearly intended as a satirical comment on Mas's equivocal position on independence, other aspects of his characterisation lessen the satirical impact. For example, his relationship with right-hand man Oriol Pujol often comes close to slapstick buffoonery as the two play out their differences. The sight of the two men enthusiastically dancing 'Mas style' also raises a complicit smile rather than inviting ridicule. In fact, many of the Catalan figures are portrayed as naively enthusiastic and somewhat dim-witted, and this is how much of the comedy of the programme is generated. While a more biting form of satire might invite us to wonder whether these people are fit to be in office, here – as noted above – the main effect is to humanise politicians and decrease the sense of distance between them and the community, which is one reason why some political figures have actually appeared as themselves on the programme. We could therefore apply to *Polònia* the following comments on the portrayal of American presidential candidates on *Saturday Night Live*: 'the skits are about them as people more than as leaders. Viewers are led to laugh but not disdain, to appreciate affectionately but not really criticize. These are portrayals of human foibles, not sketches that suggest some inherent weakness in the person as a leader' (Jones, 2008: 43).

Drawing on the work of Christy Davies, Carmelo Moreno has analysed responses to the Basque satirical programme *Vaya semanita* in terms of the distinction between humour derived from characters who are 'dim-witted' and those who are 'suspiciously canny' (Moreno, 2012). Both can be exposed to ridicule, but as Moreno notes, categorising different political groups as either one or the other can have particular effects. In the case of *Vaya semanita*, 'the PP is the allegedly astute social group that the playful story-line of the program suspiciously casts as wanting to change, from its position of power, the collective imagination of the Basque community' (Moreno, 2012: 179). *Polònia* manifested the same tendencies in its autumn 2012 episodes (when the PP was in power in Madrid), portraying Rajoy and other members of the government as seeking to block Catalonia's every move, while also cynically making ordinary Spaniards bear the brunt of the government's mismanagement of the economy. For example, in one episode

(27 Sept) Rajoy creates an 'evil twin' of himself who is designed to give all the bad news, while he concentrates on the good. His 'cunning plan' backfires when he realises that this puts him out of a job, since there is no good news to give. Another good example is the portrayal of José Ignacio Wert, the Education minister whose aim was to reduce the teaching of Catalan and make sure all school children were learning how to be 'proper Spaniards'. A range of sketches play on his cunning, including a parody of the computer game Angry Birds ('Angry Werts'), and a recurring Austin Powers spoof which sees Wert transformed into the character Dr Evil complete with his own 'Mini-Wert'.

While the 'evil plans' of Rajoy, Wert and other members of the Spanish government often backfire, the impression that remains is the original malicious intent, a topic which is reinforced again and again. Those who criticise *Polònia* as portraying some characters more sympathetically than others therefore have a point. As we have seen, aspects of character related to emotion play a role here: the Catalans – even Sánchez Camacho to some extent – are flesh-and-blood humans, while their adversaries in the Spanish government are cold and calculating. However, criticisms of uneven treatment do not just relate to the PP: other examples include the impression that José Montilla has been less of an object of satire than other politicians (Ferré-Pavia and Gayà-Morlà, 2011: 54), and that Artur Mas has been more favourably treated since becoming President of the *Generalitat* (Canal, 2011). Such impressions are of course subjective. As Moreno has shown with respect to *Vaya semanita*, viewers who are themselves more politically neutral are more likely to consider such programmes as balanced, whereas those who identify with a particular group are more likely to see it as being unfairly targeted (Moreno, 2012: 180). However, the way different groups are characterised does suggest a harsher criticism of the PP than other parties.

Parody

As will be apparent from the preceding discussion, it is impossible to separate parodic characterisation in *Polònia* from the accompanying parodies of more general cultural phenomena. Spoofing *Austin Powers*, Angry Birds or 'Gangnam Style' is one form of parody that draws on the audience's experiences of global culture, but in this section I want to draw attention to the programme's use of specifically Spanish and Catalan cultural forms. These often involve music, which is one of the staples of the programme, but also the use of traditional phrases or colloquial sayings.

As far as music is concerned, we have already noted that the use of song and dance often contributes to the humanisation of the characters involved. (Although this is not always the case: when Dr Wert and Mini-Wert rap together about making sure Spanish children all learn the same things 'just like they did when the General [Franco] was in charge', the force of the lyrics and the de-humanisation of Wert achieved by turning him into Dr Evil negate the comic effect of their dance routine.)[18] Music enhances the sense of the carnivalesque that is an important component of parody and sometimes of satire (Thompson, 2008). It also connects the audience to the characters – and to each other – through a recognition of their shared cultural heritage. It is interesting, therefore, to note the use in *Polònia* of musical forms more closely linked to other parts of Spain than to Catalonia.

In the episode first shown on 27 September 2012, after Mas had called elections, one of the sketches involves Oriol Junqueras (ERC) and Joan Herrera (ICV) trying to persuade Artur Mas to consider them as potential coalition partners. They do so using the traditional Spanish format of 'La Tuna', a group of strolling musicians – normally students – dressed in matching embroidered capes, who set out to woo the women of their locality by singing under their balconies accompanied by guitars and tambourines. In this case, they are wooing Mas, trying to convince him that they should work together to demand independence (or whatever he wants to call it), and that he need not be afraid of a pact with the Left. In the end, Mas lowers down a rope and hoists Junqueras on to his balcony, but cuts it before Herrera can climb too. A traditional song associated with 'La Tuna' is the logical choice of music to provide a metaphor for the process of pre-election negotiations between political parties.

Later in the same episode, another popular Spanish song forms the basis for a sketch about the number of parties now 'jumping on the bandwagon' of independence (the phrase is almost literally the same in Catalan: 'enfilar-se al carro'). Mas is seen driving a horse and cart at some speed with Duran Lleida beside him. Duran warns him he is going too fast (towards independence) and will cause an accident, but Mas tells him he has no right to speak because he has only just 'got on the wagon'. At this point, Carod-Rovira pops up behind them to point out that he 'invented the wagon'. Next to appear is Montilla, who states that he is qualified to lead a push for independence because of his comments about Catalonia's disaffection with Spain, but Mas makes it clear that 'only the most important president in the history of Catalonia can drive this cart'.[19] This is of course a cue for Jordi Pujol to stake his claim to this title – and to having been in favour of independence all along. Together, the five politicians then sing a song based on the well-known 'Corre, corre, caballito' ('Run, run, little horse'), sung by child star Marisol in the Spanish film *Un rayo de luz* ('A Ray of Light', 1960). The Spanish refrain is maintained while the other lyrics are adjusted to form a rousing ditty urging everyone forward to independence. The final lines mention the fact that at least Pere Navarro has not jumped on the same bandwagon. This is a cue for a shot of Navarro alone astride a stubbornly unmoving donkey, which he is urging on by using another refrain from a popular Spanish Christmas song ('Arre borriquito', 'Giddy up little donkey'): 'Go on, federalism, go on!'. Again, given that the phrase 'enfilar-se al carro' has been interpreted literally to provide the basis of the joke, 'Corre, corre, caballito' and the visual references to the film in which it appears are a logical choice.

It could be regarded as ironic that Spanish rather than Catalan musical forms are referenced in these skits on independence, but these are still very much part of the musical heritage of most Catalans. They therefore foster a sense of mutual recognition and shared culture, as of course do more local and more global forms that are a part of Catalans' cultural repertoire. Furthermore, as I have suggested, a linguistic joke sometimes dictates the choice of music and so the feeling of recognition is engendered initially by language. Taking colloquial phrases and sayings literally is a hallmark of *Polònia*'s brand of humour, and this too can be regarded as a form of parody. Each phrase is treated as a text that is then 'ironically transcontextualised', in a form that mirrors literary parody (Day, 2008: 94; Hutcheon, 2000: 32).

An example of this that has no connection with music is the on-going gag involving 'la puta i la Ramoneta' (literally, 'the whore and Ramoneta'). This comes from the colloquial saying 'fer la puta i la Ramoneta', which means to act hypocritically, saying one thing while actually thinking or doing another.[20] *Polònia* first used this phrase in 2010 in a sketch where Artur Mas is seen in his office throwing around a football with two ladies, one middle-aged, the other young and acting provocatively. Oriol Pujol interrupts him and asks what he is doing and he says he is 'playing "la puta i la Ramoneta"'. Pujol ushers the ladies out of the office, at which point it transpires of course that the younger lady is actually Ramoneta. In August 2012, the writer Quim Monzó used the same phrase in an interview to refer, among other things, to CiU's unclear stance on independence (E. González, 2012). The phrase was used again that same month by Jordi Pujol in a magazine interview, in which he said the time for 'la puta i la Ramoneta' was now over because of the real threat to Catalonia's identity and autonomy (Vilaweb, 2012b).

This presumably prompted the makers of *Polònia* to devise a sketch aired on 13 September 2012 in which members of CDC are seen at the funeral of their long-time companions *la Puta* and Ramoneta. Mas gives a eulogy in which he reveals that they were lost in an accident 'on the way to Ithaca' – a synonym for the journey towards independence derived from the 1975 song 'Ítaca' by Lluís Llach – and laments the fact that they will no longer be available to help in the job of convincing business owners. Oriol Pujol then reads a passage from *Convergència*'s Holy Book in which the duo exhorts the party to be nice to their enemies in case there comes a time when you have to make a pact with them. As Mas and Pujol leave the chapel, Pujol asks whether the ladies really are dead and Mas replies that they are even more defunct than the *pacte fiscal*. However, at the end of the sketch the camera zooms in on one of the open coffins, from which a thrusting hand emerges, accompanied by archetypal horror-genre music – and so we await the ladies' resurrection at a later date.

This playfulness with colloquial language complements and extends the way specific linguistic features are used in characterisation, although Xus Ugarte comments that the use of broader forms of linguistic parody has varied over the course of the series' history, perhaps because of the use of different scriptwriters (Ugarte Ballester, 2011: 2). Ugarte is also critical of the relatively limited and predictable level of this linguistic play (Ugarte Ballester, 2011: 6). However, like the use of music, one of the principal effects of linguistic parody in *Polònia* is to draw viewers into an identification with a particular cultural community – in this case, a bilingual speech community with its own set of recognisable characteristics. *Polònia* speaks to an audience that collectively speaks like its characters – but does that mean the audience also thinks like *Polònia*'s characters, or can easily be persuaded to do so?

Discussion

Marçal Sintes claims that '*Polònia* establishes an agenda and, furthermore, subjects the personalities and actions of politicians who have this agenda to 'priming' or framing. That is to say, certain aspects are highlighted in a way that favours one interpretation over others' (Sintes i Olivella, 2010: 52).[21] This is true, but does not mean that viewers are brainwashed into accepting this interpretation. Carme Ferré-Pavia and Catalina Gayà-Morlà have conducted a study of the influence of *Polònia,* and although it was published before the period we have examined here, their research – based on focus groups and a survey – came to two conclusions that are particularly relevant for the present discussion. Firstly, the majority of *Polònia*'s viewers consider themselves well-informed, and are therefore not using *Polònia* as a substitute for 'hard news'. (In fact, as David Marc jokes in his Foreword to the volume *Satire TV,* it may be that loyal viewers of satirical shows watch the news specifically in order to be able to follow the gags! (Marc, 2008: Kindle loc. 67; Ferré-Pavia and Gayà-Morlà, 2011: 55).) Secondly, viewers of the programme overwhelmingly agreed that it could not of itself change people's opinions (55–6). Ferré-Pavia and Gayà-Morlà therefore conclude that

> Our research refutes the concerns that television infotainment might affect voting preferences. Although some changes in attitude and perceptions are certainly evident, we have also shown how political satire humanizes politicians, generates debate and enhances viewer interest in politics. (Ferré-Pavia and Gayà-Morlà, 2011: 59)

Their one caveat is that viewers who were already cynical about politicians might feel that *Polònia*'s depiction of their weaknesses confirms the correctness of this viewpoint (Ferré-Pavia and Gayà-Morlà, 2011: 56). Nevertheless, they found no evidence that such satire can generate political apathy or cynicism where it did not already exist.

Much the same as with the documentaries on independence, then, it seems that political satire is likely to influence viewers' political opinions only to the extent of confirming those they already hold. Moreover, as Peter Keighron puts it, 'the comedy aspect of satire is only as powerful as the truth aspect. Satire is, almost by definition, a distorted representation of reality but – to work as satire, to work as comedy – it still has to hold to the truth line' (Keighron, 1998: 142). Satire must necessarily represent a recognisable truth even if it is above all trying to be funny, because it is the recognition of truth within the distortion that most effectively stimulates our laughter. Even so, television satire may be made with a specific intent to persuade: in this case, as Holbert et al. show, the force of this intent is generally considered by viewers to be no more objectionable than that of a political opinion piece in a newspaper (Holbert et al., 2013: 180).

However, we also need to look at the specific case of *Polònia*'s sketches on independence from the point of view of their contribution to the normalisation of the idea of independence itself. To quote British comedian Mark Steel, what a satirist can do is to 'make people who already agree with certain ideas [. . .] feel more confident about their ideas' (Keighron, 1998: 140). This stimulates a feeling of not being alone in their convictions. *Polònia*'s 'parodic info-satire' may not always come from a directly pro-independence point of view, but in its satire of anti-independence arguments, the Spanish government's ineptitude, and instances of anti-Catalanism, it provides pro-independence viewers with ammunition for their own views. The in-group that constitutes the show's audience is already constructed as living in a distorted version of the Catalan reality – *Polònia* – that marks them as deviant in the eyes of the rest of Spain. The show can therefore build on this to foster the kind of confidence in belonging to a community of like-minded people that is vital for any active push towards independence.

Polònia, like other satirical comedy programmes, is unable directly to persuade its audience to act in a particular way, but draws on the performative resources of epideictic rhetoric 'to increase the intensity of adherence to common beliefs and values that bind a community' (Morreale, 2008: 104). In doing so it 'stirs or strengthens in audience members a disposition to act', a disposition that is activated by the more deliberative rhetoric of fact-based political argument (Perelman and Olbrechts-Tyteca, 1969: 50; cited in Morreale, 2008: 106; see also Moy et al., 2005: 124). By helping to build a community of feeling around Catalonia's 'difference' from the rest of Spain, *Polònia* also helps to encourage them to listen to messages from other sources about how they should act on that difference.

As Mònica Terribas pointed out when challenged over the lack of political neutrality displayed by *Polònia* 'these programmes are about entertainment and parody', so 'you can't apply to these cases the same criteria as for news programmes' (Anonymous, 2011).[22] As we have seen, whether it is ethical for *Polònia* to take a particular stance on independence is largely a moot point, since – as with the documentaries – its capacity to change anyone's mind on the issue is severely limited. In any case, the observer's judgement of what is and is not ethical will depend on their own degree of neutrality or partisanship, and their position in the relevant power-making networks.

Nevertheless, both the documentaries and *Polònia* engage in affective priming that heightens their audience's sense of collective identity and has the potential to dispose them to act to protect this. They also further normalise – or 'de-dramatise', as Passola puts it – the subject of independence itself (Avui.cat, 2009). As Robert Entman says, '"telling people what to think about" is how one exerts political influence in non-coercive political systems' (Entman, 2007: 165). With a subject as serious as independence, merely encouraging people to think about it when they would not have done so before can have profound consequences. If Catalans also become more convinced that a significant number of others feel the same way they do, the situation may reach a tipping point, since people base what they do partly on what they expect others to do (Hale, 2008: 27–8; Laitin, 2007). It is little wonder, then, that some Spaniards are so profoundly upset by some of *Televisió de Catalunya*'s offerings. However, to condemn them as unethical is simply to obscure the real issue: the on-going struggle for communication power between state and autonomous institutions. With independence on the agenda, the stakes in this battle are higher than they have ever been.

Chapter 6

The Future
Imagining Independence

The documentaries that we looked at in the previous chapter concentrate mainly on the arguments surrounding independence and, therefore, on the cost/benefit analysis relevant to Catalonia's immediate situation. In contrast, this chapter will examine a group of cultural products that imagine the future: how Catalonia might become independent, and what kind of independent state it might turn out to be. While nationalism is always predicated on the need for continuity of the nation along lines that are consistent with the past and present (Mock, 2012: 47–8; Smith, 1991: 96), there is often no need to articulate this future in any very explicit way – only to be diligent about identifying any threats to it. In contrast, a secession movement introduces the possibility of a future that is consistent yet different: the nation-become-state. As we saw in chapter 4, Catalans have not generally been convinced that a Catalan state is a desirable option, instead conforming to what Hale sees as the normal preference for 'Regions', which is *'to be part of a cooperative union,* a union in which that Region is incorporated on favourable terms' (Hale, 2008: 70). Nevertheless, novels such as *Victus* and *Lliures o morts* hint at the idea that statehood would actually have been a preferable alternative in the past. Similarly, fiction can function as a tool for persuading today's Catalans that a state will provide them with a better future, and for allaying their fears about the risks involved in achieving this.

At the time of writing, there are plans for films that will tackle this subject, of which two seem likely to be particularly significant: *L'Endemà* ('The Day After') directed by Isona Passola, and *Trencant cadenes* ('Breaking Chains') by Antoni Verdaguer. *L'Endemà* will take the form of a documentary focussing on how an independent Catalonia could thrive, following on from *Cataluña-Espanya*. In contrast, *Trencant cadenes* is a feature film based on a fictionalised 'extension' of current events (its working subtitle is 'When the dream becomes reality'). Both projects are reliant on crowdfunding, and by the time it started shooting in late 2013, *L'Endemà* had managed to raise

300,000 Euros (http://lendema.cat). However, it is not in the audio-visual sector but in print that there is already a body of works that tackle these subjects.

One of these is a publication called *Polònia independent* – a spin-off from the television show – that imagines Catalonia just after independence (Lucas et al., 2013). Obviously, this revolves around the same figures with which the show's viewers are so familiar, as the satire could not function with invented personalities. The book begins with Artur Mas declaring independence, although he still struggles to say the words in more than a whisper and has to be egged on by Junqueras (Lucas et al., 2013: 5). It then imagines the institutions, economy and culture of an independent Catalan republic in which 'Mas Style' has become an unofficial national anthem, and today's politicians and celebrities all have new roles that are nevertheless characterised by the foibles they have shown in the past.

In 2010, *Polònia*'s creator Toni Soler published a novel which also imagined a future Catalonia, although not in this case an independent state but part of a federal Spain (Soler, 2010). The plot of *L'última carta de Companys* ('Companys' Last Letter') is partly science fiction, as it revolves around a power-crazed female vice-president of the *Generalitat* who in 2015 becomes aware of the invention of a time-machine, which she uses to rescue former president Lluís Companys just before his execution in 1940. While this is initially presented as a patriotic quest, it soon becomes clear that her actual interest lies in finding a hidden store of gold that was appropriated by the Catalans on its way to Moscow at the start of the Civil War.[1] The sub-text here is a condemnation of the federal system operating in this future Spain, which keeps Catalonia subordinate to the central state. One of the vice-president's aims is to force Spain to agree to a confederal arrangement that would allow Catalonia more power on the world stage (Soler, 2010: Kindle loc. 1633). However, at the end of the novel it is the Spanish state that holds all the cards, taking control of both the gold and the time-machine, and leaving the vice-president (and Catalonia) completely marginalised. Her dream of international recognition evaporates as her potential foreign allies redirect their attention back to Spain. As her assistant reminds her, 'States always help one another, and so do the economic lobbies. But the *Generalitat* has to fight alone' (Soler, 2010: Kindle loc. 4167).[2] Bringing back Companys functions as an allegory for what would happen if today's Spain ever experimented with federalism: both attempts are doomed to failure.

Another cynical view of Catalonia's political situation is provided by Marc Moreno in *Independència d'interessos* (Moreno, 2013). The title has a double meaning, seeming at first glance to indicate something that is independent of the influence of particular interests, but actually referring to

Catalan independence as an issue that is conditioned by a quest for personal and collective power. The novel is set during the time of the *consultes populars* in the real-life town of Matadepera, which in the novel is about to hold its own vote. A chance finding of a medieval legal document puts a new slant on the consultation, since if Matadepera votes in favour this would fulfil a condition in the document that would mean much of the land and property in the area passing from the control of the Church to the descendent of the original owner (who was one of the historic rulers of Barcelona). The convoluted plot involves blackmail, kidnapping, corruption, an extra-marital affair and a murder. Local members of CiU and the PP are seen to be manipulating the vote both for their own reasons and in response to a blackmail attempt related to this document. At one point this leads to the farcical situation of CiU recommending a vote against independence while the leader of the local PP urges a vote in favour. The intrigue culminates not only in the arrest of those responsible for the blackmail and murder but also the cancellation of the consultation. The absurdity of the plot coupled with the use of real places, events and political parties implies a general criticism of the egotism and corruption inherent in contemporary politics, even around such an apparently idealistic matter as the independence debate.

These books all take advantage of current issues surrounding Catalonia's political relationship with Spain, but in this chapter I am particularly interested in three novels that specifically imagine the process by which Catalonia becomes independent: *Crònica de la independència* ('The Chronicle of Independence') by Patrícia Gabancho, *A reveure, Espanya* ('Au Revoir, Spain') by Jordi Cussà, and *Tres en ratlla* ('Three in a Row') by Santi Baró. The first two of these are written from a point in the future from which the protagonists can look back on these events (2037 in the case of *Crònica* and 2038 for *A reveure*). In contrast, *Tres en ratlla* only narrates the events that occur over the course of the day on which independence is declared. All three authors opt for a unilateral declaration of independence by the Catalan parliament as the mechanism by which the process of secession begins.

I have referred to all three of these works as novels, but Patrícia Gabancho has another term for hers: a journalistic fiction (Gabancho, 2009: 10). Gabancho is best known for her contributions to print and broadcast journalism and her extended essays on Catalan society, politics and culture. It is probably for this reason (and not wishful thinking!) that *Crònica de la independència* was listed as non-fiction in the categories used at the Sant Jordi book fair of 2009, in which the book was the best seller. Gabancho claims that her book is first and foremost journalism because she wanted to make it as plausible as possible, and coherent with the realities of the Catalan situation at the time she was writing (ibid.). It is also structured around interviews that form part of a research project (carried out by Gabancho's own son), and contains a number of fictional press articles. Despite this clear influence of journalistic techniques, I will use the term 'novel' to describe the work since the term is certainly broad enough to encompass it.

A reveure, Espanya was written by Jordi Cussà, an experienced novelist as well as a poet and theatre director (Cussà, 2010). Like Gabancho's *Crònica* it is principally structured around two different moments in time: 2018, when independence is declared, and 2038, when the granddaughter of the female president of the *Generalitat* who made that declaration decides to find out more about it. There are therefore similarities in the way each step in the process is revealed. Both investigators are young and live outside Catalonia: Gabancho's son Daniel is a teenager at the time of independence and subsequently chooses to study and work in Canada, while in *A reveure* the president's granddaughter Sophie is a postgraduate student who was brought up in an independent Scotland. Their family connections in Catalonia but relative ignorance of recent history mean that they can ask sensible questions of those around them while still needing to be told basic details. This narrative device therefore ensures that the reader also has all the information s/he needs to understand how independence was achieved.

Tres en ratlla, on the other hand, is a straightforward linear narrative (Baró, 2012). The exact year is unspecified but the declaration of independence appears to take place not long after the demonstration of July 2010, which is the last real-life event that is cited. The process is witnessed by Sergi, a long-time supporter of independence, and Anna, the friend he had been secretly in love with for many years but who is now married with children. Other protagonists include the president of the *Generalitat,* the leader of the 'Independence Party', the Spanish Prime Minister and Minister of Defence, and members of the Catalan and Spanish security forces. Rather than two time frames, then, this novel revolves around two very different spheres of action: Sergi and Anna's participation in the popular demonstrations of the day (representing civil society), and the machinations of the relevant Catalan and Spanish institutions (representing the political sphere).

All three novels suppose the same basic mechanism by which Catalonia becomes independent. In *Crònica,* the president of the *Generalitat* in 2010 is Miquel Roca, the real-life former General Secretary of CDC and leader of the Catalan group in the Spanish parliament. Roca is to make a speech and then call for a vote on opening negotiations with the Spanish government for some kind of referendum on Catalonia's relationship with Spain. However, to the surprise of most of the members of parliament, he instead calls for a vote on a unilateral declaration of independence, insisting that negotiations are 'a political dead end' and a unilateral declaration is 'the only possible way forward' (Gabancho, 2009: 100, 102).[3] This would be followed by a referendum to confirm the support of the people of Catalonia. The motion is passed by 83 votes to 52. The Spanish government threatens to suspend Catalonia's autonomy, but the threat is simply met by a statement that since Catalonia is now independent Spain no longer has any jurisdiction over it. Meanwhile, the EU steps in and insists that Spain negotiate the process of separation in good faith (Gabancho, 2009: 61).

A reveure sees a unilateral declaration by fictional president Blanca Martorell Cervantes, whose name appears to be a homage to two great writers – Joanot Martorell, the Valencian author of *Tirant Lo Blanch* (Tirant the White), and Miguel de Cervantes – thus signalling the mixed cultural heritage of both the president herself and most of the people she represents. As in *Crònica*, the idea of a negotiated referendum is dismissed as unworkable (Cussà, 2010: 30). Instead, a large parliamentary majority of parties in favour of independence is used as the basis for a swift unilateral declaration, to be followed by a referendum that would legitimise the decision. Spain's reaction is to close the border with Catalonia and consider military action, an option that is discarded after these words from King Felipe (son of the current King Juan Carlos): 'if we have to use the army to win it, then this war has already been lost' (Cussà, 2010: 42–3).[4] Interestingly, Blanca persuades the parliament to accept the continuation of the monarchy rather than declaring a republic, for reasons which form part of the main plot of the novel and will be discussed later.

Tres en ratlla narrates a process quite similar to that used in *Crònica,* in the sense that the vote for a unilateral declaration is hidden from the Catalan parliament (and the Spanish government) until the last minute. Here, the Independence Party has put forward a motion in favour of independence which the majority Nationalist Party has said it will not support. The Spanish government is therefore unconcerned by this development as the motion will be defeated. However, behind the scenes the president of the *Generalitat* has devised a plan by which if there is sufficient public support for the motion, he will change the party's line and allow each member a conscience vote. Aware of Spain's likely reaction if the motion is passed, he secretly puts in place a strategy to avoid physical conflict by asking Catalonia's police force – the *Mossos d'Esquadra* – to be prepared to surround the barracks of the Civil Guard and other elements of the forces of law and order on Catalan soil that report to the Spanish state. On the day of the vote, the civic organisation *Acció Cultural* (whose leaders are complicit in the plan) calls Catalans onto the streets to ask the president to change his mind and allow a free vote for his party. As people pour into the park that surrounds the parliament building and eventually take over the surrounding streets, president Cardús (a nod to the real-life pro-independence intellectual Salvador Cardús?) waits until the last possible minute before authorising the conscience vote. The result is decisive: 90 votes in favour to 31 against (Baró, 2012: Kindle loc. 1429).

The Spanish government realises too late what is happening and their first reaction is to resort to military intervention. However, the Spanish forces in Catalonia are penned in and it will take time to deploy others. The best they can do initially is to send armed military helicopters to fly low over the demonstrators in the centre of Barcelona. Realising that the Spanish army might try to enter the city, many of the demonstrators disperse to the main entry points to block their way. Meanwhile, one of the Civil Guard commanders has intimidated the leader of the squad of *Mossos* outside his headquarters into letting them pass, taking a small force of armoured vehicles towards the park. When they arrive they find their way blocked by protesters supported by armed *Mossos*. After a tense moment, one of the vehicles tries to break through the cordon and ends up veering out of control, killing four civilians and wounding many more. The Civil Guards are surrounded by the *Mossos* in a tense stand-off and there is now no choice but for the Spanish government to declare all-out war or to back down. Despite the presence of protesters in Madrid who are urging the government to send in the military, a compromise is reached: Catalonia will call off the *Mossos* and hold a proper referendum to ratify the declaration of independence, while Spain promises that there will be no further military intervention. The Spanish Prime Minister and the team that have been advising him throughout the crisis are strangely satisfied – even happy – with this decision, as if they knew that this was morally the right thing to do (Baró, 2012: Kindle loc. 2566). Although *Tres en ratlla* focuses more closely on the potential for conflict than the other two novels, the general message is the same in all three: any conflict, whether institutionally legitimised or caused by rogue agents, is short-lived and produces no more than a handful of casualties. Common sense quickly prevails.

Emotion versus Reason

The three novels, then, have a similar approach to the overall question of independence: a unilateral declaration by the parliament is the safest and most logical choice and should be followed by a referendum; the legitimacy of this approach will eventually be accepted, leading to a peacefully-negotiated separation. However, this similarity does conceal differences in the way each version of the process is narrated, which once again revolve around questions of rationality versus emotion. *Crònica* contains few references to sentiment and concentrates on the rational reasons for independence and the logical steps that would be necessary for an independent Catalonia to function afterwards. In complete contrast, *Tres en ratlla* – partly because of its more traditionally novelistic character – narrates the process as a fundamentally emotional one, using Sergi and Anna as the litmus tests of this: their relationship is rekindled at the same time as their beloved country becomes independent. *A reveure* exists somewhere in the middle of these two extremes, since Sophie's quest to learn more about the declaration of independence eventually reveals that this apparently rational process hid dark webs of influence that were driven by people's deepest emotions. Both *seny* and *rauxa* were therefore necessary for independence to be achieved. This section will concentrate on the latter two novels and their portrayal of this emotional component.

Tres en ratlla is structured around historical parallels which afford its characters' sentimental nationalism the same kind of legitimacy we saw in the novels of '1714'. In this case, however, the focus is on a different event: the popular revolt in Barcelona of 7 June 1640 that led to the 'War of the Reapers' that lasted until 1659. The day became known as the *Corpus de Sang,* or 'Bloody Corpus', because it took place at the feast of Corpus Christi. In Baró's novel, the events also take place on 7 June and there are continuous references to the parallels with the popular uprising of 1640 and the crucial role of the people in achieving independence in the present. The link is first made by the president of *Acció Cultural* in the email she sends to call its supporters onto the streets: 'We know that with the same response the citizens gave to the Bloody Corpus on that previous 7 June in 1640, or the demonstration on 10 July 2010, our country will become a free, sovereign nation' (Baró, 2012: Kindle loc. 265).[5] When this response is forthcoming, the narrator returns to the comparison to describe the 'flood' of young Catalans pouring out of Barcelona's universities towards the park, which resembled the day in 1640 'when thousands of reapers [. . .] took Barcelona' (Kindle loc. 482).[6] This is something of an exaggeration, as the initial revolt involved hundreds not thousands of reapers who caused localised disturbances rather than 'taking' the city as a whole (Elliott, 1963: 446–51). References to the *Corpus de sang* continue throughout the novel, including the singing by the crowd of part of the national anthem derived from it once independence has been declared, and the reproduction of the full text of the anthem when it is sung by members of the Catalan parliament (Baró, 2012: Kindle locs 1464 & 1691).

The most emotionally-charged reference, however, is a speech given by a farmer using a megaphone from the cab of his tractor. (The scene is reminiscent of Shakespeare's Henry V rallying his troops at Agincourt). The farmers have used their agricultural machinery to block the main highway near Lleida and Spanish troop carriers are advancing towards them. Speaking in a thick North-Western Catalan, the farmer invokes the events of the *Corpus de Sang* to ensure that his colleagues stand firm: 'It is a long time since that 7 June of 1640 when they had to cut their chains instead of golden ears of corn, but even though it's a long time ago, the same spirit continues intact generation after generation, and since Madrid has not lost the old habits of insults, pillage, arrogance, and denial of the people's claims, we must ensure that the spirit of that 7 June is reborn and repel the invaders!!! We are the new reapers!!! Long live free Catalonia!!!' (Baró, 2012: Kindle loc. 2367).[7] In the end, there is no repeat of the bloodshed of 1640, but the novel makes it clear that the people are determined not to be cowed into submission by the threat of violence.

Sergi and Anna embody this same spirit. When the call from *Acció Catalana* comes through, Sergi remembers that Anna works for Vodafone and can send texts to everyone on that network. His reason for getting back in touch with her after several years, then, is to persuade her to circulate information about the protest, which Anna does even though this might result in her losing her job. She then joins him at the protest even though her family is worried about her and her husband is not a supporter of independence. As the emotional rollercoaster of the day unfolds, Sergi and Anna realise their latent love for one another, which is motivated as much as anything by their shared love for Catalonia. Anna's husband Pepe, on the other hand, does not support Catalan independence and is portrayed rather crudely as the stereotype of an uneducated immigrant who is incapable of thinking for himself and votes for a 'Spanish nationalist' party (within which Sergi includes both the PP and the socialists) (Baró, 2012: Kindle locs 2603 & 601). This kind of crude ethnic stereotyping also raises its head when the narrator comments that some members of the socialist party – who had been ordered to vote against independence, and did so – were actually happy with the outcome, 'especially those whose lineage bears a Catalan surname, engraved there in fire' (Baró, 2012: 1431).[8] Despite their 'betrayal' of the nation, their hearts are still seen to be true to the cause for which their ethnic heritage has prepared them.

Tres en ratlla is by far the most 'primordialist' of the three novels in its approach to fictionalising independence, narrating a process that is implied to be the culmination of centuries of oppression and the result of an act of collective love for the country. Indeed, a post-script by the author describes it as 'a portrait of a real image of a landscape that must by necessity come into being' (Baró, 2012: Kindle loc. 2697).[9] *A reveure, Espanya*, on the other hand, is more complex, even though the author's dedication at the start of the novel makes it clear that he hopes writing it will help make independence a reality. The intrigue of the novel revolves around two unusual factors in the otherwise logical progression towards independence: the election of ERC's Blanca Martorell to the presidency by an unprecedented consensus, and her decision to persuade parliament to keep the monarch as Head of State rather than declaring a republic. Sophie's investigative instincts lead her to probe into both of these and uncover the motivations behind them.

During the period leading up to the unilateral declaration, Catalan politics goes through an unprecedented upheaval, resulting in the dissolution of CiU into its two component parts and the splitting of the PSC into a sovereigntist and a non-sovereigntist socialist party (Cussà, 2010: 28–9). ICV decides to abandon its confederal position in favour of independence, and ERC renounces the idea of a referendum, backing instead the idea of a unilateral declaration after elections giving a large pro-independence majority in the parliament (Cussà, 2010: 29–31). Blanca Martorell of ERC emerges from this process as the preferred candidate to lead the new pro-independence consensus. However, Sophie later uncovers the real reason for this unanimity, which is that key players had been blackmailed into manoeuvring their party or faction towards support for the pro-independence platform and then electing Blanca as the presidential candidate. While Blanca is concerned that they suspect her of orchestrating this, others realise that there is another hand at work. At a reunion gathering of the main players twenty years to the day after the declaration of independence, no one believes Blanca was to blame.

On the other hand, Blanca was directly responsible for the choice of retaining the monarchy, and this is bound up with a secret of her own. Blanca had never told her daughter (Sophie's mother) who her father was. He is eventually revealed to be none other than King Felipe, the result of a brief affair when he and Blanca were students in America in the 1990s. Blanca's insistence on retaining the monarchy therefore has a personal motivation, which lies behind her open commitment to the rational argument that keeping the monarchy was a simple matter of expediency (Cussà, 2010: 35). However, it then emerges that some of the guests at the anniversary reunion are now receiving further threats asking them to use their influence to break the link with the monarchy and declare a republic.

The blackmailer is finally revealed to be a lifetime friend and former lover of Blanca's, who owns the neighbouring *mas* (country property). Jaume Llorets explains that his family's history of sacrifice for Catalonia had left him obsessed with seeing Catalonia become independent in his own life-

time, and his wealth and connections allowed him to pull strings in order
to do so (Cussà, 2010: 155). He is also in love with Blanca – in fact he loves
her 'as much or more than Catalonia' – and now wants to see her elected
Head of State (Cussà, 2010: 157).[10] Llorets had originally roped Blanca's
daughter into the plot, revealing to her in the process that King Felipe was
her father. Now, acting alone, he is determined to finish what he had started
twenty years ago.

Three messages emerge from Llorets' explanation of his actions in the
final pages of the novel. The first appears to be firmly addressed to today's
politicians, and is a call for the kind of selfless unity of purpose apparently
exemplified by Catalonia's leaders in the 1930s. In contrast, after the dictatorship and the disappointments of the transition to democracy, 'everyone
went crazy trying to keep and increase their own particular portion of
power, and the ship was just going round and round in port' (Cussà, 2010:
156).[11] The second is that rectifying this failing is a noble enough cause
that the end justifies the means: 'if you think about it carefully you'll see
that everyone wins and . . . it had to be done'.[12] Finally, Jaume says that
'there is always a personal factor' as well as a 'strictly patriotic' one, thus
legitimising the marriage of reason and emotion that had led him to the
drastic step of blackmail.[13] Blanca's reaction seals the legitimacy of these
messages ' "You're mad, Jaume Llorets", she murmured between two tears,
one of affliction and the other of joy. "We should have got married a century
ago" ' (Cussà, 2010: 157).[14] Like *Tres en ratlla*, then, *A reveure, Espanya* posits
a direct relationship between love of country and love for a particular person
– albeit one who shares your views on this crucial issue. Once again we seem
to be in the same territory as *Victus* and *Lliures o morts* with their emphasis
on love for family as the basis of love for community and, therefore, nation.

Crònica de la independència

Gabancho's *Crònica de la independència* is very different in approach, and one
of its most interesting features is its discussion of Catalonia's place in the
world as an independent state. In fact, the book starts with the transcript
of an interview with the Minister for Citizenship during which Daniel asks
her about the multicultural make-up of the new Catalonia and issues to do
with immigration. It is only after this chapter that the subject turns to the
process of achieving independence. The high profile of the topic is not
surprising given Gabancho's own previous work on immigration (e.g.
Gabancho, 2001). However, it also points to the fact that her main preoccupation is to show what Catalonia is like after independence, especially the

way that this has altered the relationship between identity, language and multiculturalism (Gabancho, 2009: 10).

Gabancho's imagined Catalonia exists in a new era that one might describe as 'post-globalisation'. She paints a picture of a world in which many of the barriers that had been removed by globalisation have now been re-erected: the movement of goods and people is rigidly controlled and the world has been divided into different macro-regions with very different needs and approaches. Catalonia forms part of a European zone that includes an independent Scotland, Flanders and Wallonia, as well as the remains of Spain, and in which collaboration is if anything even stronger than before. As a result, it is the EU that sets policy on human movement, restricting mass tourism and virtually eliminating immigration through stricter controls and by offering no recognition or practical support whatsoever to illegal immigrants: 'they don't exist' (Gabancho, 2009: 226).[15] Nevertheless, for those who arrive legally conditions are better and citizenship is more easily achieved. They also benefit from a multicultural Catalonia, in which diversity at the private and community level is encouraged, even to the point of tolerance of 'ghettos' (140–1). Nevertheless, all citizens know and use the Catalan language alongside any other they may employ with their family or community. The issue of Catalan identity has been relegated to secondary importance since independence, but Catalan culture thrives and has become hegemonic in an organic fashion rather than by being imposed (175–6). As the President of Catalonia puts it on the last page of the novel: 'If you want to be from here, you're from here. It's that easy' (275).[16]

Paradoxically, then, the result of globalisation has been 'compartmentalisation' rather than the complete elimination of borders and barriers (Gabancho, 2009: 23). Gabancho justifies this compartmentalisation by showing how it has allowed societies to tackle their problems on their own terms, as well as bringing global benefits such as protecting the environment. In her new world, mass consumerism has been halted, trade barriers have been re-erected and there is no longer an obsession with constant economic growth. As one of Daniel's interviewees puts it,

> We are closed in on ourselves as a way of defending ourselves from globalisation, which was leading us to disaster. Now we control everything. When we need something we open the door, put out our hand and bring it in, and that goes for a product, a material or a person. Otherwise, nothing moves.[17] (196)

Of course, this approach is anathema to those who see borders as negative things that should be broken down, and who therefore approve of globalisation's role in doing so. This stance is actually articulated in the novel by a commentator who is reported in a fictional press clipping from 2010 as opposing Catalonia's bid for independence:

> In the globalised world of the twenty-first century it is naïve to talk about independence: the crisis made it very clear that no government, however many flags it waves, controls the reins of the economy or can use the law to shape the essential evolution of society. The world no longer permits borders.[18] (146)

Gabancho is explicitly refuting this assumption in her portrayal of a successful society that functions precisely because of strengthened borders and greater controls, whether the latter are located at the European or the Catalan level.

Gabancho's view of globalisation seems to exemplify some of the current academic debates around the cultural, political and economic implications of globalisation for stateless nations. As Ryan Griffiths and Ivan Savić point out, sub-national regions benefit economically from direct access to markets outside the context of their own nation-state, which would seem to indicate that possession of a state is no longer a requirement to attain the best possible economic outcomes (Griffiths and Savić , 2009: 431). On the other hand, smaller economies tend to fare less well in this competitive environment, which means that integration into a larger economic unit does have its advantages (ibid.). This is why membership of an entity such as the European Union often comes to substitute for membership of the current nation-state in the strategies of separatist parties. Taken together, these factors have led many to assume that 'globalization increases the appeal of secessionism and decentralization short of secession, and [. . .] secession should in turn reinforce globalization, possibly requiring secessionist parties to move to the free-market right' (Sorens, 2004: 730; see also Rodríguez-Pose and Sandall, 2008: 58). One could indeed argue that one of the reasons why the discourse of CDC has shifted towards a sovereigntist stance is that as the economy becomes increasingly globalised, the option of secession better fits their business-orientated economic perspective than it did previously. Conversely, however, Sorens cautions against assuming that left-wing separatism is doomed to disappear, since there is no necessary link between neo-liberal economic policy and support for globalisation (ibid.). This means that even though parties such as ERC and the Scottish National Party embrace much of the free-market logic of global trade that is central to the EU, this is not incompatible with left-liberal or social-democratic domestic welfare policies that might require a relatively high level of taxation and 'big government'.

Cultural concerns provide another motivation for secession, since 'the need to distinguish between "us", "we", and "the others" grows as contacts and communications increase' (Lundestad, 2004: 271). Paradoxically, as globalisation progresses, so does fragmentation, especially in the form of a heightened attachment to a particular identity. Critics of this trend complain that it often leads to entrenched positions that preclude democratic compromise (Weinstock, 2006). However, Vince Marotta sees identity-based boundaries as complex and ambivalent, since they 'can be oppressive and limiting, but they can also provide an ethical basis for respecting the otherness of the other' (Marotta, 2008: 299). The problem, therefore, 'is not boundaries in themselves, but how they are used, the type of boundaries and who imposes boundaries and why' (ibid.).

For Gabancho, the re-imposition of boundaries – whether cultural, economic or political – is a necessary corrective to the runaway forces of globalisation. Her vision combines elements normally associated with both the left and right wing of politics. So, for example her future Catalonia champions a republican-style commitment to an 'achieved' citizenship 'based in agency and difference' (Dahlgren, 2007: 59), while at the same time denying basic welfare to illegal immigrants – an idea more normally associated with the right. Neoliberalism has been rejected in favour of a reduction in consumption and the abandonment of the imperative for continuous economic growth, but workers doing the same job are paid differently in accordance with their individual productivity (Gabancho, 2009: 191). When Daniel interviews the Minister for Economic, Financial and Commercial Affairs, he is told that this unorthodox combination came about as the result of a total reorientation of economic thinking stimulated by the crisis of 2008 (ibid.). Nevertheless, he also says that money was the Catalans' primary motivation for secession, at a time when 'the world was already totally global' and 'the Spanish market was incidental' (184–5).[19]

Whether seen from the perspective of the benefits of access to global markets unrestricted by Spanish policies, or a need to rein in the more perverse socioeconomic effects of globalisation, the answer for Catalonia as far as separatists are concerned is in both cases the same: independence. The key issue seems to be the same as it was for Alex Salmond when he stated that 'an independent Scotland will embrace the interdependence of the modern world, but we would do so on <u>our own terms</u>' (Salmond, 2012: my emphasis). Whether or not all readers would share Gabancho's view of the preferred political, economic and cultural profile of an independent Catalonia, the key message is that Catalans can now make their own decisions – including the decision to share power with the European Union. Her post-global Europe still faces important challenges, but Catalonia is an equal partner in working towards their solution.

Hale posits that 'separatist politics is largely the process by which Regions' perceptions are influenced as to the risk involved in union and separation' (Hale, 2008: 75). Gabancho, Cussà and Baró all engage in this form of politics through their fictional representations of Catalan independence, reassuringly playing down the risk involved in separation while also highlighting some of the penalties Catalonia pays for its union with Spain. Their messages follow the same basic trajectories as we found in the novels and films/television programmes analysed in the previous two chapters, effectuating similar calls to action. The collective heroism of the people of Barcelona and their leaders during the siege of 1714 is reproduced in the tales of the steadfastness with which the civil and political protagonists of the three novels work towards their goal; the fragmentation of Catalanist political forces must be, and can be, overcome for the sake of the people they represent. The use or threat of force by the Spanish government becomes a graphic illustration of Catalonia's subordinate position within the state, with the implication that Catalans are being asked to consider whether they really want to continue living under an arrangement in which this threat can be made, no matter how remote the possibility of it being carried out. Economic prosperity and the well-being of all gives the rational motivation for choosing independence, while love for family, friends and community provides the necessary emotional stimulus to act on this conviction.

There are also indications of the kind of ambivalence that Mock sees as fundamental to nationalist attitudes towards ethnicity and historical authenticity, which are encapsulated in the way in which the three novels diverge. As we have seen, *Tres en ratlla* feeds directly off primordialist discourses of historical continuity, and even reveals the lasting presence of ethnic categorisation in judgements about who might or might not be 'loyal' to the nation. This temptation to 'distinguish insiders from outsiders' rests on an ethnic conception of the nation that provides 'a satisfying construct of identity' (Mock, 2012: 44). On the other hand, 'the signifiers that determine ethnic communities must shift in the process of nation formation to account for modern institutions and instrumentalities' (ibid.). It is this process that *Crònica* takes to the extreme, completely disavowing ethnicity as a signifier to the extent that this constitutes what Mock calls 'radical inauthenticity' (ibid.). A *reveure* has elements of both: one character's 'intellectual eroticism' is described as 'genetically Catalan', and

Sophie's sense of deep connection with the Catalan language is explained in very Herderian terms: it 'emanates from the depths of time, and is the eternal collective mother' (Cussà, 2010: 48, 78).[20] On the other hand, a man of Gypsy origin proudly states that no other country has ever treated Gypsies as well as the new Catalonia, while a contrast is made in another case between two men who are putting forward different points of view at the celebrations of the twentieth anniversary of independence: one of them is demanding a federation of Catalan states in a Catalan thick with Castilian influences, while the other holds a placard proclaiming (in Spanish) 'Long Live Spain!' but speaks grammatically perfect Catalan (Cussà, 2010: 54). The diverse nature of the new state is stressed through further references to people of African, Latin American, European and Asian origin who are now 'absolutely committed to the sentiments and referents of the State of Catalonia' (Cussà, 2010: 51).[21]

These novels all take their cue from contemporary debates and concerns, but add an extra creative dimension that feeds the reader's imagination. They remind us of the fundamental role played in nationalism by collective dreams of a better world: a new 'golden age' to come. However, encouraging members of a stateless nation to make such dreams a reality implies much more than the rehearsal of rational arguments about the risks and potential rewards of secession for the individual, since these cannot speak directly to 'the strong emotional dimension of belonging which involves commitment and identification with the group' (Guibernau, 2013: 6). Literature – on the other hand – can do so, and moreover it tends to elicit emotional responses based primarily on empathy rather than egoism (Hogan, 2011: 22–3, 68). It therefore speaks to the reader first and foremost of that which unites him/her with the protagonist(s). Even *Crònica de la independència*, which is the novel that least directly appeals to collective sentiment, can engage the readers' empathy with the cast of characters it presents: imagined future members of their own renewed nation. If emotion is 'experienced as transformation of dispositions to act' (Barbalet, 2001: 27), then the kind of empathic emotion stimulated by these novels has the potential to arouse the same transformation as the affective priming used in the audio-visual products examined in the previous chapter. Gabancho dedicates *Crònica* 'to those who make dreams into reality' (Gabancho, 2009: 13):[22] as readers we are perhaps meant to know that she hopes that includes us.

Conclusion

There are two interweaving currents in the political discourses and cultural phenomena that have been analysed in this volume. On one hand, we see the evolving construction of a simplified message about independence designed to generate consensus; on the other, the realities of the fragmentation, ambivalence, and social complexity that belie this simplification. Nevertheless, as time goes on the idea that the secessionist message is a self-evident truth becomes ever stronger, as pro-independence social actors increasingly refine their ability to construct meaning (Castells, 2009: 10). The only discourse of equivalent strength is that of Spanish unionism, which – especially in its right-wing form – is easily rejected, not just by those who support independence but by a wide spectrum of Catalans who object to the way it attempts to mark them as 'bad' Spaniards. 'Collective dignity and self-respect' and 'expectations of mutual reciprocity (vis-à-vis the majority group)' are fatally undermined by Spanish nationalists' attacks on the Catalans' public image and key national symbols (Lluch, 2012: 440).

The effect of the increasing polarisation of these two discourses can be seen in the fact that, by the end of 2013, two apparently contradictory trends were emerging in Catalan politics. The political landscape seemed to have taken a new turn, with ERC now close to – or even ahead of – CiU in surveys of voting intentions (Noguer, 2013a; Sastre, 2013). The surveys suggested ERC would gain a similar number of seats to those that would be lost by CiU. This would appear to indicate that Mas had not been able convincingly to play the role of separatist leader and that voters with a strong commitment to independence were therefore switching to ERC. As *El País* put it,

> The leaders of CiU have been discreetly warning of this for months: 'If Rajoy won't negotiate with Mas, one day he will have to do so with Junqueras in even more complicated circumstances'.[1] (Noguer, 2013a)

The surveys also indicated an increasing polarisation of Catalan voters, with the 'anti-nationalist' *Ciutadans* set to win more seats, possibly even becoming the third force in the parliament (Noguer, 2013a). The overall picture, then, was one of fragmentation of the pro-independence vote and a widening division between the pro- and anti-independence camps.

On the other hand, one of the same surveys also showed that, given the choice, the majority of Catalans would vote neither for independence nor the status quo, but a 'third way' between the two (Noguer, 2013b). While 46% would choose independence in a straight yes/no vote, the figure would drop to 31% if also offered an alternative that would exclusively give Catalonia more powers within the Spanish state: in fact, 40% of voters would choose this other option. The proposed referendum question drafted in December 2013 by a joint working party of CDC, UDC, ERC, ICV, CUP and EUiA[2] did indeed include this 'third way' as an option, although more because of the need to find a consensus among these parties to take the referendum forward than as a reflection of the will of the people. The question had two parts: 'Do you want Catalonia to become a state? If so, do you want that state to be independent?'.[3] This would give voters three options, since a 'no' vote to the first question would indicate an acceptance of the status quo, 'yes' to both parts would be a vote in favour of independence, and 'yes' then 'no' would indicate a wish to find some other way forward, such as a federal or confederal solution. However, at the time the question was devised there was no party able properly to represent this last viewpoint in the Catalan parliament, and no clarity about what a 'third way' might involve. The very term 'third way' marks this 'other' option as somehow radical or deviant.

This suggests that the secessionist message made hegemonic through the efforts of political and civil pro-independence forces may appear to be working to unite a greater number of Catalans behind the option of independence, but their true desires are more ambivalent. This is unsurprising given that remaining part of Spain was the clear majority position in Catalonia only a decade ago. Furthermore, Henry E. Hale argues that it is natural for all 'Regions' to prefer to remain within the central state, although only if that does not adversely affect the life-chances of their residents (Hale, 2008: 70). Jaime Lluch expresses the same idea slightly differently when he characterises sub-state nationalists as belonging to a 'moral polity' whose continued desire to remain within the state depends on 'plurinational reciprocity' (Lluch, 2012: 456). The lack of willingness by the Spanish government to provide such reciprocity is one of the main explanations for the lack of representation of a credible 'third way' within the Catalan party structure.

These kinds of survey results are seized upon by opponents of Catalan independence to discredit the idea that the majority of Catalans support secession. Indeed a counter-discourse is emerging that speaks of a silent –

or 'silenced' – majority in Catalonia whose views are marginalised by the polarised terms of the current debate. Thomas Jeffrey Miley describes this as an issue of 'blocked articulation' affecting certain sections of the Catalan electorate – 'particularly, working-class Castilian-speakers' – on all matters dealt with by the Catalan parliament, not just independence (Miley, 2013a: 13–14; Miley, 2013b). The present study has only considered the evolution of pro-independence arguments and sentiment, and not the arguments of dissenting groups, and so it would be inadvisable to draw conclusions here about the existence or characteristics of this silent/silenced majority/ minority. However, Miley's identification of working-class Spanish speakers as the main under-represented constituency does feed in to the debate on the role of ethnicity in the Catalan secession movement, and it is this subject to which we now turn in conclusion.

Uncertainty Reduction and Risk Evaluation: Ethnicity and its Alternatives

This book has suggested that there is much to be gained by viewing Catalan nationalism as inherently ambivalent about its ethnic foundations, as suggested by Steven Mock. Furthermore, ethnicity does not work well for Catalans as an uncertainty-reducing mechanism, partly because Catalanist rhetoric explicitly rejects ethnicity as a resource for constructing national identity, and partly because Catalan ethnicity is itself uncertain. Nevertheless, we have seen from both political rhetoric and cultural phenomena how other elements have come to substitute for ethnicity in the national imagination. When Thomas Hylland Eriksen suggested that ethnicity can have 'functional equivalents' he put particular emphasis on place and kinship (Eriksen, 2004), and these do indeed seem to be key to contemporary notions of Catalonia as a 'state in waiting'.

Although a shared sense of place would appear to demand very specific referents, it is actually the more intangible of the two notions. As I suggested in the Introduction, the idea that Catalonia's territorial borders might substitute for ethnic ones is problematic because of the unresolved issue of how independence for the current Autonomous Community of Catalonia would affect its political and cultural relationship with the other Catalan-speaking areas of Spain and France. However, this does not prevent place being used metonymically or synechdochically to signify a community that retains a sense of territory through an emotional connection rather than political borders. As Eriksen points out, 'territoriality is metaphorical since the nation is an abstract place' (Eriksen, 2004: 55). This is clear from some of the cultural products we have analysed. *Adéu, Espanya?* and *Hola, Europa!* use landscapes and cityscapes to stimulate a particular affective response in their viewers based on their positive feelings towards these places. Novels such as *Victus, Lliures o morts* and *Tres en ratlla* describe historically and politically significant locations that speak to their readers as Catalan citizens as well as members of the nation. On the other hand, *A reveure, Espanya,* set in the Catalan countryside, describes a traditional country property (*mas*) as a site of political action that affects the whole nation, perhaps hinting at a more primordial connection of Catalan identity with the countryside rather than the city.

Nevertheless 'fictive kinship' appears to be more important than place as a substitute for ethnicity in Catalonia's national mythscape (Eriksen, 2004: 59). In fact, Martha Nussbaum subsumes place under kinship when she comments that

> patriotic love is particularistic. It is modelled on family or personal love of some type, and, in keeping with that origin or analogy, it focuses on specifics: this or that beautiful geographical feature, this or that historical event. (Nussbaum, 2013: 208–9)

'Family or personal love' is a key feature of both the political discourse surrounding independence – in which love of family becomes a positive motive for supporting secession – and explorations of the nature of the nation in cultural products. It is explicitly portrayed in *Victus, Lliures o morts, Tres en ratlla* and *A reveure, Espanya* as the basic building block that underpins love of community. Nor is this love exclusive, as is best exemplified by Martí Zuviría's unusual adopted family.[4] Rather, family and community are defined by the act of loving itself, which focuses not just on the large-scale 'specifics' noted by Nussbaum, but also on the shared trivia of everyday existence, which denote 'being in the same boat and living in the same world' (Eriksen, 2004: 57; see also Vázquez, 2013: 20–2). *Polònia*, for example, reminds Catalans of how much they have in common in their daily experience despite their heterogeneous cultural heritage.

Eriksen points out that it is this kind of everyday interaction over long periods of time that engenders a sense of trust (Eriksen, 2004: 56). As we have noted, trust in political institutions is at a very low ebb at the moment, not just in Catalonia but Spain as a whole (Vázquez, 2011). Indeed, Catalan calls for independence are partly inspired by a desire for a more trustworthy democracy. Marc Moreno portrays some of the reasons for this lack of trust in *Independència d'interessos*, while Patrícia Gabancho tries to get round the problems it causes by bringing back a more trusted figure from the past – Miquel Roca – as the protagonist of the drive for independence in her 'journalistic fiction'. Meanwhile, *Victus* specifically points the finger at the political classes' ineptitude, crediting the Catalan public with the steadfastness and determination they lack, while *Tres en ratlla* tries to reconcile the two by describing a 'pincer movement' of institutional and civil action for independence. Despite the rhetoric of popular revolt, the use of a unilateral declaration of independence in all three of the 'imagined futures' we examined in chapter 6 suggests that an institutionally-driven bid for secession is considered the only practical way forward, however much this might be driven by 'bottom up' pressure. The sub-text here, then, is that Catalonia's leaders can be trusted to do the right thing in the end, no matter if there are – as most blatantly in *A reveure, Espanya* – some dubious machinations along the way.

J. M. Barbalet draws a distinction between trust, which 'gets by with inconclusive evidence', and confidence, 'which requires substantial evidence' (Barbalet, 2001: 83). He posits that action is more likely to occur when it has a basis in confidence, rather than simply trust, because 'confidence, in bringing a possible future into the present, provides a sense of certainty to what is essentially unknowable, so that assured action with regard to it may be engaged' (Barbalet, 2001: 88). Barbalet argues that confidence is therefore 'a central affect or emotion for praxis' (ibid.), which implies that the stimulation of this emotion ought to be a central concern for those who would like to mobilise the public behind a bid for independence. Indeed, we have seen this at work in such things as the construction of narratives of 'ordinary' heroism, the refutation of 'discourses of fear', and the portrayal of better futures, all of which engage emotional as well as rational means of boosting confidence in civil solidarity and political leadership. They also point to an underlying preoccupation with achieving a 'tipping point', at which the choice to support independence can be made with the confidence of knowing that it is the most likely preference of other members of the community (Laitin, 2007: 58). Confidence-boosting activities linked to the assurances offered by kinship therefore reduce uncertainty in a similar way to the 'rule of thumb' provided by ethnicity (Hale, 2008: 48).

In the case of Catalonia, the sense of kinship that substitutes for ethnicity is very broadly defined. In fact, it would be so broad as to be meaningless if it was not for the simultaneous maintenance of ingroup/outgroup boundaries, and it is perhaps here where we most obviously see the ambivalence of which Steven J. Mock speaks. Socio-political imperatives in today's Catalonia demand 'a radical inauthenticity' in nationalist thinking (Mock,

2012: 44): the construction of the ingroup as a matter of purely voluntary belonging. Although kinship and place can substitute for ethnicity in this process, these are harder to press into service in definitions of the outgroup: if anyone can be 'kin', how can we identify with certainty those who are not? Definitions of the outgroup are therefore based primarily on the more automatic shorthand offered by ethnic categorisation. Thus 'Spain', and by extension 'Spaniards', are characterised as (by nature) politically incompetent, inefficient, centralising, inward-looking, domineering and disrespectful (for examples, see Castro, 2013: passim). These stereotypes draw on a long tradition of differentiation of the Catalan and Spanish (or Castilian) character, and are used in current circumstances to suggest that the Spanish state is innately exploitative. It is here that we most obviously see the continued relevance of ethnicity: not as an uncertainty-reducing mechanism, but as a 'means by which people turn uncertainty into risk', leading them to stress 'the dangers of exploitation in a union seen to be dominated by members of other ethnic communities' (Hale, 2008: 79).

The difficulty with this method of separating ingroup and outgroup is that there are residents of Catalonia who could on this basis be characterised as part of the Spanish outgroup (because they have roots in the rest of Spain and have not taken on important signs of Catalan identity such as preferring to speak Catalan). However, those who have not visibly joined the Catalan ingroup are not immediately characterised as members of the outgroup. Rather they are seen as members of the ingroup who need to be persuaded to act as such. As Reicher and Hopkins suggest, in the construction of social identity 'the process of consensualization and the state of dissensus are entirely compatible – more than that, they are interdependent [. . .]: we only bother arguing because we expect to agree' (Reicher and Hopkins, 2001: 102). It is therefore perfectly possible for dissenters to remain part of the ingroup. Nevertheless, as we saw in *Tres en ratlla*, it can still be tempting to categorise those who refuse to be persuaded as ethnically incapable of seeing the benefits of independence.

Emotion, Loyalty and Identification

The preceding discussion suggests that emotions such as confidence, trust, pride, attachment to place and love of kin combine to produce an overarching national sentiment that now has a renewed importance for those who identify as Catalan. Indeed, Montserrat Guibernau argues that identification has a stronger emotional component than an inherited identity. This is because of the element of personal choice, which binds us more closely to the community with which we wish to identify (Guibernau, 2013: 3, 6). Political mobilisation to protect that community is therefore just as likely to occur even though, to an observer, the objective ties may appear weak (Guibernau, 2013: 92). Similarly, Sara Ahmed describes identification not as a result of love for a particular object but as 'a form of love' in itself: 'it is an active kind of loving', which results in a transformation of ourselves (Ahmed, 2004: 126). Silvina Vázquez uses similar terms when speaking specifically of the way Catalans talk about their nation: 'through the bonds of identification, that which has been adopted *by* the person *becomes* the person' (Vázquez, 2013: 21).[5] No wonder, then, it is so deeply wounding to be accused of hiding purely selfish motives behind love for one's nation.

Mock suggests that a necessary first step in solving ethnic conflicts is to stop trying to discredit nationalists' claims about the historical legitimacy of their nation – since this will not change their minds in any case – and instead properly acknowledge the validity and depth of their national sentiment (Mock, 2012: 281–2). It could certainly be argued that if the Spanish governments of the 1970s and 80s had recognised that Catalan nationalism was as much about sentiment as politics, relatively minor concessions could have been made that would have averted – or at least diminished – the current secession crisis, even if some of the short-term circumstances after 2005 (e.g. the economic crisis) had been much the same. Instead, the 'solution' revolved around a form of legal and administrative autonomy that gave Catalonia more tools to construct itself as 'different' (the most significant of these being its quasi-parallel media networks and its competencies in linguistic, educational and cultural policy), without at the same time reinforcing the reasons why Catalans might wish to identify with Spain (Balfour and Quiroga, 2007: 160). If, as Guibernau suggests, the devotion triggered by voluntary – or 'democratic' – loyalty is potentially stronger than that which comes with loyalty to an inherited identity, then the inherited dual Spanish and Catalan identity of the majority of Catalans is not enough in itself to prevent shifts in the balance of these allegiances over time (Guibernau, 2013: 137).

This, it seems, is where the role of the pro-independence sector of Catalonia's cultural and intellectual elites, and the communication power they enjoy, has the most influence. Firstly, they are able to remind Catalans that identifying with Catalonia is a form of 'democratic loyalty', partly by stressing the active role of 'the people' throughout Catalonia's history, but also by constructing Spanish nationalism as a form of 'authoritarian loyalty' which involves 'reverence for a particular narrative, the preservation of the status quo and the defence of traditionalism' (Guibernau, 2013: 137). Secondly, they are able effectively to stimulate the emotional components of this loyalty in a way that politicians find more difficult because of general cynicism about their trustworthiness. As we have seen, heightened emotional states have consequences for decision-making, acceptance of new information and arguments, and the likelihood (or otherwise) of active participation. The multi-dimensionality of the networks in which the cultural elites move, and the multimodality of the communication system they employ, extend the reach of their influence and help them to intersect with expressions of civic activism that draw on contemporary and traditional popular culture. Together, they help turn separatist politics into emotive spectacle.

Clearly, what has been described in this book is an evolving situation that has the potential to take a number of different turns, as long-standing and transient factors continue to interweave. Whatever happens, Catalonia will remain an important object of study for our understanding of nationalism and secession movements in democratic nation-states, and maybe even as an example of the creation of a new European state. Further research is needed especially in the area of Catalonia's civil pro-independence movement and its use of the internet and social media. Any study of this or other developments that includes the analysis of cultural products can only function as a complement to other approaches grounded in more scientific methodologies. Nevertheless, culture and communication are key components of the current situation and it has been my aim here to make sure that their importance is not overlooked – not least because they remind us of the emotional impact of this political conflict and its direct personal relevance to millions of individuals.

Notes

Introduction

1 'Si un objectiu prioritari ha de tenir un govern català és la defensa, l'enfortiment i la projecció d'allò que fa que, a través dels segles, Catalunya hagi estat Catalunya: la seva llengua, la seva cultura, la vivència de la seva història, el sentiment i la consciència de col·lectivitat, la defensa dels seus drets polítics, la voluntat de ser . . . '.

2 'la butxaca i el cap, és a dir, el desig de viure millor'.

3 'inespecífic però molt sentit'.

4 Compare, for example, the 34% of respondents cited as describing Catalonia as a nation in 1996 (McRoberts, 2001: 164, 168) with the 51% in 2005 (*El Periódico*, 9 October 2005, p. 2; survey conducted by GESOP).

5 Hale points out that the unconscious nature of ethnic categorisation means that any of us can occasionally lapse into racial stereotyping despite all our efforts not to do so (Hale, 2008: 48).

1 Political Parties and Civil Pro-Independence Groups

1 What Scotland Thinks, 'Do you agree that Scotland should be an independent country?', http://whatscotlandthinks.org/questions/should-scotland-be-an-independent-country-1#table, accessed 5 August 2013.

2 'A bird in the hand'. (The phrase literally means 'fish in the basket'.)

3 'el federalismo debe ser el modelo definitivo de nuestra organización territorial'.

4 'Espanya com a *nació política*'; 'una demanda de major reconeixement'.

5 Figures taken from http://3anys.ara.cat, accessed 29 November 2013.

6 'ARA vol contribuir al debat, parlant de tot sense dogmes i sense límits, perquè Catalunya aposti pel futur amb tota la seva ambició i energia, i esdevingui aviat una de les societats europees amb més prosperitat i benestar, capaç de generar riquesa immaterial i material per als seus ciutadans, de manera permanent i sostenible.' From ARA's Founding Manifesto, available on http://arames.ara.cat/manifest/, accessed 29 November 2013.

7 'Manifestació 2.0'.

8 'la plena recuperació col·lectiva de la identitat de la nació catalana' (Article 2).

9 'Aquesta sentència confirma que la llengua catalana no pot disposar d'un marc jurídic propi i tanca la via a la igualtat de drets lingüístics a Espanya. A partir d'ara, per garantir aquests drets cal plantejar un canvi de marc legal de fons –ja sigui mitjançant una reforma de la Constitució Espanyola o per la creació d'un

nou Estat català dins de la Unió Europea– que parteixi dels ciutadans de Catalunya i que respecti el seu dret de decidir sobre un eix tan central per a la vertebració social i cultural com és la llengua catalana.'
10 'els objectius unificadors i homogeneïtzadors castellans'.
11 'l'actual procés de destrucció econòmica i de genocidi cultural'.

2 The Path to a Pro-Independence Consensus

1 'Ethnic' in the sense that, at the time, CiU voters primarily identified with Catalonia and PSC voters with Spain (Ferran Sáez, 2011b: 257).
2 For a list of all the entities that backed the editorial, including the twelve original newspapers, see http://www.lavanguardia.com/politica/noticias/20091126/53831586056/lista-de-adhesiones-al-editorial-conjunto-de-12-diarios-catalanes-en-defensa-del-estatut.html, accessed 15 December 2013.
3 'un esforç fiscal també similar'.
4 'Desde bebés a ancianos. De Girona a las tierras del Ebro. Nacidos en Cataluña o en África. La variedad dominó la manifestación de ayer en Barcelona'.
5 'El Parlament de Catalunya constata la necessitat d'arribar a un pacte fiscal per a Catalunya fora del sistema de règim comú i de la negociació multilateral'. Resolució 275/IX del Parlament de Catalunya, sobre l'orientació política general del Govern (BOPC 150, 06.10.2011).
6 'El poble està preparat, i necessitem que el govern i les institucions facin un pas endavant, perquè volem un país lliure i sobirà, volem la independència'.
7 'El poble de Catalunya té, per raons de legitimitat democràtica, caràcter de subjecte polític i jurídic sobirà'.
8 'no és cosa d'ara mateix [. . .]. Al contrari: és el resultat d'un llarg, constant i ben documentat procés de desengany.'

3 Political Discourse: The Triumph of Rationality?

1 For example, she does not consider the idea that there are costs associated with membership of the Spanish state, and fails to critique what she calls the 'accommodating' nature of the State (Bartkus 1999: 180, 231).
2 'nou catalanisme de benestar'.
3 'Adéu al nacionalisme, visca la nació!'.
4 'Només cal voler viure millor tu i els teus.'
5 'La sola cosa que t'estalvia haver de donar explicacions de per què ets com ets, fas el que fas, parles com parles i vols el que vols, és tenir estat'.
6 'Estimar Espanya des de Catalunya, ser i sentir-se *també* espanyol a Catalunya, *més* o *molt més* espanyol que català a Catalunya –potser fins i tot *només* espanyol–, és perfectament compatible amb defensar la independència de Catalunya.'
7 'tot independentisme és consubstancialment nacionalista'.
8 'Ara el projecte nacional català pot ser engrescador no només per a aquelles persones que se senten catalanes, i per tant maltractades, sinó pels que se senten espanyols i ciutadans de Catalunya, i per tant maltractats; perquè el maltracte

també el senten, no nacionalment per la imposició de la nació espanyola, sinó pel maltracte econòmic, fiscal, i, al capdavall, pel domini de majoria sobre minoria'; 'els espanyols els discriminen com a catalans, encara que ells mateixos no se'n sentin'.

9   See *Súmate*'s manifesto on http://www.sumate.cat/p/manifiesto.html (accessed 2 October 2013).

10 'No se tenía ni una idea aproximada de cuál iba a ser el resultado final del proceso de descentralización'.

11 'porque la naturaleza de los nacionalismos catalán y vasco era ajena a la estructura del Estado'.

12 'realidades históricas, resultado de largos procesos de consolidación y vertebración de la propia personalidad o identidad cultural diferenciada'.

13 This argument is made, for example, by interviewees in the documentaries *Cataluña-Espanya* (Passola, 2009) and *El Laberint* (Mercader, 2010).

14 'la pretensió, a més, de tenir-hi un lloc a la cabina de comandament de la nau, s'ha estavellat un cop i un altre contra les roques de la intolerància, l'uniformisme i el centralisme ciclopis. No hi ha res a fer que no sigui canviar de nau, de mar i de port de destí. Qualsevol altra ruta està condemnada al naufragi, de sempre, i això ja se sap abans de salpar. El pròxim vaixell que noliegem ha de ser nostre del tot, des del número identificador de l'embarcació, fins a la bandera que hi onegi. I si hem de compartir amb algú la cabina de control, aquest «algú» no pot ser altre que la Unió Europea, no pas Espanya.'

15 'La comparació entre beneficis i costos socials és molt més favorable en el cas d'un millor encaix federal de Catalunya a Espanya i a Europa, que no pas en el cas de la independència.'

16 'No se'ns escapen les dificultats del que proposem i la sensació real fins avui d'un cert fracàs en aquest propòsit. D'una banda, perquè l'esquerra espanyola majoritària no ha volgut jugar a fons aquesta carta, i, de l'altra, perquè la dreta espanyola és profundament nacionalista i s'atrinxera quan li convé en l'immobilisme constitucional.'

17 'No els dic que no a les terceres vies, però resulta que la tercera via és el que hem fet sempre, i si som on som és perquè les terceres vies no han funcionat'.

18 Law 4/2010, 17 March, Articles 6, 13 and 35.

19 'a state of our own'.

20 'un refugi còmode per no haver de dir les coses pel seu nom'.

21 'el viratge més ràpid de la seva història. En gran mesura, forçat per la pressió ciutadana, però sobretot per l'avançament d'uns comicis que els ha enxampat amb un projecte poc definit i sense musculatura social i un líder encara en construcció'.

22 We should note, however, that Vázquez's survey was published in 2011: there has been more media debate on the exact form of independence since then.

23 'un tipus de discurs pragmàtic, que no s'interroga sobre el com, ni el quan, i encara menys sobre el per què de la independència'.

24 These arguments are expressed by many interviewees in the film *Cataluña-*

Espanya (Passola, 2009) and the documentary *Adéu, Espanya?* (Genovès, 2010).

25 '[el] concepte de «dret a decidir», que malgrat la seva ambigüitat o indefinició teòrica sí que ha estat capaç d'incorporar al llenguatge polític l'apel·lació a l'autoreconeixement com a *demos*, això és, com a subjecte de decisió política, de manera intel·ligible'.

26 One very positive side-effect of this is the near-absolute rejection by the pro-independence movement of any violent form of protest or struggle. (This also serves to distance the Catalans from the more extreme versions of Basque nationalism represented in the Spanish (and global) psyche by the terrorist group ETA).

4 Past/Present Heroes and the Future Catalan State

1 The Kingdom of Spain was formed by the Crowns of Castile and Aragon as the result of the dynastic union of Isabella of Castile with Ferdinand of Aragon in 1469. The basic territory of the Crown of Aragon comprised the Kingdoms of Aragon and Valencia as well as the Principality of Catalonia, and Mallorca. The Crown of Castile included, among others, the Kingdoms of Castile, Toledo, Galicia, Leon, and later Navarre, and the territories in the South of Spain that had been 'reconquered' from the Muslims.

2 Santa Eulàlia, a Christian martyr, is one of the patron saints of Barcelona.

3 'serè i lúcid'; 'l'activitat callada i eficaç'.

4 The information on Moragues' life is taken from Pladevall i Font, 2007.

5 'cap altre català no va patir uns afronts semblants'.

6 'un homenatge rutinari'.

7 'fou menys conflictiu, més hàbil i va saber guardar la vida sense perdre la reputació'.

8 'Moragues ha estat reconegut i en cert sentit «adoptat» per grups de patriotes no enquadrats en organismes oficials que l'han convertit en un símbol del patriotisme reivindicatiu, enfront de Rafael Casanova «l'heroi oficial»'.

9 'aquest prohom pansit'.

10 The Latin title contains two opposing ideas relevant to the novel, as it means both 'conquered' and 'nourishment' (or 'way of life').

11 I will refer to the two protagonists by their first names to show that all comments relate to the fictionalised versions rather than the real people on which they are based.

12 'No tinc la resposta al fet d'haver-la escrit en castellà, hi ha factors irracionals en el procés creatiu [. . .] Vaig escriure cent pàgines en català i no funcionava; quan la vaig tornar agafar en castellà, la història va rutllar'.

13 'No es tracta de convèncer el convençut sinó que aquesta novel·la podria donar a conèixer a Espanya fets que ignora'.

14 'La majoria tenien esperit patriòtic i sabien que les llibertats catalanes estaven en perill'.

15 Francesc Macià i Ambert (1658–1713) was a real-life leader of the *Miquelets* known as Bac de Roda. (See also note 34.)

16 'qualsevol pràctica que tingués per objectiu l'escarni públic mitjançant el terror. Ell, com els altres fusellers dels regiments de miquelets, no era precisament un angelet, però sempre seguia un codi d'honor'.

17 'Nosaltres pensem que la memòria col·lectiva dels països es construeix a través dels seus herois'.

18 'En la Catalunya del 2012, i els anys que venen, l'esperit d'Amill ha de ser molt present'.

19 '[. . .] la acumulación de banalidades. No hay nada más significante que la suma de un millón de insignificancias'.

20 'Qui sap si no havia trobat l'eixida del seu patiment i podria convertir la seva pena infinita en la fúria militar que el país reclamava'.

21 Literally 'a good strike with the sickle'. The anthem refers to a previous conflict, the War of the Reapers that began in 1640.

22 '[. . .] no ho havia perdut tot. Tenia un fill i una bandera. «Potser no som lliures, però de ben segur que tampoc no som morts»'.

23 'cuanto más oscuro sea nuestro crepúsculo más dichoso será el amanecer de los que están por venir'.

24 'por encima de todos pienso en don Antonio, don Antonio de Villarroel Peláez, renunciando a la gloria y el honor, la familia y la vida, y todo por una fidelidad insensata para con hombres sin nombre. Él, un hijo de Castilla, con todo lo bueno de esa tierra áspera, sacrificándose por la defensa de la misma Barcelona. Y ¿cuál fue su paga? Un dolor infinito, un olvido eterno.'

25 'si aspiras a que tu país te ame tienes que estar dispuesto a sacrificarte por él'.

26 'contes per a infants'.

27 'explicar la realidad es desmitificar'.

28 'El que tinc clar de l'obra és que els catalans hem sobreviscut fins ara gràcies al valor simbòlic de la resistència del setge del 1714, perquè hi va haver un comportament que va treure tota la rauxa d'un poble'.

29 'las libertades catalanas, que eran algo perfectamente tangible, un régimen opuesto al horror que se les venía encima'.

30 'el 1714 és el gran gir narratiu de l'historia de Catalunya' [. . .] 'precisament ara estem a punt d'arribar al segon gir narratiu [. . .] i espero que aquest cop serà per acabar bé.'

31 'un oficial del gobierno, responsable'.

32 'Un català desarmat és un mig català!'; 'el vincle entre els catalans i les seves armes tenia un sentit quasi espiritual, vinculat a la pertinença a un poble lliure dotat de Constitucions i lleis pròpies'.

33 'deja muy claro el papel "poco afortunado de las clases dirigentes catalanas, con actos que son casi de traición"'.

34 *Lliures o morts* carries echoes of this schema in its narration of the betrayal of Bac de Roda by a supposed friend, Josep Riera de Vallfogona (which is of course also based on historical events) (de Montserrat and Clotet, 2012: Kindle loc.

3785). Other motifs of betrayal in the novel relate to the abandonment of the Catalans by the English, and the treacherous Countess Mercè de Moncalp.

35 'su patriotismo falso y vacuo'.

36 'trajimos el huevo de la serpiente a casa y lo arrullamos hasta que nació la víbora'.

37 'No un acto de rebeldía, sino un desacatamiento sordo'.

38 'el gran protagonismo de las clases populares en la defensa de Barcelona, por el que siempre se ha pasado de puntillas'.

39 'Si no recibo nada antes del día 1 de octubre del 2004 me pensaré que pasan de mí. Entonces no les pediré otra vez a las buenas, les vendrá a pedir que lo traduzcan toda mi organización i no creo que muy simpaticamente [sic].'

40 '¡Di que eres español o te encierro!'

41 'Políticament, per desgràcia, sóc . . .'

42 'sóc un nen molt violent, ja que a casa parlem en català i miro TV3'.

43 'el primer hombre libre'.

44 'un mártir del nacionalismo catalán'; 'exalta la lucha independentista'.

45 'el propio Èric Bertran no tiene sus orígenes en Cataluña'.

5 Stimulating Affect: Catalan Television and the Independence Debate

1 President of the Basque Autonomous Community.

2 'Catalonia' is spelt here as it would be in Spanish, with 'Spain' as it would be in Catalan.

3 'En definitiva, *La pelota vasca* es un documental en el que el punto de vista nacionalista domina sobre cualquier otro más por la incidencia en los temas, los conflictos y las inquietudes de los nacionalistas que por un porcentaje claramente superior de personajes procedentes o adscritos a esa ideología. [. . .] no importa lo que entra en la sala de edición sino lo que sale de ella; la creación de sentido que se hace con el material en el montaje.'

4 'la España grande'.

5 'dispara al cervell, no dispara al cor'.

6 'codicia insaciable', 'insolidaridad egoísta', 'persecución del castellano'.

7 On ets, Espanya? No et veig enlloc.
No sents la meva veu atronadora?
No entens aquesta llengua que et parla entre perills?
Has desaprès d'entendre an els teus fills?
Adéu, Espanya! (Translation by Ronald Puppo.)

8 'els noruecs així ho volien'.

9 'España siempre ha sido un laberinto, con moros o con cristianos, y dudo mucho que salga de ese laberinto'.

10 'qüestions del discurs de la por'.

11 'el que fa [. . .] és que la gent reflexioni sobre el tema [. . .] que perdi el por'.

12 'que només està en la ment dels independentistes'.

13 'no quiere convencer a nadie de nada'.

14 http://www.susancalman.com/blog/politics-in-scotland-is-sometimes-not-that-funny, accessed 16 July 2013.

15 Another important contribution is provided by *Alguna pregunta més?* ('Any More Questions?', known as *APM?*), which transferred from radio to television in 2004. It includes hidden camera work, 'bloopers', and 'zapping' ('channel hopping') videos which humorously combine different clips, using either the original sound or new dubbing. Its main target is trash TV itself (Miguélez-Carballeira, 2012: 190), but anti-Catalanism and the independence debate are also favourite topics.

16 'El programa de TV3 permet, doncs, a un públic convertit en voyeur, penetrar en la personalitat i en els motius de l'actuació de personatges molt cèlebres, però que, ateses la teatralitat i la retòrica pròpia de la política mediatitzada, té l'aguda sensació de desconèixer, de no saber gran cosa realment. Té la sensació que se li veta l'accés, que se l'obliga a quedar-se a l'altra banda de la porta. El Polònia obre aquesta porta de bat a bat. [. . .] El Polònia desemmascara la política mitjançant la màscara. Com dèiem més amunt, obre a l'audiència els espais amagats de la política.'

17 'volem ser independents'; 'Oriol, vam dir que això no ho diríem!'.

18 'Igual que en esos años que mandaba el General'.

19 'Aquest carro només el pot conduir el president més important de la història de Catalunya'.

20 The etymology of the phrase itself is extensively discussed in an article on the website 'Etimologies paremiològiques': http://etimologies.dites.cat/2012/09/fer-la-puta-i-la-ramoneta.html.

21 'El *Polònia* estableix una agenda i, a més, sotmet els personatges i les accions dels polítics d'aquesta agenda al *priming* o enquadrament, o sigui, en ressalta certs aspectes de manera que s'afavoreix i es propicia una determinada interpretació i no d'altres.'

22 'son programas de entretenimiento y parodia', 'no se puede aplicar en estos casos los mismos criterios que en los informativos'.

6 Imagining Independence

1 This has some basis in historical fact: three-quarters of the gold reserves of the Bank of Spain were transferred to Moscow at the start of the Civil War (ostensibly for safe-keeping, but they were in fact used to pay for Russian arms supplies and military aid). However, there is no evidence that any of this ended up in Catalan hands.

2 'Els Estats sempre s'ajuden entre ells, i els lobbies econòmics també. La Generalitat, en canvi, ha de lluitar sola'.

3 'carreró polític sense sortida'; 'l'únic camí possible'.

4 'si l'hem de guanyar amb l'exèrcit, aquesta guerra ja l'hem perdut'.

5 'Sabem que amb una resposta ciutadana com la del Corpus de Sang d'aquell

altre 7 de juny de 1640 o la manifestació del 10 de juliol de 2010, el nostre
país esdevindrà una nació lliure i sobirana'.

6 'talment aquell altre 7 de juny, dia del Corpus del 1640, quan milers de segadors exaltats contra l'ultratge de la Cort van prendre Barcelona'.

7 'Queda lluny aquell Set de Juny de lo 1640 quan va convenir segar cadenes en
lloc d'espigues d'or, però malgrat que queda tan lluny, l'esperit continua
intacte generació rere generació, i com que los vells costums d'ultratge, d'espoli, d'arrogància i de negació a les reivindicacions d'un poble no los perden
los de Madrid, hem de fer renéixer l'esperit d'aquell Set de Juny per fer fora los
invasors!!! Natros som los nous segadors!!! Visca Catalunya lliure!!!'

8 'sobretot els que porten el cognom català gravat amb foc com a llinatge'.

9 'un retrat d'una imatge real d'un paisatge que a la força ha d'arribar'.

10 'm'estimo la Blanca tant o més que Catalunya'.

11 'tothom perdia la xaveta per conservar i ampliar la parcel·la de poder particular,
i la barca només traçava cercles dins del port'.

12 'si t'ho rumies bé veuràs que tots hi hem sortit guanyant i . . . que s'havia de
fer'.

13 'sempre hi ha un factor personal, a més de l'estrictament patriòtic'.

14 '–Ets boig, Jaume Llorets –va murmurar entre dues llàgrimes, una d'aflicció i
l'altra d'alegria–. Ens havíem d'haver casat fa una centúria.'

15 'No existeixen, no són'.

16 'Si vols ser d'aquí, ets d'aquí. Tan fàcil com això.'

17 'Estem tancats sobre nosaltres mateixos per defensar-nos d'una globalització
que ens portava al desastre. Ara ho controlem tot. Quan necessitem quelcom
obrim la porta, traiem la mà i ho portem cap aquí, i això val per un producte,
una matèria o una persona. Altrament, no es mou res.'

18 'En el mundo globalizado del siglo XXI hablar de independencia es una inge-
nuidad: la crisis dejó bien claro que ningún gobierno, por más banderas que
haga ondear, controla los resortes de la economía o dibuja con leyes el devenir
esencial de la sociedad. El mundo ya no admite fronteras'.

19 'el món ja era global del tot', 'el mercat espanyol era anècdota'.

20 'erotisme intel·lectual [. . .] genèticament català'; 'prové de la cova dels temps
i és la mare col·lectiva eterna'.

21 'absolutament compromesos amb els sentiments i els referents de l'Estat de
Catalunya'.

22 'als qui fan realitat els somnis'.

Conclusion

1 'Los dirigentes de Convergència i Unió llevan meses advirtiéndolo en voz baja:
"Si Rajoy se niega a negociar con Mas algún día tendrá que hacerlo con Oriol
Junqueras en condiciones aún más complicadas".'

2 Esquerra Unida i Alternativa (United and Alternative Left).

3 'Vol que Catalunya esdevingui un estat? En cas afirmatiu, vol que aquest estat sigui independent?'

4 John Sinclair in Bosch's *1714* has an equally eclectic set of companions, including his wife Mariana, who is the daughter of a wealthy Catalan and an Afro-Cuban slave (Bosch, 2008).

5 'a partir del llaç d'identificació, allò que ha estat apropiat *per a* la persona es torna *en l*a persona'.

Bibliography

(Agències) (2013), 'Mas: "Si som on som és perquè les terceres vies no han funcionat"'. *El Punt Avui* [Online], 26 September, http://www. elpuntavui. cat/noticia/article/3-politica/17-politica/680550-mas-si-som-on-som-es-perque-les-terceres-vies-no-han-funcionat.html, accessed 1 October 2013.

6, Perri, Squire, Corinne, Treacher, Amal & Radstone, Susannah (2007), 'Introduction', in 6, P., Radstone, S., Squire, C. & Treacher, A. (eds.) *Public Emotions* (Basingstoke: Palgrave Macmillan), 1–33.

A. D. (2012), 'La fiscal m'acusava d'amenaçar un hotel i era un joc d'ordinador'. *Diari d'Andorra* [Online], 8 November, http://www.diariandorra.ad/index.php?option=com_k2&view=item&id=21218&Itemid=276, accessed 29 May 2013.

Ahmad, Sajjad (2013), 'The Instrumentalist Perspective on Nationalism: Case Study of Catalonia', *Journal of European Studies*, 29 (1): 70–82.

Ahmed, Sara (2004), *The Cultural Politics of Emotion* (Edinburgh: Edinburgh University Press).

Albert, Víctor et al. (2012), 'Crida a la Catalunya federalista i d'esquerres' [Online]. http://federalistaidesquerres.cat/?p=20-more-20, accessed 1 October 2013.

Albertí, Santiago (2006), *L'Onze de setembre* (Barcelona: Albertí Editor).

Alexandre, Víctor (2007), *Èric i l'Exèrcit del Fènix* (Barcelona: Proa).

Anonymous (2011), 'El PP pide a TV3 que tome "medidas" contra las sátiras de "Polònia" y "Crackòvia"'. *El Mundo* [Online], 30 April, http://www.elmundo.es/elmundo/2011/04/29/barcelona/1304104302.html, accessed 19 September 2012.

Anonymous (2012), 'Catalunya hauria d'estar confiscant béns de l'Estat'. *El Singular digital* [Online], http://www.elsingulardigital.cat/cat/imprimir. php?IDN=88286, accessed 10 April 2013.

Anonymous (2013a), 'ERC pide a Telemadrid que rectifique tras equiparar nazismo y nacionalismo catalán'. *El Mundo* [Online], 2 May, http://www. elmundo.es/elmundo/ 2013/05/02/barcelona/1367510836.html, accessed 10 December 2013.

Anonymous (2013b), 'What 2014 Vote Needs: More Jokes'. *The Herald* [Online], 31 March, http://www.heraldscotland.com/news/home-news/what-2014-vote-needs-more-jokes.20661780, accessed 16 July 2013.

ARA (2012), 'Artur Mas, sobre la manifestació de la Diada: "Anímicament hi seré, però físicament no hi puc anar"'. *ARA* [Online], 6 September, http://www. ara.cat/politica/artur_mas-entrevista_Catalunya_Radio_0_769123160.html, accessed 26 August 2013.

Assemblea Nacional Catalana (2011), 'Declaració de la conferència nacional per l'estat propi', [Online], http://www.assemblea.cat/?q=node/31, accessed 14 August 2013.

Assemblea Nacional Catalana (2013), 'Estatuts de l'Assemblea Nacional Catalana', [Online], http://assemblea.cat/sites/default/files/documents/Text%20refós %20Ponència%20revisió%20ESTATUTS%2019–01-13%20%2B% 20AGED%20color%2020130418%200h50%20v2%2024mg2013.pdf, accessed 20 August 2013.

Avui.cat (2009), '10.000 persones ja han vist la pel·lícula "Cataluña-Espanya"'. *Avui* [Online], 1 May, http://www.elpuntavui.cat/noticia/article/5-cultura/19-cultura/287237—10000-persones-ja-han-vist-la-pelmlicula-cataluna-espanya-.html, accessed 10 November 2010.

Balcells, Albert (1996), *Catalan Nationalism: Past and Present* (London: Macmillan).

Balcells, Albert (2008), *Llocs de memòria dels catalans* (Barcelona: Proa).

Balfour, Sebastian & Quiroga, Alejandro (2007), *The Reinvention of Spain: Nation and Identity since Democracy* (Oxford: Oxford University Press).

Barbalet, J.M. (2001), *Emotion, Social Theory and Social Structure: A Macrosociological Approach* (Cambridge: Cambridge University Press).

Barbeta, Jordi (2013), 'La "tercera vía" de Duran: pacto fiscal, soberanía cultural y nueva Constitución'. *La Vanguardia* [Online], 25 Sptember, http://www.lavanguardia.com/ politica/20130925/54389995338/duran-madrid-apoyos-someter-consulta-estatus.html, accessed 1 October 2013.

Baró, Santi (2012), *Tres en ratlla* (Barcelona: Random House Mondadori).

Bartkus, Viva Ona (1999), *The Dynamic of Secession* (Cambridge: Cambridge University Press).

Bel, Germà (2013), *Anatomia d'un desengany* (Barcelona: Destino).

Bell, Duncan S. A (2003), 'Mythscapes: Memory, Mythology, and National Identity', *British Journal of Sociology*, 54 (1): 63–81.

Belzunces, Marc (2008), 'Suport social a la independència de Catalunya (1991–2008)' (Barcelona: Cercle d'Estudis Sobiranistes). [Online], http://www.cercleestudissobiranistes.cat, accessed 5 August 2013.

Bertran, Èric (2006), *Èric i l'Exèrcit del Fènix. Acusat de voler viure en català* (Barcelona: Proa).

Bertran, Uriel et al. (eds) (2007), *Independència 2014* (Barcelona: Dux).

Billig, Michael (1995), *Banal Nationalism* (London: Sage).

Bosch, Alfred (2008), *1714* (Barcelona: La Butxaca).

Bourdieu, Pierre (1986), *Distinction: A Social Critique of the Judgement of Taste* (Abingdon: Routledge).

Bourdieu, Pierre (1991), *Language and Symbolic Power* (Cambridge, MA: Harvard University Press).

Boyd, Carolyn P. (2008), 'The Politics of History and Memory in Democratic Spain', *Annals of the American Academy of Political and Social Science*, 617 (1), 113–148.

Brenan, Gerald (1960), *The Spanish Labyrinth: An Account of the Social and Political Background of the Civil War* (Cambridge; New York: Cambridge University Press).

Breuilly, John, Hechter, Michael, Sasse, Gwendolyn & Hale, Henry E. (2011), 'Sixth *Nations and Nationalism* debate: Henry E. Hale's The Foundations of Ethnic Politics: Separatism of States and Nations in Eurasia and the World', *Nations and Nationalism*, 17 (4): 681–711.

Brubaker, Rogers (2004), *Ethnicity without Groups* (Cambridge, MA: Harvard University Press).

Brubaker, Rogers (2009), 'Ethnicity, Race and Nationalism', *Annual Review of Sociology*, 35: 21–42.

Brubaker, Rogers & Cooper, Frederick (2000), 'Beyond "Identity"', *Theory and Society*, 29 (1):1–47.

Butchart, Garnet C. (2006), 'On Ethics and Documentary: A Real and Actual Truth', *Communication Theory*, 16 (4): 427–452.

Butlletí Oficial del Parlament de Catalunya (2011), 'Informe de la Comissió d'Estudi d'un Nou Model de Finançament basat en el Concert Econòmic' (Barcelona: Parlament de Catalunya), issue number 175.

Cabana, Francesc (2007), 'Perspectiva econòmica del catalanisme', in Cabana, F., Pujol, J., Termes, J. & Villatoro, V. (eds.) *El catalanisme, motor del país* (Barcelona: Proa/Centre d'Estudis Jordi Pujol), 17–42.

Cabeza San Deogracias, José & Paz Rebollo, María Antonia (2011), 'Formas de condicionar la verdad con el uso del montaje en *La pelota vasca*', *Revista Latina de Comunicación Social*, 66 (1): 1–30.

Canadell, Joan (2013), 'The Catalan Business Model', in Castro, L. (ed.) *What's Up With Catalonia?* (Ashfield, MA: Catalonia Press), 197–9.

Canal, Jordi (2011), 'El independentismo en Cataluña: comedia, farsa, astracanada'. *El Imparcial* [Online], http://www.elimparcial.es/nacional/el-independentismo-en-cataluna-comedia-farsa-astracanada--91686.html, accessed 16 July 2013.

Cardús, Salvador (2010), *El camí de la independència* (Barcelona: La Campana).

Cardús, Salvador (2013), 'What Has Happened to Us Catalans?', in Castro, L. (ed.) *What's Up With Catalonia?* (Ashfield, MA: Catalonia Press), 95–100.

Carod-Rovira, Josep-Lluís (2003), *El futur a les mans* (Barcelona: Angle Editorial).

Carod-Rovira, Josep-Lluís (2008), *2014* (Barcelona: Mina).

Carod-Rovira, Josep-Lluís (2009), 'Adéu al nacionalisme, visca la nació!'. [Online], http://www.vilaweb.cat/media/attach/vwedts/docs/conferencia_carod_41109.pdf, accessed 6 November 2009.

Carranco, Rebeca & Vallespín, Ivanna. (2010), 'Dos horas sin moverse del sitio'. *El País*, 11 July, 14.

Cassadó, Xavier (dir.) (2010), *Divendres* (TV3). 3 June.

Cassino, Dan & Lodge, Milton (2007), 'The Primacy of Affect in Poltical Evaluations', in Neuman, W. R., Marcus, G. E., Crigler, A. N. & Mackuen, M. (eds.) *The Affect Effect: Dynamics of Emotion in Political Thinking and Behaviour* (Chicago: University of Chicago Press), 101–123.

Castells, Manuel (2009), *Communication Power* (Oxford: Oxford University Press).

Castellví i Obando, Francesc de (1998–2002), *Narraciones Históricas desde el año 1700 al 1725* (Madrid: Fundación Francisco Elías de Tejada y Erasmo Pèrcopo).

Castro, Liz (ed.) (2013), *What's Up with Catalonia?* (Ashfield, MA: Catalonia Press).

Centre d'Estudis d'Opinió (2005), 'Baròmetre d'opinió política (Juny)'. (Barcelona: Generalitat de Catalunya).

Centre d'Estudis d'Opinió (2011), 'Baròmetre d'opinió política, 2a onada'. (Barcelona: Generalitat de Catalunya).

Centre d'Estudis d'Opinió (2013a), 'Baròmetre d'opinió política, 2a onada'. (Barcelona: Generalitat de Catalunya).

Centre d'Estudis d'Opinió (2013b), 'Baròmetre d'opinió política, 1a onada'. (Barcelona: Generalitat de Catalunya).

Cerdán, Manuel (dir.) (2011), *Cataluña: Violencia Callejera* (Telemadrid).

Chilton, Paul (2004), *Analysing Political Discourse: Theory and Practice* (London; New York: Routledge).

Colino, César (2009), 'Constitutional Change Without Constitutional Reform: Spanish Federalism and the Revision of Catalonia's Statute of Autonomy', *Publius: The Journal of Federalism*, 39 (2): 262–288.

Condeminas, Daniel (2010), '"Adéu, Espanya?" i la magnèsia'. *Bloc del Degà* [Online], http://www.cpac.cat/articledega.php?id=23, accessed 6 December 2012.

Consejo Territorial (2013), 'Hacia una estructura federal del estado' (Partido Socialista Obrero Español), [Online], http://estaticos.elperiodico.com/resources/pdf/6/9/1373129660596.pdf, accessed 10 December 2013.

Conversi, Daniele (1997), *The Basques, the Catalans and Spain: Alternative Routes to Nationalist Mobilisation* (London: Hurst).

Cornell, Stephen & Hartmann, Douglas (1998), *Ethnicity and Race: Making Identities in a Changing World* (Thousand Oaks, CA: Pine Forge Press).

Crameri, Kathryn (2000), 'Banal Catalanism?', *National Identities*, 2 (2): 145–157.

Crameri, Kathryn (2008), *Catalonia: National Identity and Cultural Policy, 1980–2003* (Cardiff: University of Wales Press).

Crameri, Kathryn (2011), '"We need another hero": The Construction of Josep Moragues as a Symbol of Independence for Catalonia', *National Identities*, 13 (1): 51–65.

Crameri, Kathryn (2012), 'History Written by the Losers: History, Memory, Myth and Independence in Twenty-First Century Catalonia', in Martín-Estudillo, L. & Spadaccini, N. (eds.) *Memory and Its Discontents: Spanish Culture in the Early Twenty-First Century*, Hispanic Issues On Line 11: 35–51.

Crespi-Vallbona, Montserrat & Richards, Greg (2007), 'The Meaning of Cultural Festivals: Stakeholder Perspectives in Catalonia', *International Journal of Cultural Policy*, 13 (1): 103–122.

Crexell, Joan (1985), *El monument a Rafael Casanova* (Barcelona: El Llamp).

Cussà, Jordi (2010), *A reveure, Espanya* (Berga: L'Albí).

Dahlgren, Peter (2007), 'Civic Identity and Net Activism: The Frame of Radical

Democracy', in Dahlberg, L. & Siapera, E. (eds.) *Radical Democracy and the Internet: Interrogating Theory and Practice* (Basingstoke: Palgrave Macmillan), 55–72.

Danés, Lluís (2012). 'Anunci de la manifestació de l'11 de setembre 2012', [Online], http://www.youtube.com/watch?v=9guzU9dWsiU, accessed 16 August 2013.

Day, Amber (2008), 'And Now . . . The News? Mimesis and the Real in *The Daily Show*', in Gray, J., Thompson, E. & Jones, J. (eds.) *Satire TV* (New York: New York University Press), 85–103.

de Montserrat, David & Clotet, Jaume (2012), *Lliures o morts* (Barcelona: Columna).

Dentith, Simon (2000), *Parody* (London: Routledge).

Díaz i Esculíes, Daniel (2005), 'L'independentisme català durant l'autarquia franquista', *El Temps d'Història*, 46: 21–25.

directe!cat (2010), ' "Cataluña-Espanya" tomba "La Noria" d'Artur Mas'. *directe!cat* [Online], http://www.directe.cat/xoc-de-trens/63171/cataluna-espanya-tomba-la-noria-d-artur-mas, accessed 6 January 2012.

Dowling, Andrew (2009), '*Autonomistes, Catalanistes* and *Independentistes*: Politics in Contemporary Catalonia', *International Journal of Iberian Studies*, 22 (3): 185–200.

Dowling, Andrew (2013), *Catalonia Since the Spanish Civil War: Reconstructing the Nation* (Brighton, Chicago, Toronto: Sussex Academic Press).

Earl, Jennifer & Kimport, Katrina (2011), *Digitally Enabled Social Change: Activism in the Internet Age* (Cambridge, MA: MIT Press).

EFE. (2012), 'Sánchez Piñol: "Con la novela 'Victus' recibiré bofetadas de todos los lados" '. *elEconomista.es*, [Online], 10 October, http://ecodiario.eleconomista.es/libros/noticias/4310753/10/12/Sanchez-Pinol-Con-la-novela-Victus-recibire-bofetadas-de-todos-los-lados.html, accessed 25 April 2013.

El Periódico (2012), 'El independentismo bajaría al 40% si Catalunya saliera de la Unión Europea'. *El Periódico* [Online], 4 November, http://www.elperiodico.com/es/noticias/elecciones-2012/encuesta-independencia-catalunya-continuidad-union-europea-2241628, accessed 30 August 2013.

Elliott, John H. (1963), *The Revolt of the Catalans* (Cambridge: Cambridge University Press).

Entman, Robert M. (2007), 'Framing Bias: Media in the Distribution of Power', *Journal of Communication*, 57 (1): 163–173.

Eriksen, Thomas Hylland (2004), 'Place, Kinship and the Case for Non-Ethnic Nations', *Nations and Nationalism*, 10 (1/2): 49–62.

Eriksonas, Linas (2004), *National Heroes and National Identities: Scotland, Norway and Lithuania* (Brussels: Peter Lang).

Estrada, Isabel (2010), 'The Recuperation of Memory in Regional and National Television Documentaries: The Epistemology of *Els* [sic] *Fosses del Silenci* (2003) and *Las Fosas del Olvido* (2004)', *Journal of Spanish Cultural Studies*, 11 (2): 191–209.

Europa Press (2010a), 'Jorge Fernández lamenta el "publireportaje" de TV3 sobre la independència'. *Avui+* [Online], 5 June, http://www. elpuntavui. cat/noticia/article/-/17-politica/264157—jorge-fernandez?cks_mnu_id=75-N&cks_darrers_mnu_id=75:459, accessed 5 June 2010.

Europa Press (2010b), 'PSC, PP y Ciutadans acusan a Terribas de defender una "tesis única" en TV3'. *El Mundo* [Online], 19 June, http://www.elmundo.es/elmundo/2010/06/18/barcelona/1276861724.html, accessed 19 June 2010.

Fancelli, Agustí (2007), 'El "català emprenyat" en el Parlament'. *El País* [Online], 28 September, http://elpais.com/diario/2007/09/28/catalunya/1190941645_850215.html, accessed 4 October 2013.

Fernández Díaz, Roberto (1993), *Manual de historia de España. La España moderna: Siglo XVIII* (Madrid: Historia 16).

Fernàndez, Josep-Anton (2008), *El malestar en la cultura catalana* (Barcelona: Empúries).

Ferré-Pavia, Carme & Gayà-Morlà, Catalina (2011), 'Infotainment and Citizens' Political Perceptions: Who's Afraid of *Polònia?*', *Catalan Journal of Communication and Cultural Studies*, 3 (1): 45–61.

Freixenet Guitart, Oriol (2010), 'Dels Cors Clavé als 'lipdub''. [Online], http://www.omnium.cat/ca/article/cultura-dels-cors-clave-als-lipdub-4001.html, accessed 15 August 2013.

Fusi, Juan Pablo (2000), *España: La evolución de la identidad nacional* (Madrid: Temas de hoy).

Gabancho, Patrícia (2001), *Sobre la immigració. Carta a la societat catalana* (Barcelona: Columna).

Gabancho, Patrícia (2009), *Crònica de la independència* (Barcelona: Edicions 62).

Gallifa Martínez, Albert (2000), 'Un monument contemporani per al general Moragues', *L'Avenç*, 249 (July): 79–80.

Ganyet, Josep Maria (2013), 'Keep Calm and Speak Catalan', in Castro, L. (ed.) *What's Up with Catalonia?* (Ashfield, MA: Catalonia Press), 67–74.

García, César (2010), 'Nationalism and Public Opinion in Contemporary Spain: The Demobilization of the Working Class in Catalonia', *Global Media Journal (American Edition)*, 10 (17).

Genovès, Maria Dolors (dir.) (2010), *Adéu, Espanya?* (TV3).

Genovès, Maria Dolors (dir.) (2013), *Hola, Europa!* (TV3).

Gifreu, Josep (2003), *La potenciació de l'espai cultural i audiovisual català* (Barcelona: Generalitat de Catalunya).

Giménez, Pere (2010), 'L'Ara sortirà amb un tiratge de 100.000 exemplars'. *Comunicació21* [Online], http://comunicacio21.cat/2010/10/l'ara-sortira-amb-un-tiratge-de-100-000-exemplars/, accessed 29 November 2013.

Giordano, Benito & Roller, Elisa (2002), 'Catalonia and the "Idea of Europe": Competing Strategies and Discourses within Catalan Party Politics', *European Urban and Regional Studies*, 9 (2): 99–113.

González, Enric (2012), 'Quim Monzó (Interview)'. *Jot Down* [Online], August, http://www.jotdown.es/2012/08/quim-monzo-catala/, accessed 19 July 2013.

González, Sara (2012), 'El PSC es compromet a defensar el dret a decidir'. *ARA*

[Online], 29 October, http://www.ara.cat/especials/eleccions25n/PSC-compromet-defensar-dret-decidir_0_800919976.html, accessed 2 October 2013.

González, Sara (2013), 'Diputats crítics podrien deixar el grup abans de la votació'. *ARA* [Online], 19 November, http://www.ara.cat/premium/tema_del_dia/Diputats-critics-podrien-deixar-votacio_0_1032496798.html, accessed 25 November 2013.

Griffiths, Ryan & Savić, Ivan (2009), 'Globalization and Separatism: The Influence of Internal and External Interdependence on the Strategies of Separatism', *Perspectives on Global Development and Technology*, 8 (2/3): 429–454.

Guibernau, Montserrat (1999), *Nations without States: Political Communities in a Global Age* (Cambridge: Polity).

Guibernau, Montserrat (2004), *Catalan Nationalism: Francoism, Transition and Democracy* (London: Routledge).

Guibernau, Montserrat (2013, *Belonging: Solidarity and Division in Modern Societies* (Cambridge: Polity).

Guibernau, Montserrat (2014), 'Prospects for an Independent Catalonia', *International Journal of Politics, Culture, and Society*, 27 (1): 5–23.

Hale, Henry E. (2008), *The Foundations of Ethnic Politics* (Cambridge: Cambridge University Press).

Hart, Graeme (dir.) (2013), *Rory Goes to Holyrood* (BBC Scotland). 13 June.

Hermans, Dirk, De Houwer, Jan & Eelen, Paul (1994), 'The Affective Priming Effect: Automatic Activation of Evaluative Information in Memory', *Cognition and Emotion*, 8 (6): 515–533.

Hewitt, John & Vazquez, Gustavo (2010), *Documentary Filmmaking: A Contemporary Field Guide* (New York; Oxford: Oxford University Press).

Hodgart, Matthew (2010), *Satire: Origins and Principles* (New Brunswick, NJ: Transaction Publishers).

Hogan, Patrick Colm (2011), *What Literature Teaches Us About Emotion* (Cambridge: Cambridge University Press).

Holbert, R. Lance, Tchernev, John M., Walther, Whitney O., Esralew, Sarah E. & Benski, Kathryn (2013), 'Young Voter Perceptions of Political Satire as Persuasion: A Focus on Perceived Influence, Persuasive Intent, and Message Strength', *Journal of Broadcasting and Electronic Media*, 57 (2): 170–186.

Huddy, Leonie, Feldman, Stanley & Cassese, Erin (2007), 'On the Distinct Political Effects of Anxiety and Anger', in Neuman, W. R., Marcus, G. E., Crigler, A. N. & Mackuen, M. (eds.), *The Affect Effect: Dynamics of Emotion in Political Thinking and Behaviour* (Chicago: Chicago University Press), 202–230.

Hutcheon, Linda (2000), *A Theory of Parody: The Teachings of Twentieth-Century Art Forms* (Urbana: University of Illinois Press).

Intereconomía (dir.) (2012), *Fenix 11 23: La nueva película de la propaganda independentista catalana.* [Online], http://www.intereconomia.com/video/telediario-intereconomia/fenix-11-23-nueva-pelicula-propaganda-independentista-catalana-201211, accessed 30 April 2013.

J.V. (2012), 'Sánchez Piñol remou el 1714'. *El Punt Avui*, 11 July, p. 29.

Jenkins, Richard (1997), *Rethinking Ethnicity: Arguments and Explorations* (London: Sage).

Joan, Joel & Lara, Sergi (dir.) (2012), *Fènix 11*23* (Arriska Films).

Jones, Jeffrey P. (2008), 'With All Due Respect: Satirizing Presidents from *Saturday Night Live* to *Lil'Bush'*, in Gray, J., Thompson, E. & Jones, J. P. (eds.) *Satire TV* (New York: New York University Press), 37–63.

Junqueras i Vies, Oriol (1998), 'L'Onze de setembre de 1714 en la cultura catalanista del segle XIX', *Manuscrits*, 16: 305–318.

Keating, Michael (2000), *The New Regionalism in Western Europe* (Cheltenham: Edward Elgar).

Keating, Michael (2001), *Plurinational Democracy: Stateless Nations in a Post-Sovereignty Era* (Oxford; New York: Oxford University Press).

Keating, Michael & Bray, Zoe (2006), 'Renegotiating Sovereignty: Basque Nationalism and the Rise and Fall of the Ibarretxe Plan', *Ethnopolitics*, 5 (4): 347–364.

Keating, Michael & Wilson, Alex (2009), 'Renegotiating the State of Autonomies: Statute Reform and Multi-Level Politics in Spain', *West European Politics*, 32 (3): 536–558.

Keating, Michael, Loughlin, John & Deschouwer, Kris (2003), *Culture, Institutions and Economic Development: A Study of Eight European Regions* (Cheltenham: Edward Elgar).

Keighron, Peter (1998), 'The Politics of Ridicule: Satire and Television', in Wayne, M. (ed.) *Dissident Voices: The Politics of Television and Cultural Change* (London: Pluto Press), 127–144.

King, Stewart (2005), *Escribir la catalanidad: Lengua e identidades culturales en la narrativa contemporánea de Cataluña* (Suffolk & New York: Tamesis).

Lago, Ignacio, Montero, José Ramón & Torcal, Mariano (2007), 'The 2006 Regional Election in Catalonia: Exit, Voice and Electoral Market Failures', *South European Society and Politics*, 12 (2): 221–235.

Laitin, David D. (2007), *Nations, States and Violence* (Oxford: Oxford University Press).

Lash, Scott & Lury, Celia (2007), *Global Culture Industry: The Mediation of Things* (Cambridge: Polity Press).

Llorens Vila, Jordi (2005), 'El primer catalanisme independentista', *El Temps d'Història*, 46: 16–20.

Lluch, Jaime (2010), 'How Nationalism Evolves: Explaining the Establishment of New Varieties of Nationalism within the National Movements of Quebec and Catalonia', *Nationalities Papers*, 38 (3): 337–359.

Lluch, Jaime (2012), 'Internal Variation in Substate National Movements and the Moral Polity of the Nationalist', *European Political Science Review*, 4 (3): 433–460.

Lo Cascio, Paola (2008), *Nacionalisme i autogovern: Catalunya, 1980–2003* (Barcelona: Afers).

Lodares, Juan R. (2005), 'La comunidad lingüística en la España de hoy. (Temas y problemas de diferenciación cultural)', *Bulletin of Hispanic Studies*, 82 (1): 1–15.

López Tena, Alfons (2007), *Catalunya sota Espanya: L'opressió nacional en democràcia* (Barcelona: Magrana/Dèria).

López Tena, Alfons. (2010), 'Monarquia catalana'. *Avui*, 14 May, p.16.

Lorés, Jaume (1985), *La transició a Catalunya (1977–1984): El pujolisme i els altres* (Barcelona: Empúries).

Lucas, Manel, Lucas, Martí, Buixó, Jaume, Cot, Júlia, Jara, Oriol, Morales, Quim & Tienda, Pepe (2013), *Polònia Independent* (Barcelona: Columna).

Lundestad, Geir (2004), 'Why Does Globalization Encourage Fragmentation?', *International Politics*, 41 (2): 265–276.

Maalouf, Amin (2000), *In the Name of Identity: Violence and the Need to Belong*, trans. Barbara Bray (New York: Arcade).

MacInness, John (2006), 'Castells' Catalan Routes: Nationalism and the Sociology of Identity', *The British Journal of Sociology*, 57 (4): 677–698.

Mackuen, Michael, Marcus, George E., Neuman, W. Russell & Keele, Luke (2007), 'The Third Way: The Theory of Affective Intelligence and American Democracy', in Neuman, W. R., Marcus, G. E., Crigler, A. N. & Mackuen, M. (eds.) *The Affect Effect: Dynamics of Emotion in Political Thinking and Behaviour* (Chicago: University of Chicago Press), 124–151.

Madí, David (2007), *Democràcia a sang freda: Les interioritats de la política catalana* (Barcelona: Mina).

Maragall, Pasqual (2008), *Oda inacabada: memòries* (Barcelona: La Magrana).

Marc, David (2008), 'Foreword', in Gray, J., Jones, J. P. & Thompson, E. (eds.) *Satire TV* (New York: New York University Press).

Marfany, Joan-Lluís (1992), 'Mitologia de la Renaixença i mitologia nacionalista', *L'Avenç*, 164, 26–29.

Marfany, Joan-Lluís (2006), 'The Catalan Question Revisited: On Lodares, a Dubious 'Linguistic Community' and Imaginary Threats To It', *Bulletin of Spanish Studies*, 83 (7): 939–955.

Marotta, Vince (2008), 'The Hybrid Self and the Ambivalence of Boundaries', *Social Identities*, 14 (3): 295–312.

Marquis, Elizabeth (2012), 'Performance, Emotion, and Persuasion in *The Ground Truth*', *New Review of Film and Television Studies*, 10 (4): 425–442.

Martínez-Herrera, Enric & Miley, Thomas Jeffrey (2010), 'The Constitution and the Politics of National Identity in Spain', *Nations and Nationalism*, 16 (1): 6–30.

Marvin, Carolyn & Ingle, David (1999), *Blood Sacrifice and the Nation: Totem Rituals and the American Flag* (Cambridge: Cambridge University Press).

Mas, Artur (2003), *La Catalunya emergent* (Barcelona: Planeta).

Mas, Artur (2007), 'El catalanisme, energia i esperança per a un país millor', [Online], www.ciu.cat/media/21719.pdf, accessed 5 August 2013.

Mateos, Roger (2013), 'La consulta viatjarà al Congrés el febrer del 2014'. *ARA* [Online], 9 November, http://www.ara.cat/premium/tema_del_dia/consulta-al-Congres-PSC-negociacio_0_1026497504.html, accessed 25 November 2013

McGarry, John & O'Leary, Brendan (2007), 'Federation and Managing Nations', in Burgess, M. & Pinder, J. (eds.) *Multinational Federations* (Abingdon: Routledge), 180–211.

McRoberts, Kenneth (2001), *Catalonia: Nation Building without a State* (Don Mills, Ont. New York: Oxford University Press).

Medem, Julio (dir.) (2003), *La pelota vasca: la piel contra la piedra* (Golem Distribución).

Mercader, Jordi (dir.) (2010), *El Laberint* (TV3). 10 June.

Mató, Xevi (dir.) (2007), *Èric and the Army of the Phoenix*. [Online], http://www.youtube.com/watch?v=aIiRFSCgGu4, accessed 29 May 2013.

Miguélez-Carballeira, Helena (2012), '"La literatura es eso, Literatura": the Rhetoric of Empty Culture in Francoist and Neo-Francoist Discourses', *Journal of Spanish Cultural Studies*, 13 (2): 189–203.

Miley, Thomas Jeffrey (2007), 'Against the Thesis of the "Civic Nation": The Case of Catalonia in Contemporary Spain', *Nationalism and Ethnic Politics*, 13 (1): 1–37.

Miley, Thomas Jeffrey (2013a), 'Blocked Articulation and Nationalist Hegemony in Catalonia', *Regional & Federal Studies*, 23 (1): 7–26.

Miley, Thomas Jeffrey (2013b), 'Democratic Representation and the National Dimension in Catalan and Basque Politics', *International Journal of Politics, Culture, and Society*, [Online], link.springer.com/article/10.1007/s10767-013-9159-2, accessed 7 March 2014.

Mock, Steven J. (2012), *Symbols of Defeat in the Construction of National Identity* (Cambridge: Cambridge University Press).

Montilla, José (2007), 'Intervenció del MHP de la Generalitat de Catalunya, José Montilla, al Foro Nueva Economía (Madrid) 7/11/2007'. [Online], http://www.iceta.org/jm071107.pdf, accessed 22 August 2013.

Moore, Margaret (2001), *The Ethics of Nationalism* (New York: Oxford University Press).

Moreno, Carmelo (2012), 'Humour, Violence, and Infotainment in the Basque Country: The *Vaya Semanita* Phenomenon on Basque Public Television, 2003–2005', in Mingolarra, J. A., Arocena, C. & Sabaris, R. M. (eds.) *Violence and Communication* (Reno: Center for Basque Studies, University of Nevada/University of the Basque Country), 171–190.

Moreno, Luis (2001), *The Federalization of Spain* (London: Frank Cass).

Moreno, Marc (2013), *Independència d'interessos* (Barcelona: Llibres del delicte).

Morreale, Joanne (2008), 'John Stewart and *The Daily Show*: I Thought You Were Going to Be Funny!', in Gray, J., Jones, J. P. & Thompson, E. (eds.) *Satire TV* (New York: New York Univeristy Press), 104–123.

Moy, Patricia, Xenos, Michael A. & Hess, Verena K. (2005), 'Communication and Citizenship: Mapping the Political Effects of Infotainment', *Mass Communication and Society*, 8 (2): 111–131.

Muñoz, Jordi & Guinjoan, Marc (2013), 'Accounting for Internal Variation in Nationalist Mobilization: Unofficial Referendums for Independence in Catalonia (2009–11)', *Nations and Nationalism*, 19 (1): 44–67.

Muñoz, Jordi & Tormos, Raül (2012), 'Identitat o càlculs instrumentals? Anàlisi dels factors explicatius del suport a la independència'. Centre d'Estudis d'Opinió, *Papers de treball* (Barcelona: Generalitat de Catalunya).

Muro, Diego & Quiroga, Alejandro (2004), 'Building the Spanish Nation: The Centre-Periphery Dialectic', *Studies in Ethnicity and Nationalism*, 4 (2): 18–37.

Nagel, Klaus-Jürgen (2010), 'How Parties of Stateless Nations adapt to Multi-Level Politics: Catalan Political Parties and their Concept of the State', in Guelke, A. (ed.) *The Challenges of Ethno-Nationalism: Case Studies in Identity Politics* (Basingstoke: Palgrave Macmillan), 118–142.

Neuman, W. Russell, Marcus, George E., Crigler, Ann N. & Mackuen, Michael (eds.) (2007a), *The Affect Effect: Dynamics of Emotion in Political Thinking and Behaviour* (Chicago: University of Chicago Press).

Neuman, W. Russell, Marcus, George E., Crigler, Ann N. & Mackuen, Michael (2007b), 'Theorizing Affect's Effects', in Neuman, W. R., Marcus, G. E., Crigler, A. N. & Mackuen, M. (eds.) *The Affect Effect: Dynamics of Emotion in Political Thinking and Behaviour* (Chicago: University of Chicago Press), 1–20.

Noguer, Miquel (2013a), 'ERC confirma el "sorpasso" a CiU'. *El País* [Online], 2 November, http://ccaa.elpais.com/ccaa/2013/11/02/catalunya/1383418486_347437.html, accessed 4 November 2013.

Noguer, Miquel (2013b), 'La tercera vía vence al independentismo'. *El País* [Online], 2 November, http://ccaa.elpais.com/ccaa/2013/11/02/catalunya/1383418112_808082.html, accessed 4 November 2013.

Nussbaum, Martha C. (2013), *Political Emotions: Why Love Matters for Justice* (Cambridge, MA; London: The Belknap Press of Harvard University Press).

Òmnium Cultural (2010), 'La manifestació del 10 de juliol serà la primera marxa 2.0' [Online]. http://www.somunanacio.cat/ca/noticia/la-manifestacio-del-10-de-juliol-sera-la-primera-marxa-2-0-4285.html, accessed 19 August 2013.

Orte, Andreu & Wilson, Alex (2009), 'Multi-level Coalitions and Statute Reform in Spain', *Regional & Federal Studies*, 19 (3): 415–436.

Özkirimli, Umut (2010), *Theories of Nationalism: A Critical Introduction* (Basingstoke: Palgrave Macmillan).

Pagès i Blanch, Pelai (2005), 'El moviment d'alliberament nacional durant la transició', *El Temps d'Història*, 46: 26–30.

Pallarés, Francesc & Muñoz, Jordi (2008), 'The Autonomous Elections of 1 November 2006 in Catalonia', *Regional & Federal Studies*, 18 (4): 449–464.

Parreño Rabadán, Mònica. 2010. *El nou periodisme integrat i multiplataforma. El cas del diari ARA.* Unpublished Masters dissertation, Universitat Oberta de Catalunya.

Passola, Isona (dir.) (2009), *Cataluña-Espanya* (Baditri).

Pelayo, Andrea (2010), 'TV3 aboga por la independencia de Cataluña en un documental'. *El Mundo* [Online], 2 June, http://www.elmundo.es/elmundo/2010/06/02/ barcelona/1275494471.html, accessed 3 June 2010.

Perelman, Chaïm & Olbrechts-Tyteca, Lucie (1969), *The New Rhetoric: A Treatise on Argumentation* (Notre Dame: University of Notre Dame Press).

Pladevall i Font, Antoni (2007), *El General Josep Moragues: Heroi i màrtir de Catalunya* (Maçaners: Abadia Editors).

Plataforma per la Llengua (2010), 'La Plataforma per la Llengua rebutja la sentència del TC perquè és antidemocràtica i no respecta els notres drets lingüístics'. [Online], http://in.directe.cat/plataforma-llengua/blog/3900/la-plataforma-per-la-llengua-rebutja-la-sentencia-del-tc-perque-es-antidemocratica-i-no-re, accessed 30 August 2013.

Pons i Novell, Jordi & Tremosa i Balcells, Ramon (2005), 'Macroeconomic Effects of Catalan Fiscal Deficit with the Spanish State (2002–2010)', *Applied Economics*, 37 (13): 1455–1463.

Pujol, Jordi (2007), 'Juicio severo'. *La Vanguardia*, 1 August, p.17.

Pujol, Jordi (2011), *Memòries: Temps de construir (1980–1993)* (Barcelona: Proa).

Pujol, Jordi (2012a), *Memòries: De la bonança a un repte nou (1993–2011)* (Barcelona: Proa).

Pujol, Jordi (2012b), *Reflexió en el tombant d'un camí. 1714–2014* (Barcelona: Centre d'Estudis Jordi Pujol).

Puppo, Ronald (2011), 'The Poetry of Troubles: Maragall's "Els tres cants de la guerra" (Three songs of war) and their Translation', *Journal of Catalan Studies* [Online], 14, http://www.anglo-catalan.org/jocs/14/Articles & Reviews/Versio pdf/12 Puppo.pdf.

Reicher, Stephen & Hopkins, Nick (2001), *Self and Nation: Categorization, Contestation and Mobilization* (London: Sage).

Requejo, Ferran (2010), 'Revealing the Dark Side of Traditional Democracies in Plurinational Societies: the Case of Catalonia and the Spanish "Estado de las Autonomías"', *Nations and Nationalism*, 16 (1): 148–168.

Ridao, Joan (2005), *Les contradiccions del catalanisme* (Barcelona: L'Esfera dels Llibres).

Ridao, Joan (2006), *Així es va fer l'Estatut: De l'Estatut del Parlament a l'Estatut de la Moncloa* (Barcelona: Editorial Mediterrània).

Ridao, Joan (2007), *El pla B* (Barcelona: Mina).

Rodríguez-Pose, Andrés & Sandall, Richard (2008), 'From Identity to the Economy: Analysing the Evolution of the Decentralisation Discourse', *Environment and Planning C: Government and Policy*, 26 (1): 54–72.

Roger, Maiol (2011), 'La consulta soberanista de Barcelona registra una participación del 18,14%'. *El País* [Online], 10 April, http://elpais. com/elpais /2011/04/10/actualidad/1302423422_850215.html, accessed 13 April 2011.

Roller, Elisa & Van Houten, Pieter (2003), 'A National Party in a Regional Party System: The PSC-PSOE in Catalonia', *Regional & Federal Studies*, 13 (3): 1–22.

Ros i Ombravella, Jacint, Tremosa i Balcells, Ramon & Pons i Novell, Jordi (2003), 'Capital públic i dèficit fiscal: l'impacte sobre l'economia catalana', *Nota d'economia*, 75: 103–117.

Rubiralta i Casas, Fermí (2004), *Una història de l'independentisme polític català: De Francesc Macià a Josep Lluís Carod-Rovira* (Lleida: Pagès Editors).

Rusiñol, Pere & Cué, Carlos. (2003), 'Zapatero promete apoyar la reforma del

Estatuto que salga del Parlamento'. *El País* [Online], 14 November, http://elpais.com/diario/2003/11/14/espana/1068764421_850215.html, accessed 19 December 2013.

Sáez, Albert (2005), *El futur del nacionalisme: Cap a on va la política en el postpujolisme* (Barcelona: Columna).

Sáez, Ferran (2011a), 'Política i valors', in Castiñeira, À. & Elzo, J. (eds.) *Valors tous en temps durs: La societat catalana a l'Enquesta Europea de Valors de 2009* (Barcelona: Barcino), 194–245.

Sáez, Ferran (2011b), 'La identitat nacional com a valor', in Castiñeira, À. & Elzo, J. (eds.) *Valors tous en temps durs: La societat catalana a l'Enquesta Europea de Valors de 2009* (Barcelona: Barcino), 246–312.

Sala, Carlos (2013), 'TV3 vulneró la ley que protege la pluralidad con el reportaje «Hola Europa!»'. *La Razón* [Online], 9 May, http://www.larazon.es/detalle _normal/noticias/2194096/tv3-vulnero-la-ley-que-protege-la-pluralidad-c- .UcrDPxa CgRk, accessed 26 June 2013.

Sallés, Quico (2012), 'Ferran Requejo: «He deixat de ser idiota, ara sóc independentista»'. *Nació Digital* [Online], 29 June, http://www.naciodigital. cat/noticia/44239/ferran/requejo/he/deixat/ser/idiota/ara/soc/independentista, accessed 1 October 2013.

Salmond, Alex (2012), 'Voting Yes Will Create a New Scotland'. *The Guardian* [Online], 16 October, http://www.theguardian.com/commentisfree/2012/oct/ 16/voting-yes-create-new-scotland, accessed 1 November 2012.

Salvat, Joan (2010a) *Sense ficció* (Interview with Jordi Mercader), (TV3). 10 June.

Salvat, Joan (2010b), *Sense ficció* (Interview with M. Dolors Genovès about *Adéu, Espanya?*), (TV3). 3 June.

Salvat, Joan (2013), *Sense ficció* (Interview with M. Dolors Genovès about *Hola, Europa!*) (TV3). 7 May.

Sampedro Blanco, Víctor & Valhondo Crego, José Luis (2012), 'L'infosatira televisiva e i suoi effetti', *Comunicazione Politica*, 2012 (1): 43–56.

Sánchez Piñol, Albert (2012), *Victus* (Barcelona: La Campana).

Sanders, Willemien (2010), 'Documentary Filmmaking and Ethics: Concepts, Responsibilities, and the Need for Empirical Research', *Mass Communication and Society*, 13 (5): 528–553.

Sastre, Daniel G. (2013), 'CiU adelanta otra vez a ERC por el protagonismo de Mas'. *El Mundo* [Online], 16 December, http://www.elmundo.es/cataluna/ 2013/12/16/52ae80b522601dea0b8b4583.html?a=7193e9a10fe5108d25229 bf95c69ea50&t=1387177134, accessed 17 December 2013.

Sense ficció (2013), '"Hola, Europa!" El blog de Sense ficció' [Online]. http://blogs.tv3.cat/senseficcio.php?itemid=49923, accessed 29 May 2013.

Serra, Xavi (2012), 'L'Èric Bertran és el primer català lliure, el nostre Kunta Kinte'. *ARA* [Online], 5 November, http://www.ara.cat/cultura/Joan-LEric-Bertran- Kunta-Kinte_ 0_805119605.html, accessed 29 May 2013.

Serrano, Ivan (2013a), 'Just a Matter of Identity? Support for Independence in Catalonia', *Regional & Federal Studies*, 23 (5): 523–545.

Serrano, Ivan (2013b), *De la nació a l'estat* (Barcelona: Angle Editorial).

Simpson, Paul (2003), *On the Discourse of Satire* (Amsterdam: John Benjamins).

Sintes i Olivella, Marçal (2010), 'De la política a la política "polonitzada"', *Trípodos*, 27: 49–58.

Smith, Anthony D. (1991), *National Identity* (London: Penguin).

Sobrequés i Callicó, Jaume (2013), *Cap a la llibertat* (Barcelona: Base).

Solà, Xavier (dir.) (2012), *La nit dels ignorants* (Interview with Albert Sánchez Piñol), (Catalunya Ràdio). 28 October.

Soler, Toni (2010), *L'última carta de Companys* (Barcelona: Columna).

Sorens, Jason (2004), 'Globalization, Secessionism, and Autonomy', *Electoral Studies*, 23 (4): 737–752.

Sorens, Jason (2005), 'The Cross-Sectional Determinants of Secessionism in Advanced Democracies', *Comparative Political Studies*, 38 (3): 304–326.

Strubell i Trueta, Toni (1997), *El cansament del catalanisme* (Barcelona: La Campana).

Strubell i Trueta, Toni (2008), *El moment de dir prou: La manifesta incompatibilitat amb Espanya* (Lleida: Pagès Editors).

Strubell i Trueta, Toni & Brunet, Lluís (2011), *What Catalans Want* (Ashfield, MA: Catalonia Press).

Thompson, Ethan (2008), 'Good Demo, Bad Taste: *South Park* as Carnivalesque Satire', in Gray, J., Thompson, E. & Jones, J. (eds.) *Satire TV* (New York: New York University Press), 214–232.

Tree, Matthew (2011), *Barcelona, Catalonia: A View from the Inside* (n.p.: Cookwood Press).

Tremosa i Balcells, Ramon (2006), *Estatut, aeroports i ports de peix al cove* (Valencia: 3 i 4).

Tusell, Javier (1999), *España, una angustia nacional* (Madrid: Espasa Calpe).

Ucelay Da Cal, Enric (2008), 'Més que un club? Exploració d'un relat persistent ', *Metropolis: Revista d'informació i pensament urbans*, 71: 47–57.

Ugarte Ballester, Xus (2011), 'El Polònia de TV3: tastets paremiològics amb versions en francès i castellà', *Catalonia*, 8 (March), [Online], http://www.crimic.paris-sorbonne.fr/IMG/pdf/CATALONIA_8_Xus_Ugarte .pdf, accessed 22 July 2013.

Universitat Oberta de Catalunya/Instituto DYM (2009), 'Diagnòstic de percepcions Catalunya-Espanya: principals resultats'. (Barcelona: UOC), [Online], http://www.slideshare.net/collectiuemma/independncia-de-catalunya, accessed 10 February 2011.

Urry, John (2005), 'The Complexities of the Global', *Theory, Culture & Society*, 22 (5): 235–254.

V. F. (2012), 'Albert Sánchez Piñol: «He escrito una novela que incomodará a todo el mundo»'. *La Razón* [Online], 27 October, http://larazon.es/noticia/2494-albert-sanchez-pinol-he-escrito-una-novela-que-incomodara-a-todo-el-mundo, accessed 27 November 2012.

Valero, Joan Carles (2006), 'El boicot al cava catalán "es casi imperceptible"'. *ABC* [Online], 4 December, http://www.abc.es/hemeroteca/historico-04-12-

2006/abc/Nacional/el-boicot-al-cava-catalan-es-casi-imperceptible_
153288979322.html, accessed 13 September 2009.

Vázquez, Silvina (2011), 'Elements i significats del malestar amb la política a Catalunya. Una aproximació qualitativa a partir de la indagació amb grups de discussió' (Barcelona: Centre d'Estudis d'Opinió).

Vázquez, Silvina (2013), 'Identitat nacional i autogovern. Un estudi qualitatiu sobre les configuracions identitàries nacionals a la Catalunya contemporània' (Barcelona: Centre d'Estudis d'Opinió).

Vicens Vives, Jaume (1960), *Notícia de Catalunya* (Barcelona: Àncora).

Vicens Vives, Jaume (1992), 'The Catalans and the Minotaur', in Sobrer, J. M. (ed.) *Catalonia: A Self Portrait* (Bloomington: Indiana University Press), 97–105.

Vilaregut, Ricard. (2008), '2014 / Generació.cat / ERC: temps de transició (Book review)'. *El País*, 12 June, 'Quadern', 4.

VilaWeb (2009), 'Passola: Cataluña-Espanya dispara al cervell i no al cor'. *Vilaweb* [Online], http://www.vilaweb.tv/?video=5658, accessed 10 December 2013.

VilaWeb (2012a), 'La manifestació amb més autocars de la història'. *VilaWeb* [Online], 5 September, http://www.vilaweb.cat/noticia/4038121/20120905/manifestacio-autocars-historia.html, accessed 26 August 2013.

Vilaweb (2012b), 'Jordi Pujol: "S'ha acabat fer la puta i la Ramoneta. El govern ha de ser valent"'. *Vilaweb* [Online], 31 August, http://www.vilaweb.cat/noticia/4037049/20120831/jordi-pujol-acabat-puta-ramoneta-govern-valent.html, accessed 19 July 2013.

Ward, Paul (2005), *Documentary: The Margins of Reality* (London: Wallflower).

Watts, Ronald L. (2007), 'Multinational Federations in Comparative Perspective', in Burgess, M. & Pinder, J. (eds.) *Multinational Federations* (Abingdon: Routledge), 225–247.

Weinstock, Daniel (2006), 'Is "Identity" a Danger to Democracy?', in Primoratz, I. & Pavkovic, A. (eds.) *Identity, Self-Determination and Secession* (Aldershot: Ashgate), 15–26.

Wieting, Mark (dir.) (2007), *Ciudadanos de segunda* (Telemadrid), 9 April.

Winter, Jay (2006), 'Notes on the Memory Boom: War, Remembrance and the Uses of the Past', in Bell, D. (ed.) *Memory, Trauma and World Politics: Reflections on the Relationship between Past and Present* (Basingstoke: Palgrave Macmillan), 54–73.

Youcat (2010), 'Lipdub per la independència' [Online]: Youcat Canal. http://www.youtube.com/watch?v=muTMLuGWrp8, accessed 10 December 2013.

Index